I0819090

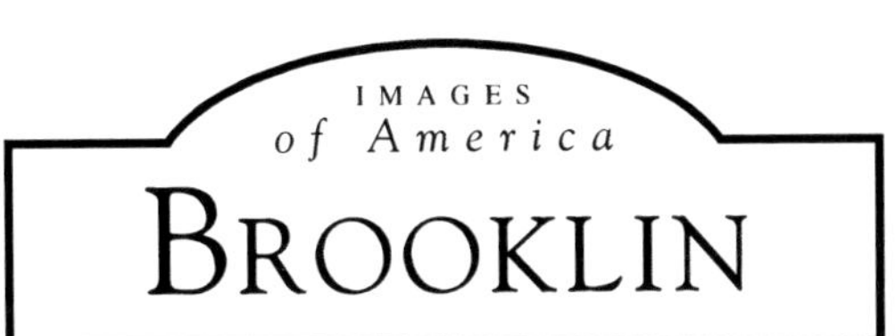
IMAGES
of America
BROOKLIN

Apreal 3 Day 1768
reckned and settled with Samull Cusanes and thar remanes due to Shadrach Watson 12 19 0

Samuell Cusoneas Det

2 pound of Coffay	0	1	13
to one galan of malases	0	0	16 0
to Cash	0	0	5 0
to one galan of malases	0	0	16 0
to one galan of malases	0	0	16 0
to one quart of malases	0	0	4 0
to 2 quartes of rum	0	0	12 6
to one galan of malases	0	0	16
to meal 5½ quartes	0	1	14 0
to 2 quarte of malases	0	0	8
to one galan of malases	0	0	16 0
to one quarte of rum	0	0	7 0
to one quarte of rum	0	0	7 0
to 2 quartes of malases	0	0	8 0
to 2 quartes of rum	0	0	12 6
to 3 galanes of malases	0	2	8 0
to 2 quartes of malases	0	0	9 0
to 4 galanes and one quart of rum	0	0	7 6
to one barrill and a half of meal	0	2	10 0
to one quarte of rum	0	0	7 6
to 2 galanes of malases	0	1	16 0
to one bushel and a half of meall	0	1	15 0
to 6 quartes of meall	0	0	6 0
to one galan of malases	0	0	18 0
to a bushel [illegible]			

This page from Shadrach Watson's Naskeag store ledger dates from 1768. The top of the page reads, "Rekoned and settled with Samull Cusanes and thar remanes due to Shadrack Watson," and the amount of 12 pounds and 19 shillings is given. Watson, John Black, and Joseph Freethy were the first permanent settlers at Naskeag.

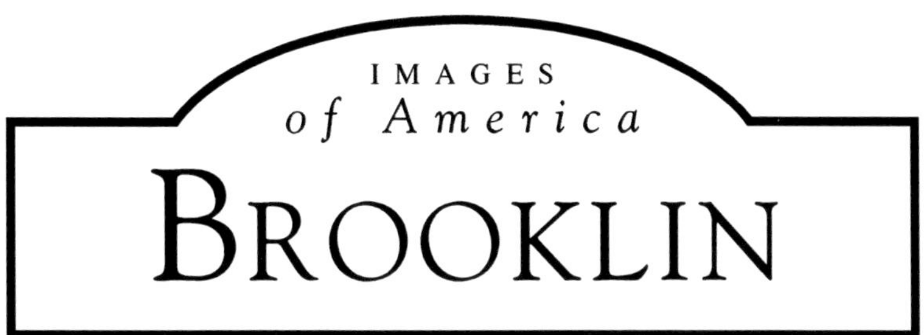

Brooklin Keeping Society

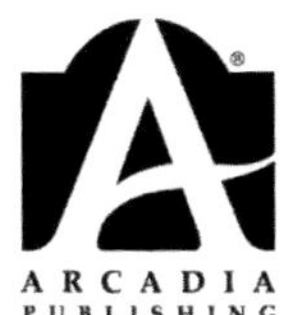

ISBN 978-0-7385-1159-7

Published by Arcadia Publishing
Charleston, South Carolina

Printed in the United States of America

Library of Congress Catalog Card Number: 2002115308

For all general information, contact Arcadia Publishing:
Telephone 843-853-2070
Fax 843-853-0044
E-mail sales@arcadiapublishing.com
For customer service and orders:
Toll-Free 1-888-313-2665

Visit us on the Internet at www.arcadiapublishing.com.

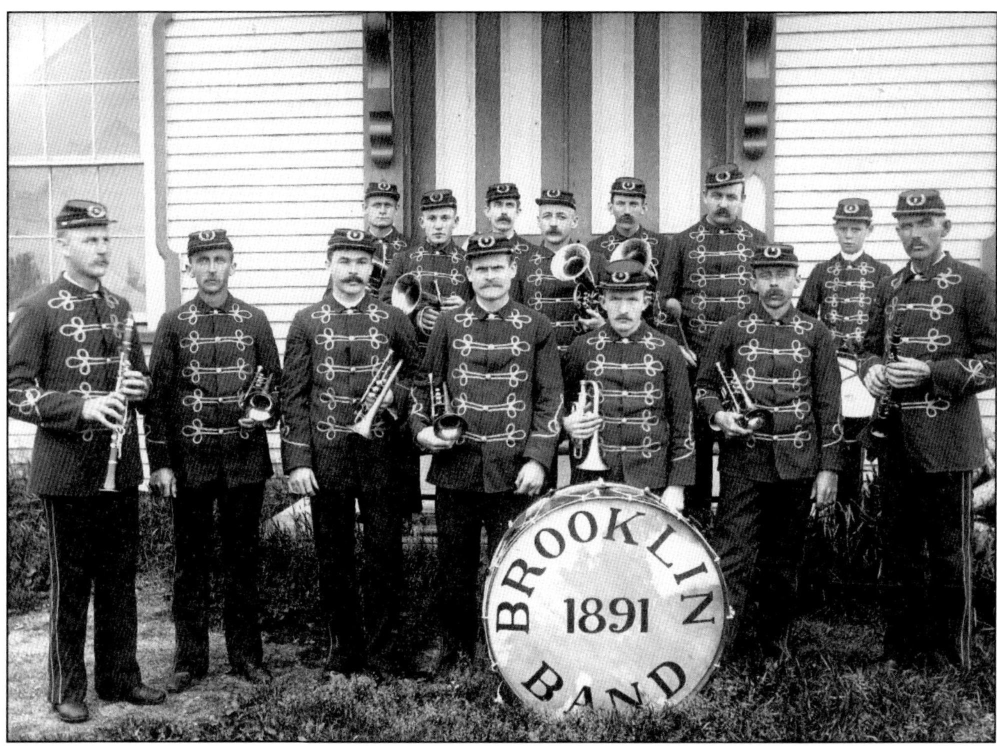

These 1891 Brooklin Band members are, from left to right, as follows: (front row) Owen Flye, Webster McFarland, Gene Stanley, Win Stanley, Arthur Bridges, and Ross Bridges; (back row) Eldorus Bridges, Edward Mayo, Almon Atherton, Rodney Smith, Harold Grindle, Ralph Bent, Tom Stanley, and Horace Pease.

Contents

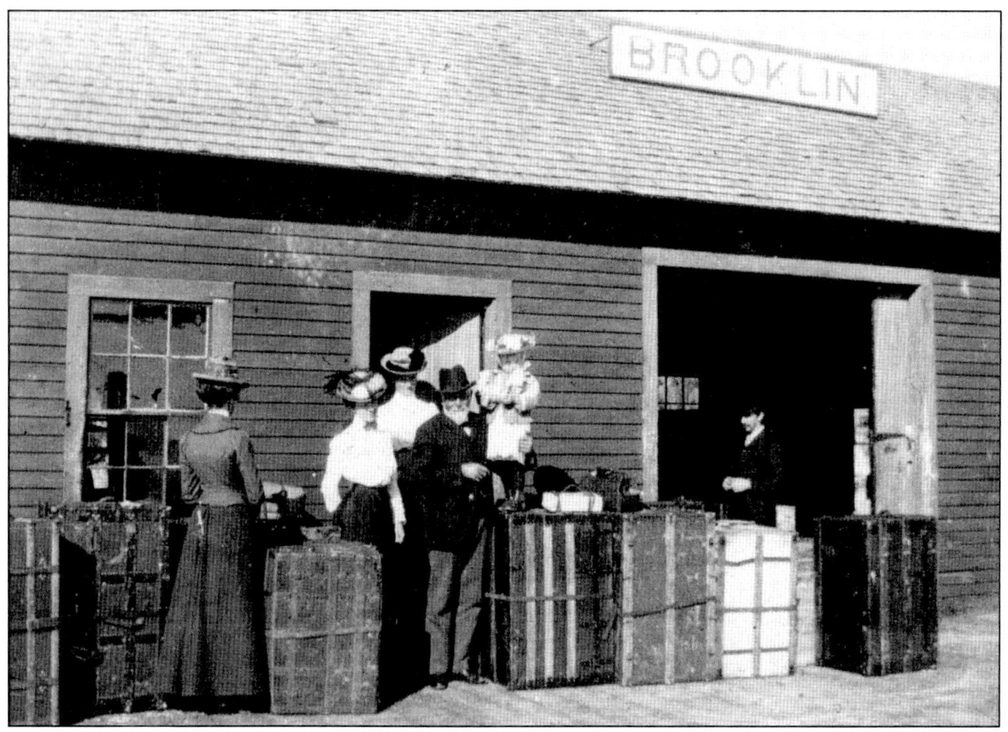

Steamships came into Brooklin Landing several times a day. From 1884, starting with the Crockett Line, to 1934, when the *Southport* made its last Brooklin trip, steamboats kept Brooklin supplied with all manner of goods. Pictured here are the large trunks used often by summer people who came with toys and pots and pans as well as clothing.

Acknowledgments

For photographs, information, and technical and literary support, the Brooklin Keeping Society would like to thank the following people and institutions: the Friend Memorial Public Library, the Penobscot Marine Museum, the Sedgwick-Brooklin Historical Society, George and Georgene Allen, Janet Allen, George and Glyneta Andrews, Joyce Barr and James Bartlett, Maynard Bray, Albert Bridges, Richard Bridges, Hilda Smith Bryant, Sherry Carter, Margot Case, Allen Cole, Carol Damon, Frank Day Jr., Paula Dougherty, Eric and Barbie Dow, Wade and Helena Dow, James and Mary Catherine Dunn, June Eaton, William Eaton, Wesley Flye, Pauline Ferris, Faith Field, Mary Wells Fowle, Basil and Frances Friend, Judy Fuller, Virginia Gersch, Adele H. Goddard, Louis and Linda Graceffa, Lorna Grant, Carlton Gray, Laurie Gray, Olney Grindall, Stanley and Eunice Hardy, Alice Hildebrand, Ernest Hildebrand, Hazel Flye Hunt, Catherine Hutchinson, Laura Johns, Cressida Keefe, Roger Kellett, George and Cynthia Knapp, Jill Knowles, Celia Laughlin, Henry and Jane Lawson, Elaine Mahoney, Brenda Means, Patricia Flye Meyers, Susanne Noessel, Donald and Connie Parson, Hope Pert, Richard Roberts, Jeryl Schriever, Patricia Schroth, Florence Sherman, Roxanne Sherman, Roxanne Sly, Gordon and Norma Smith, Robert Smith, Butch Smith, Jim and Pam Steele, Dennis and Clare Sullivan, Ethel Howard Tandy, Elaine Trowbridge, Mary Ford Weber, Allene White, Nancy Whitman, Betty Williams, Edmund Williams, and Jon Wilson.

Introduction

The very early history of Brooklin has been well documented through extensive archaeological explorations on Naskeag and Flye Point. Prehistoric people had a large village on Naskeag (the largest of any known from New Jersey to the Maritimes), which served as a major Atlantic coast trade center. In later years, the Penobscots used this shore for summer and fall camps.

The first permanent settlers came when the Brooklin area (then called Naskeag) was a territory claimed by England and considered part of Massachusetts. Under land grants from the English king, Township No. 4 was established in what is now Brooklin, Sedgwick, and part of Brooksville. When 60 families had settled and built 60 homes, when they had 300 acres under tillage, and when a meetinghouse was built and a minister installed, the town was established and given the name of Sedgwick. In 1849, particularly with the efforts of state representative John C. Tibbetts, Brooklin established its own town with the name of Port Watson. Shortly after, the name was changed to Brooklin.

Names of the first settlers were Freethey, Watson, Flye, Herrick, Black, Reed, Babson, Allen, Cousins, Carter, Jackson, Hale, Dority, and Wells. Many Brooklin residents today can trace their lineage back to these early settlers, as will be evident in the captions of this book.

The livelihood of Brooklin people came from the sea. The first recorded boat was built in early 1793, when John Allen and John Dority built the *Trail* at the head of Herrick's Bay. By 1850, more than half the men in Brooklin were working on ships, and by 1876, no fewer than 46 vessels had been built within the town limits. In the early 1800s, wood was the largest export. Before the Revolutionary War, the British wanted masts from the area's ancient tall trees. During the Civil War, Americans prized lumber for the building of towns and barrel staves for molasses storage.

In the late 1800s, Brooklin began a significant change when the steamboats came, the canning factories were built, and summer colonies and hotels sprung up in nearly every part of town. Clams were canned on Naskeag. Center Harbor was known for its lobsters, sardines, clams, fish, beans, and brown bread. Summer colonies and hotels were started at Flye Point, Naskeag, North Brooklin, Haven, and the Corner. Steamboats increased the service to Brooklin both winter and summer.

The town changed again in the 1930s. Shipping on newly improved roads was cheaper than on the steamboats, and the fish-canning businesses moved to areas closer to highways. The Great Depression depleted the summer resident business, and when the last steamship, the *Southport,* departed for Rockland in 1934, Brooklin was a changed town.

The population dwindled from 1,002 (in 1850) to 656 (in 1940) as residents moved to other areas, seeking jobs.

In Boston, homesick Brooklin residents formed the Brooklin Club. At the first meeting (in 1910), there were 62 Brooklinites in attendance to dance to the "Eggemoggin Waltz" or the "West End Two Step." The club was in existence some 30 years—from the first president, Lee H. Powers, to the last, Stillman Mayo—until October 1940.

Gradually, Brooklin rebounded. Boatyards began to boom again as the economy strengthened. Property was inexpensive, and writers, sailors, and craftsmen came to the area for the beauty and quiet of the town. WoodenBoat Publishing established a magazine and boat school, and summer visitors returned. Today, while there are no canning factories, the summer business is brisk, and boats are still built all over town. With a year-round population of 840, Brooklin has 11 boatyards in steady production. Old inns are revitalized and new hotels and restaurants have opened. It is estimated that more than 7,000 people come through the town each summer to sail, to visit family and friends, to eat lobster and blueberries, to learn boatbuilding, or just to be here.

The Brooklin Keeping Society is indebted to Lewis Watson for many of the photographs in this book. As pictures came in to the society from different people, we began to realize that many were from the same source. They were black and white, the same size, and had the same handwriting on the back to identify the subject of the photograph. It seems that Watson spent his early life in Brooklin and then lived in the Boston area. Each summer, as an adult, he would come to Brooklin for his vacation and would walk the town with his Brownie box camera and a black bag of film. He took pictures of houses and people through much of the 1920s and 1930s and, when he returned home, mailed back the photographs to people in town.

The Brooklin Keeping Society is grateful for all who donated their photographs for this book. In fact, we received many more than we could use and so made selections to represent a variety of places and people as well as for the quality of the print. We have tried to include as many families and different areas as possible.

The first seven chapters in *Brooklin* are divided according to town sections, and the titles are self explanatory. Chapter 8 features a scattering of special events or scenes that caught our attention. Chapter 9 includes people from every area. The final chapter presents a sample of the builders, owners, captains, and crews of boats both modest and grand with ties to Brooklin.

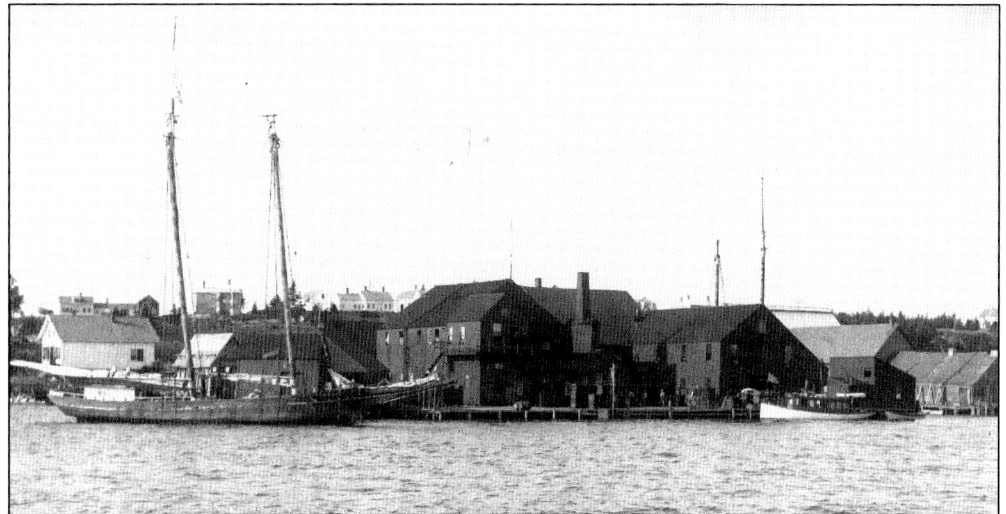

These buildings at Center Harbor have a long history in the fish-packing industry. Here, in 1870, R.A. Friend canned lobster. He was followed by McFarland & Sons and Augustine Bray (smoked pogies), the Brooklin Packing Company (clams and pogies), S.G. Stevens (sardines), A.E. Farnsworth (clams and sardines), and in 1923, W.A. Ramsdell. Steve and Charles Cousins and then E. Herrick and R. Allen packed blueberries.

One

Brooklin Corner

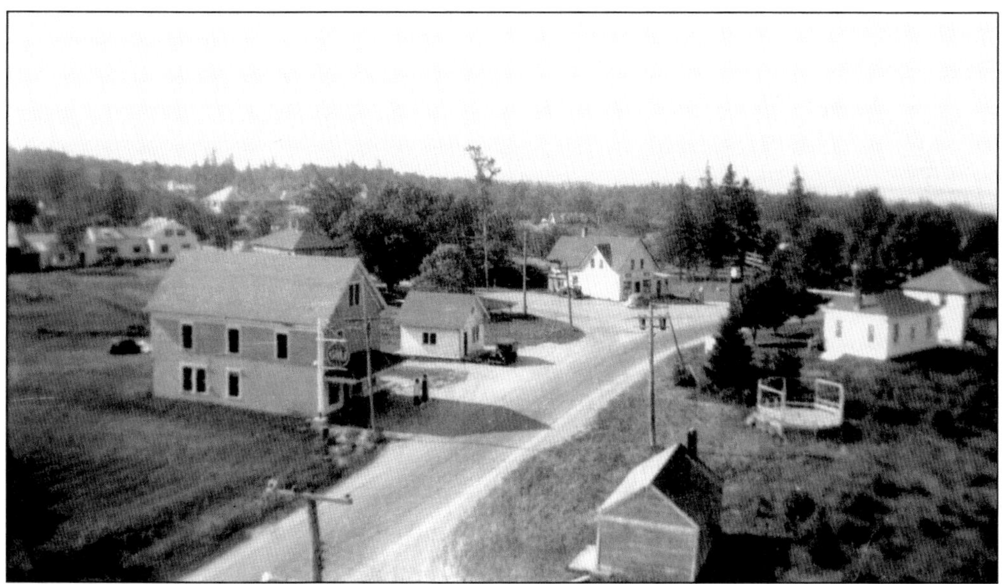

By 1949, Brooklin Corner had paved roads and a library. On the left are the Grange Store (now Hylan's), the post office (Morning Moon Cafe), and G. Frank Gott's store (the Brooklin General Store). On the right are the barbershop, the town bandstand, the Friend Memorial Public Library, and a house that was given to Katharine White by E.B. White in the 1940s. The house was torn down in the early 1950s for landscaping the library. Behind the Grange Store, the Cole house can be seen.

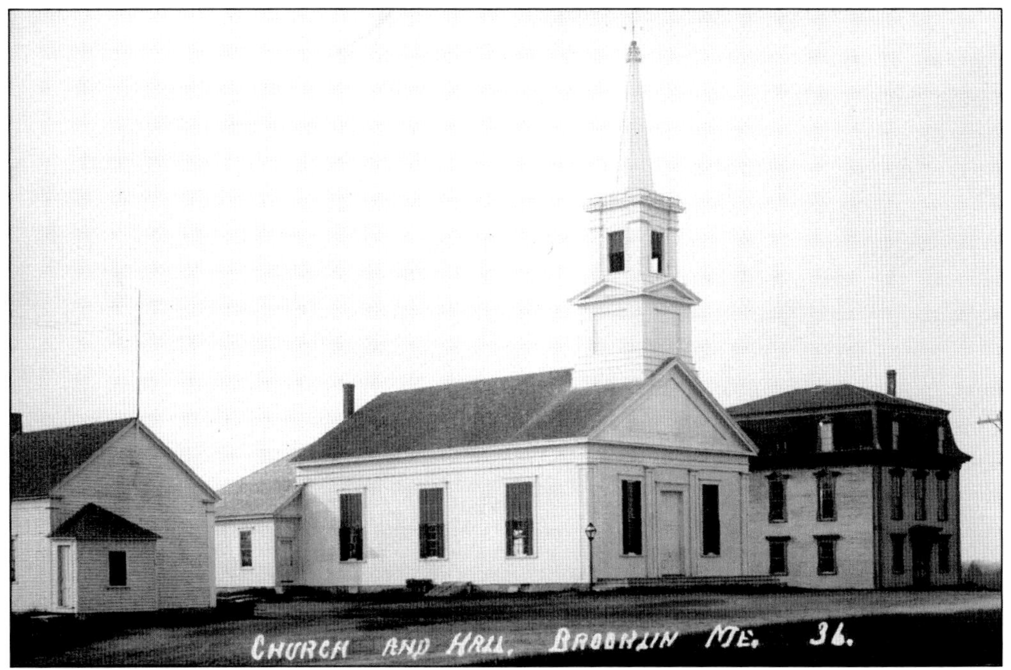

On the left is schoolhouse No. 8 (at the Corner), later used as a selectmen's office and then moved to Center Harbor. The First Baptist Church of Brooklin, designed by Thomas Lord, was built in 1854. In 1920, stained-glass windows made by Arthur Bell were dedicated to early church members. The first floor of the building to the right was used as a town hall. The second floor was Union Hall, and the third floor was the Masonic lodge.

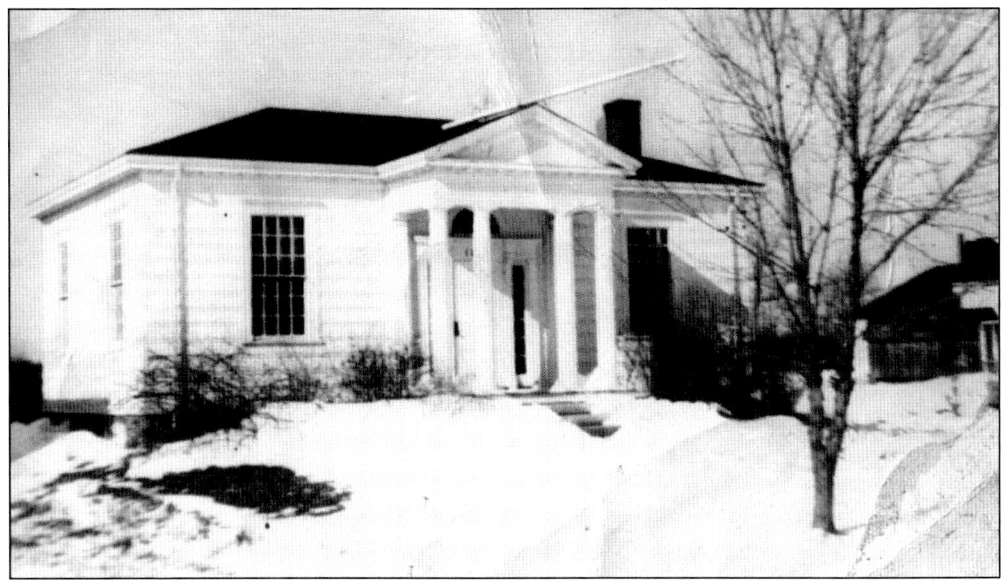

The Friend Memorial Public Library was built in 1912 on land donated by the R.A. Friend family. The architect for the original building was William N. Wilkins, the husband of Ella McFarland of Brooklin. The first librarians were Musa and Annie Dollard, with Annie in service from 1901 to 1945. In 1940, Katherine and E.B. White, Owen Flye, and others were instrumental in revitalizing the library, increasing the collections and hours of operation.

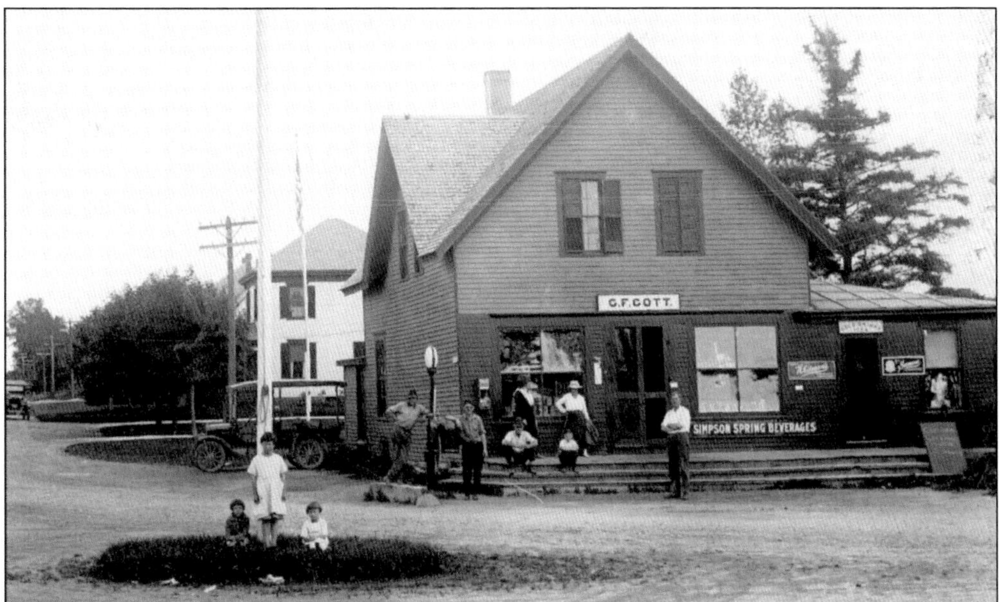

The store at Brooklin Corner is shown when it was owned by G. Frank Gott, who ran the store from 1903 to 1946. Correspondence from the Reed family indicates that Elijah Reed constructed this building in 1866 and was there until 1872. After Gott, the store was owned by Lincoln Anderson and then by Charlie Williams (1946–1968), who was followed by Al Ormondroyd (until 1978), "Clem" Clements, Vauna Haza, and Lorna Grant (the present-day owner).

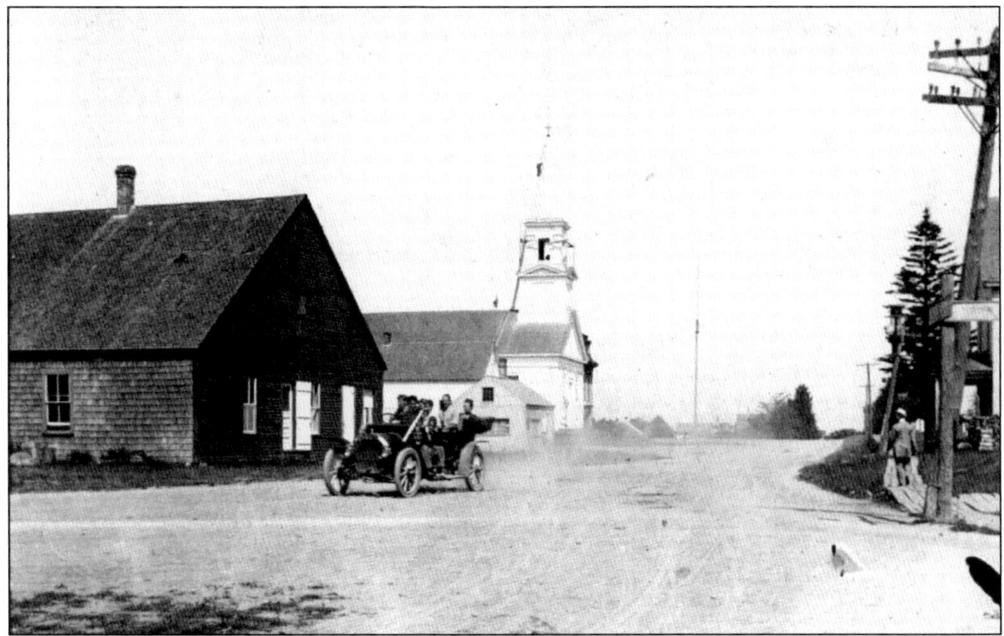

A roller-skating rink, shown here next to the First Baptist Church of Brooklin, was built by R.A. Friend in 1880. It was a favorite gathering place for Brooklin youth at the time. In a letter dated September 6, 1886, from the Rufus Wells papers, we find the following: "The Skating rink is in Operation—Rose goes every night—I have seen her about 1 hr." The rink was torn down, and the land and materials were donated to the town for the new library.

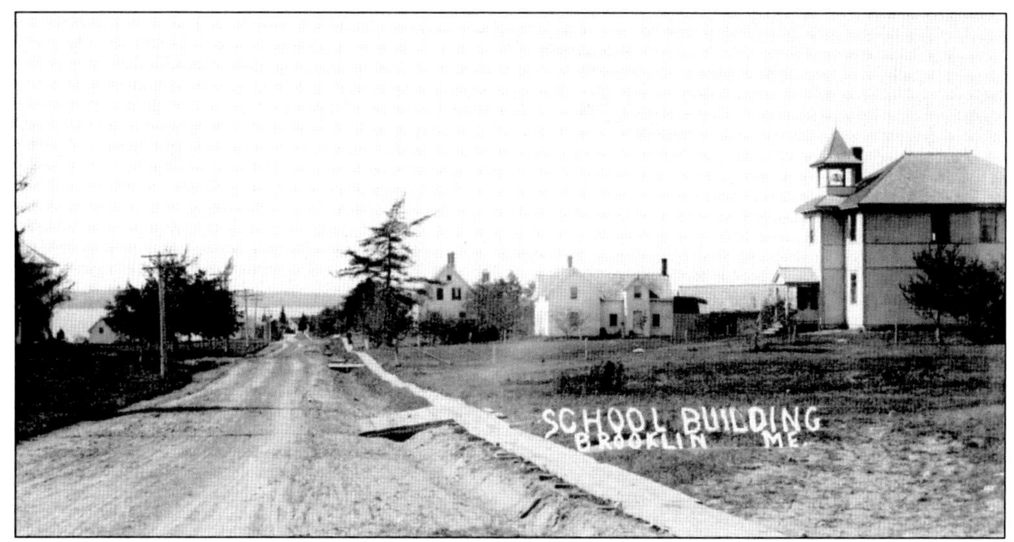

This view looks west on Reach Road from the Corner. The building on the right is the first high school (built in 1897), which burned in 1916. Owen Flye was the superintendent. The next building in view is the home of Brooksie and Earl Kane, and the next is that of Harriet and Burt Henderson. The wooden sidewalks of that era can be seen running toward Center Harbor.

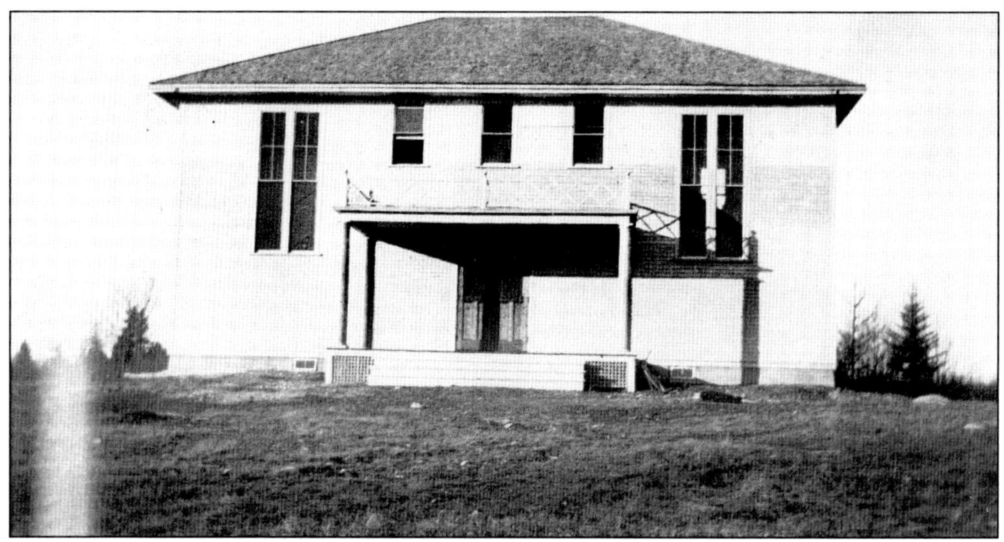

The second high school was built on the site of the first in 1917. Edward Linscott was superintendent by then. Again, in 1930, this school burned, and students had to attend classes in the town hall and chapel until the third school was built two years later.

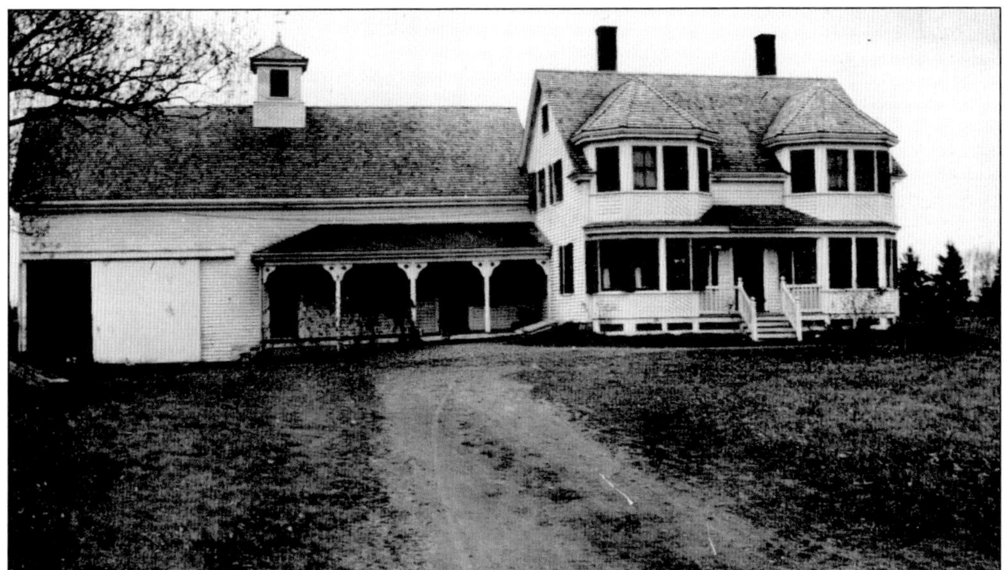

This house, the home of Roland and Alena Flye, is located behind the First Baptist Church of Brooklin and is shown as it was in the late 1800s. The collections from this house provided the impetus for the start of the Brooklin Keeping Society. In later years, it was the home of Winslow and Linnie Bowden.

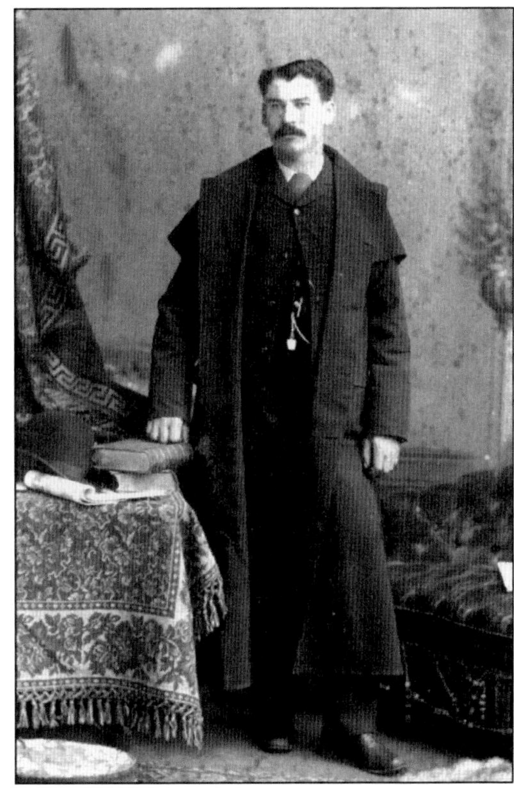

Roland Flye, the husband of Alena Gray from Sedgwick, was in charge of the draft board in Brooklin for World War I. Alena was a teacher in Brooklin and Sedgwick. Later, Roland had a business in Nova Scotia, and his letters from that era, in the Brooklin Keeping Society archives, contain much information about early Brooklin.

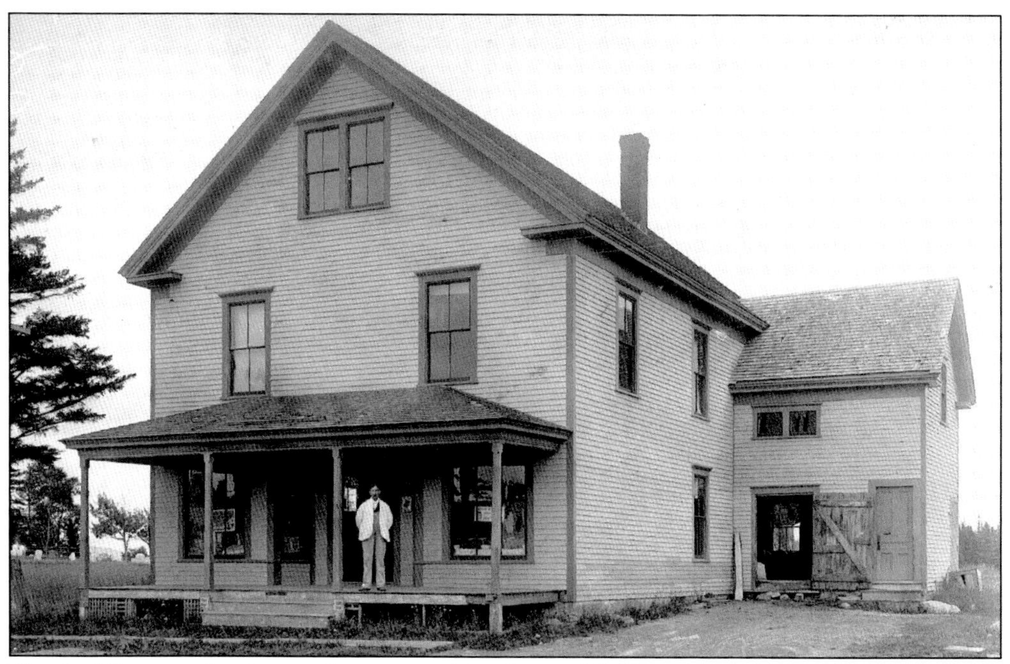

This building was the Grange Store, owned by George W. Herrick, a grandson of John Herrick, who came to Brooklin in 1785. At one time, Bill Cousins was a merchant there, as was Arthur Gray. For many years, Norton Smith owned the building and ran a hardware store and other businesses. It is now owned by Doug and Jean Hylan.

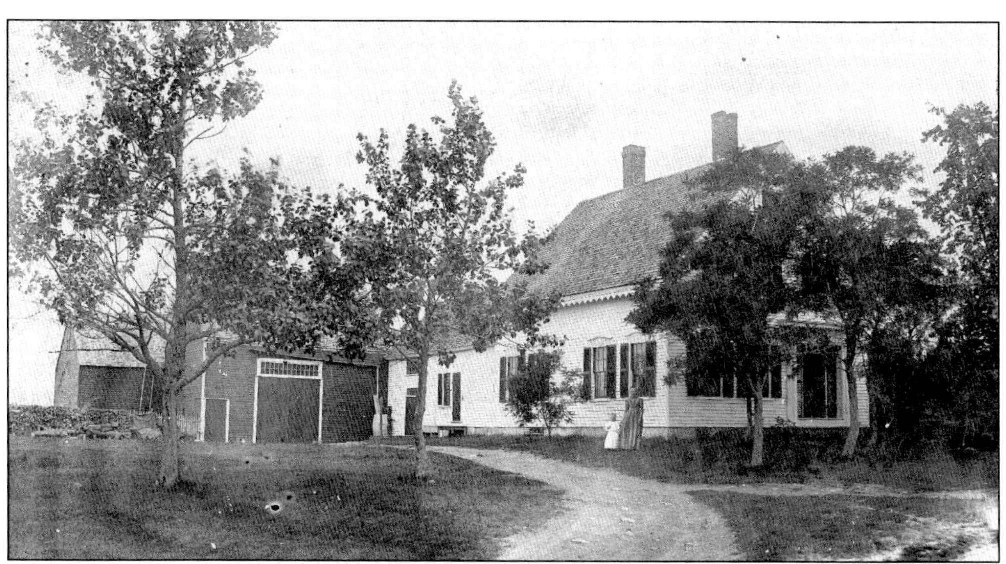

This house was built by Arthur M. Herrick (1809–1885) c. 1840 on land that was part of the original 1700s land grant to Samuel Herrick III. Arthur gave the house to his daughter Catherine and her husband, George C. Hall. Catherine is shown in front with her grandson Llewellyn S. Herrick. Today, a fifth-generation Herrick descendant owns the house.

Hattie Hall Herrick (1868–1965), the wife of George W. Herrick, was born in Brooklin. She attended Castine Normal School and taught in Surry. As a young woman, she and her children often sailed with her husband.

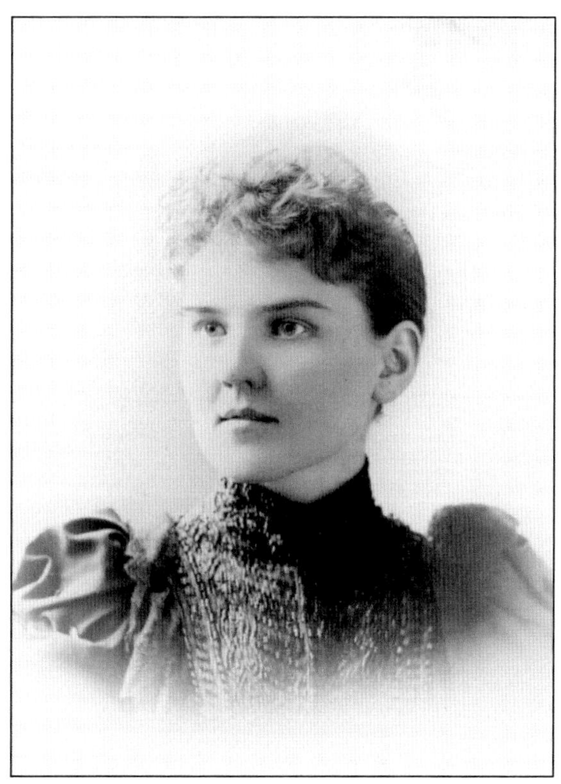

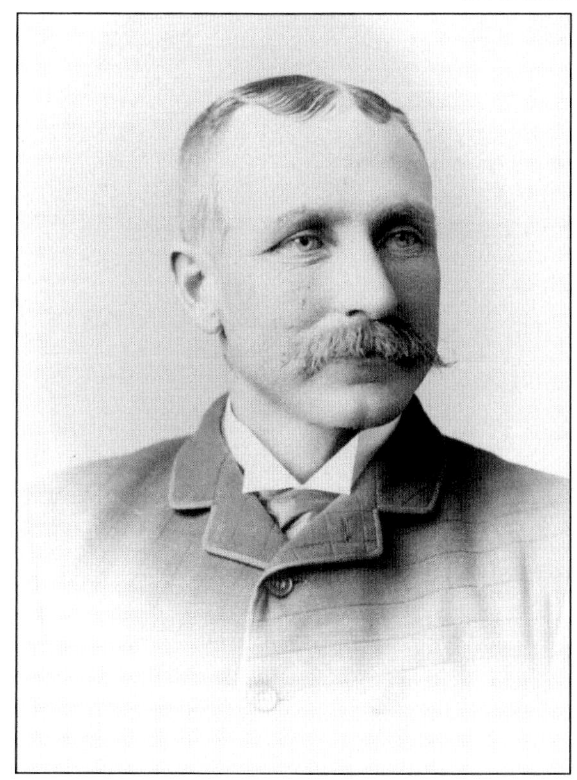

Capt. George W. Herrick (1857–1924) was born in North Brooklin. He went to sea in 1868 at age 11 and was later captain of the schooners *Almira* and *Pochasset,* which traveled up and down the eastern seaboard. After coming ashore, he owned the Grange Store and served in the state legislature for Brooklin. In 1910, he moved to Boston, where he ran a coal company.

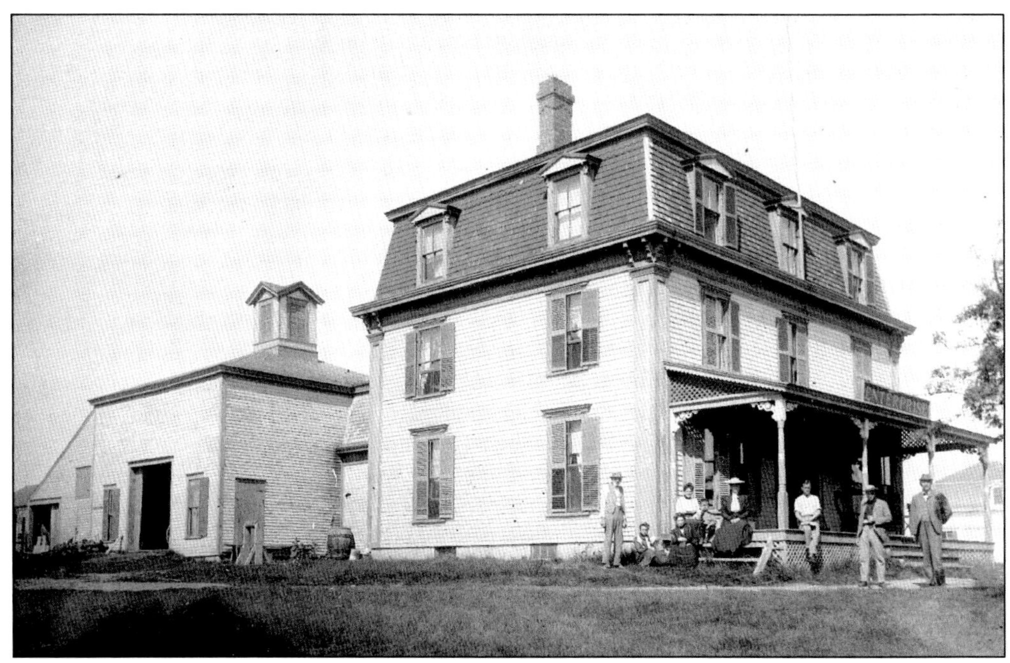

This building, constructed in 1868, was a private residence for Capt. Ahira Watson. His wife later ran it as Watson House. Then, George C. and Catherine Hall ran it as the Enterprise House. Steven D. and Charles C. Cousins called it the Brooklin House. In 1920, Isobel H. Lenman named it the Mountain Ash Inn, and it then became the Faith School of Theology under Rev. Russell Pier. Today, it belongs to the WoodenBoat School.

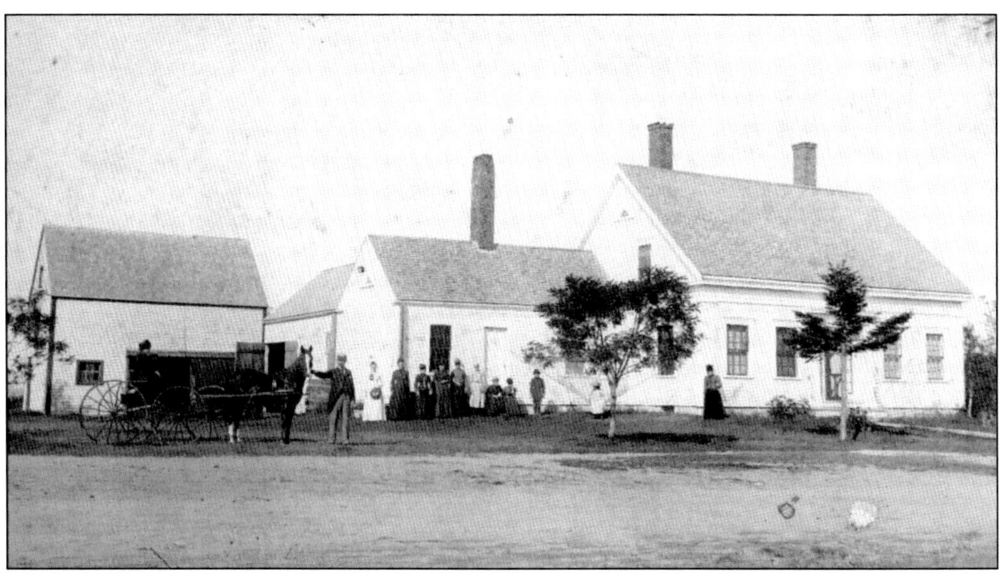

The parsonage of the First Baptist Church of Brooklin was built in 1856–1857 at cost of about $1,400. According to church records, the money was donated by "thirty three persons in varied amounts from five dollars to one hundred seventy-nine dollars." It has been continuously used as the home of the pastors of the church.

Catherine Herrick Hall (1842–1898) lived in the Arthur Herrick house and was owner, with her husband, George, of the Enterprise House, pictured on the previous page.

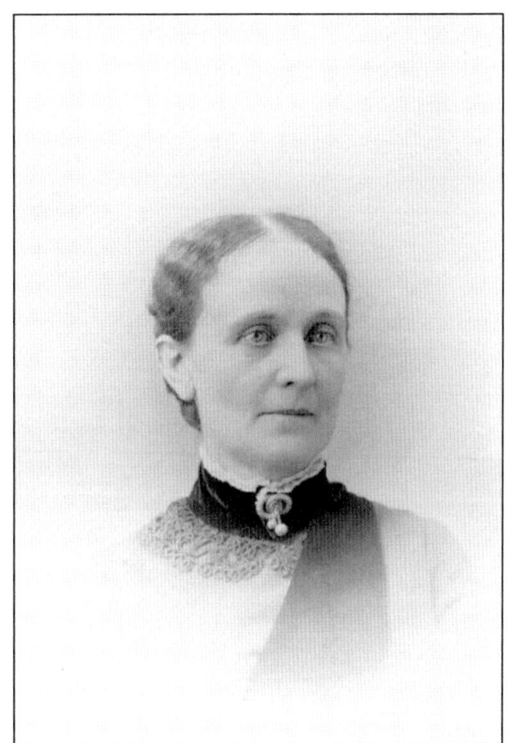

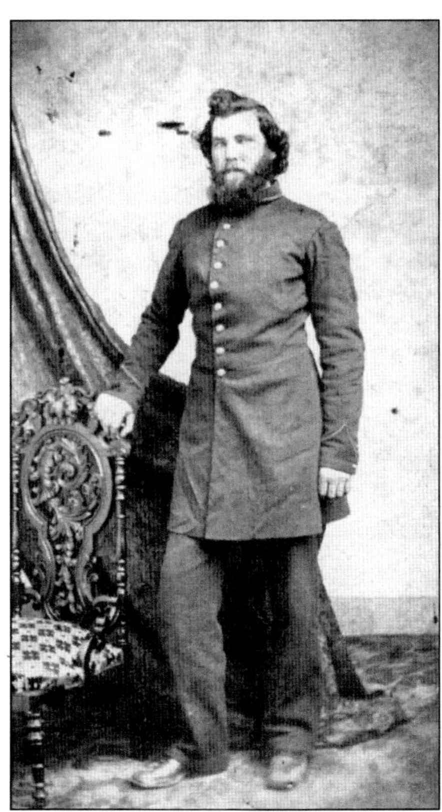

George C. Hall (1842–1923), the husband of Catherine Herrick Hall, was a Brooklin soldier in the Civil War before becoming a farmer and owner of the Enterprise House. During the war, he was taken prisoner and sent to Belle Isle in Richmond, Virginia.

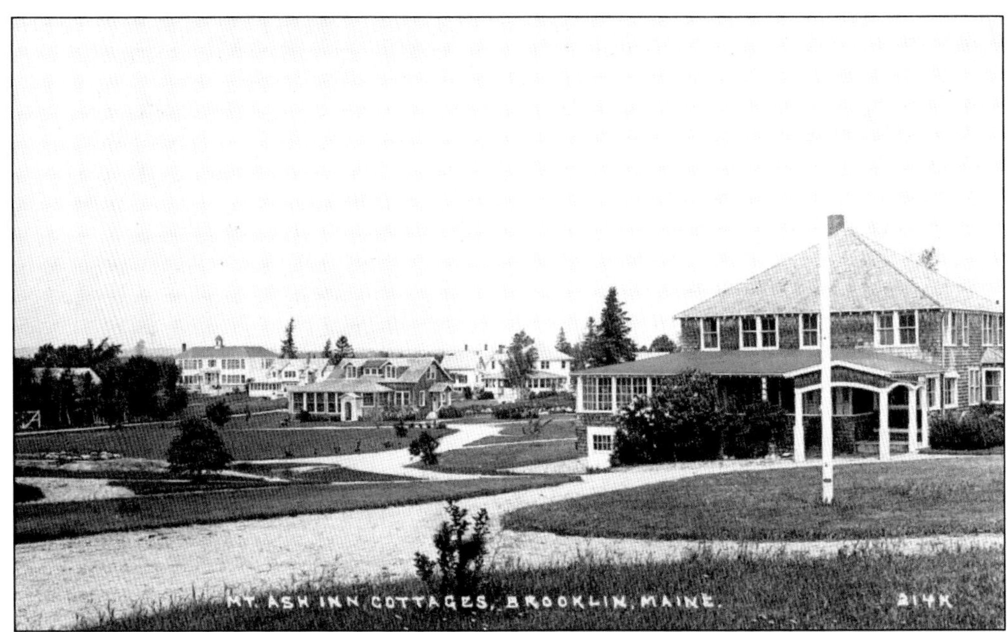

On the right is the Lilac Cottage of the Mountain Ash Inn, and in the center is the one named Clematis. In the far background are, from left to right, the third Brooklin High School (built in 1932) and the present Brooklin Inn. Today, this area is the town green, where Fourth of July celebrations are held.

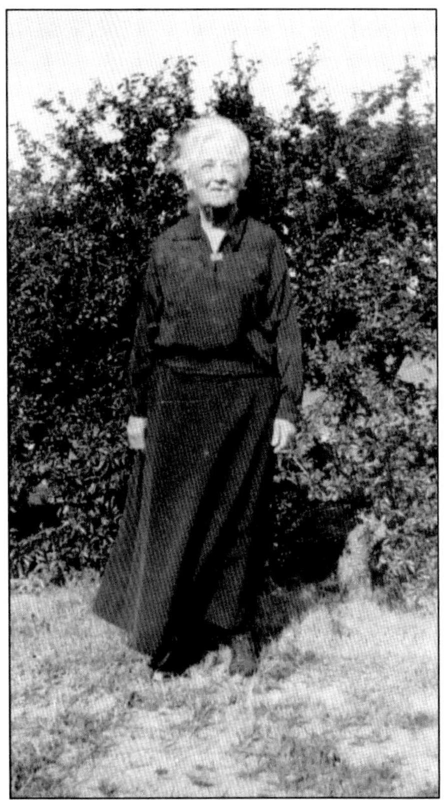

Isobel Lenman came to Brooklin from Washington, D.C. In 1920, she bought the Brooklin House building and the land behind it with a clear view to the harbor. She then added eight cottages and a saltwater swimming pool and established the Mountain Ash Inn. Many townspeople worked at the inn or enjoyed the pool and the suppers held there in the summer.

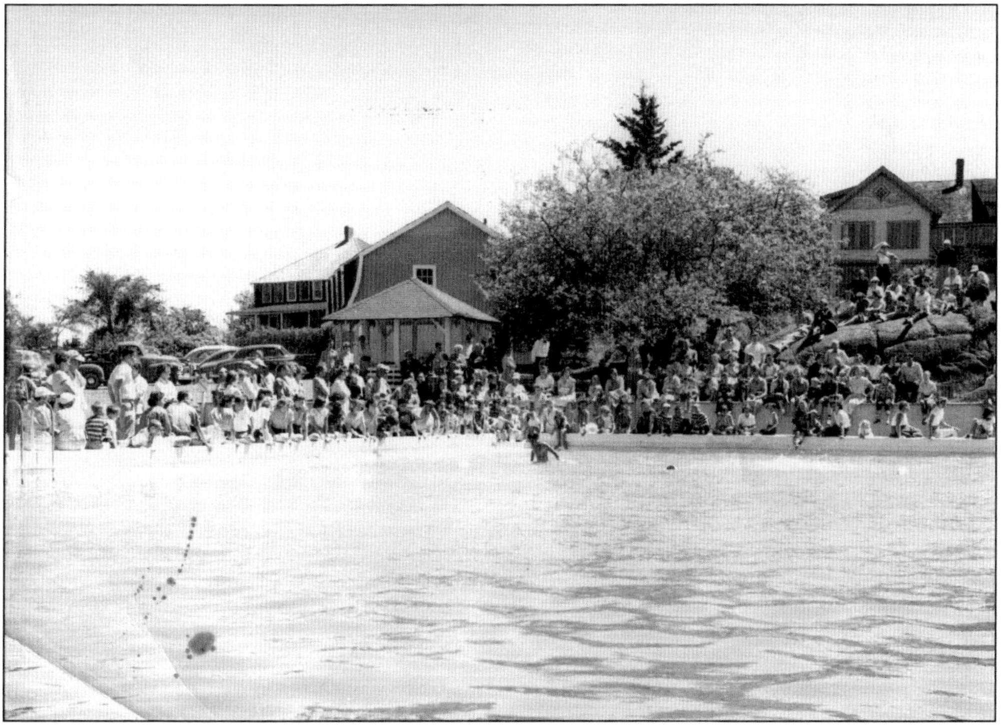

The pool at the Mountain Ash Inn was reputed to be the best saltwater swimming pool in Maine. The water was changed twice a day with the tides. In this view, folks are gathered to enjoy the waters. Behind the pool are cottages from the inn and the storage and mail building now referred to as "Old Town Hall."

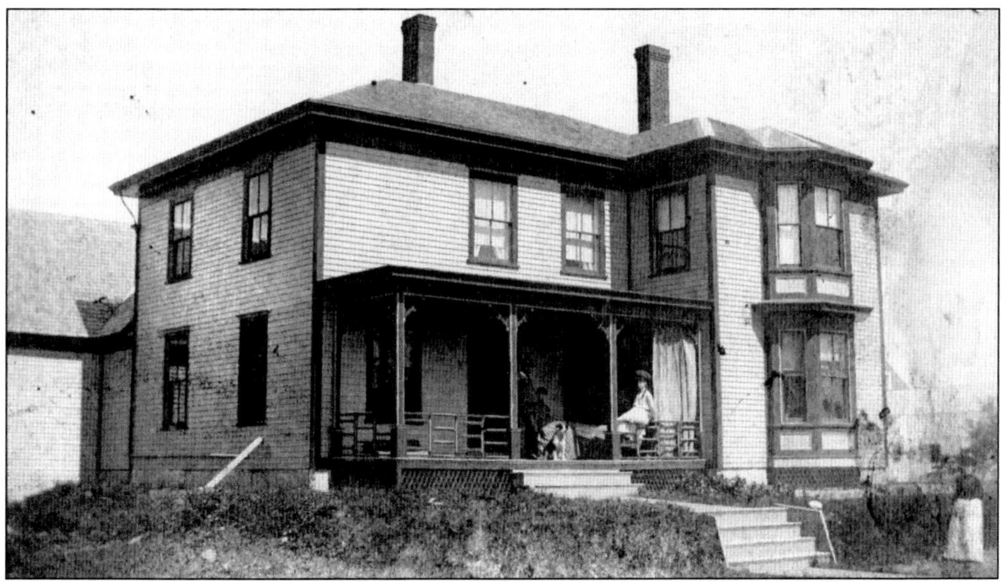

The Leslie and Charity (Freethey) Mitchell house stands at the corner of the Naskeag Point, Bay, and Reach Roads. It was previously owned by Naomi and Henry C. Allen and, at a later date, by Nancy (Mitchell) and Norton Smith.

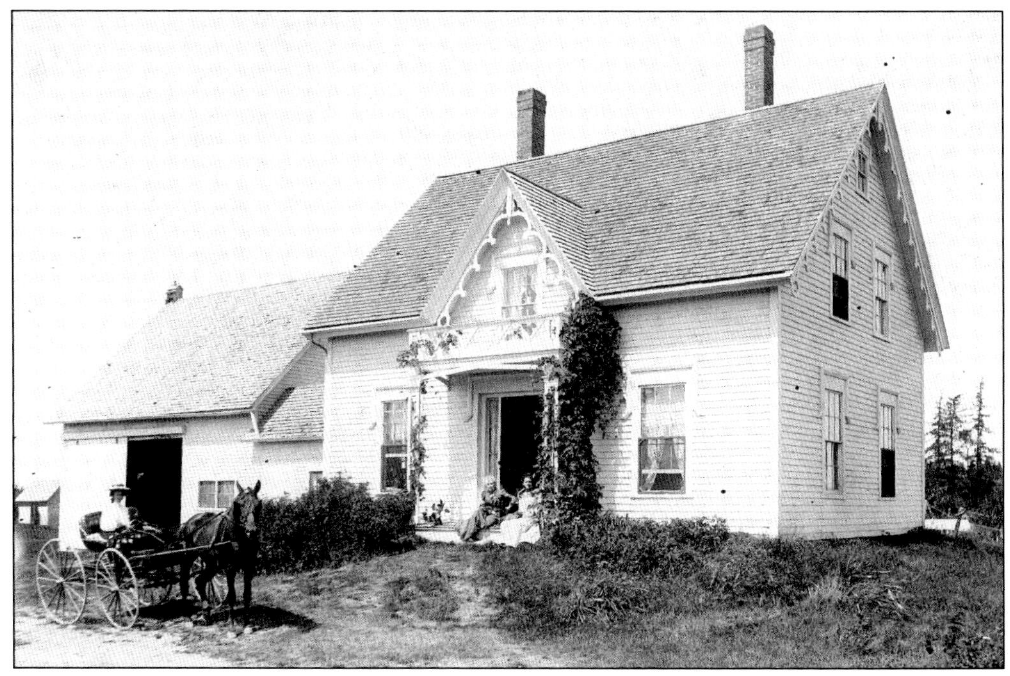

Now known as the Maples, this house in Brooklin Corner was once the Robert and Lydia Chase Tibbetts Friend house. Their daughter Gabriella married Amos Grindle, and Gabriella and Amos's daughter married George M. Allen. At one time, G. Frank Gott bought the house. His son George and George's wife, Dorothy Cole, lived there, as did Nellie Gott Gray. Today, Dorothy Jordan runs it as an inn.

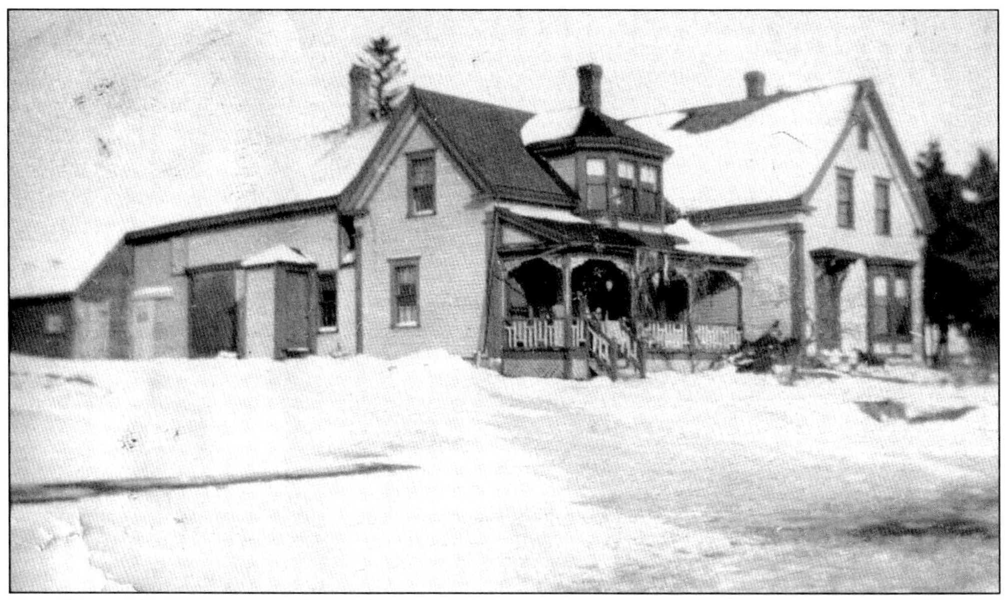

This house, heading away from the Corner toward Center Harbor, belonged to William E. and Anna (Grant) Herrick *c.* 1910. They were parents of Eva Herrick Phillips. At one time, Celia and Victor Bridges lived in an apartment there. In the 1940s, it was Arthur and Jennie Eaton's home.

Pictured here is the family of Frank and Lizzie Cole with their daughters, Rachel Cole (Cousins), standing in front, and Mary Cole (Smith), in the back. The Coles lived on the Naskeag Road, the second house from the corner, which was later the home of Mary and Wallace Smith.

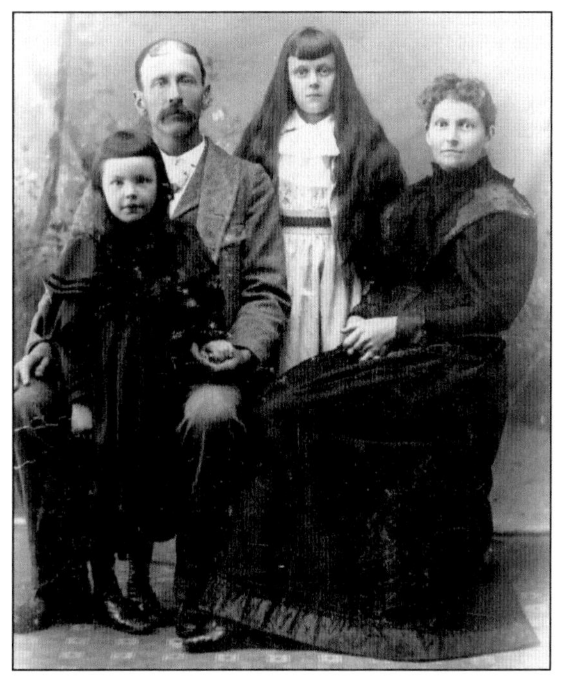

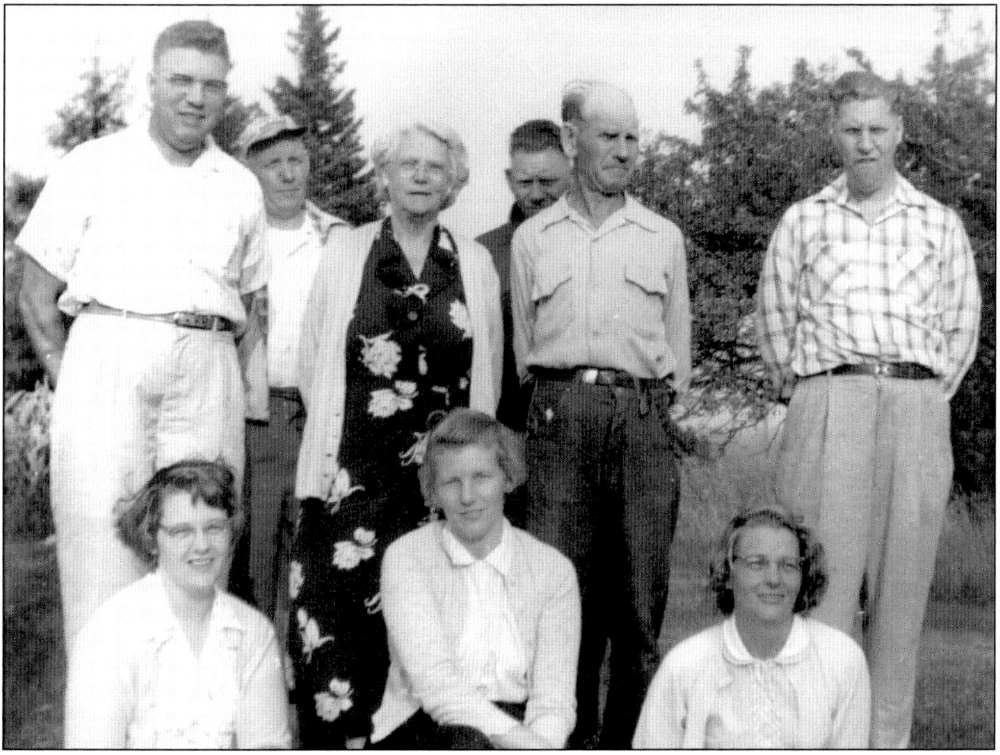

The Austin and Leona Staples family lived on the other side of Staples Corner, heading toward North Brooklin on Bay Road after the Old County Road. Pictured, from left to right, are the following: (front row) Marjorie, Alice, and Peggy Staples; (middle row) Chester, Leona, Austin, and Russell Staples; (back row) Kenneth and Arnold Staples.

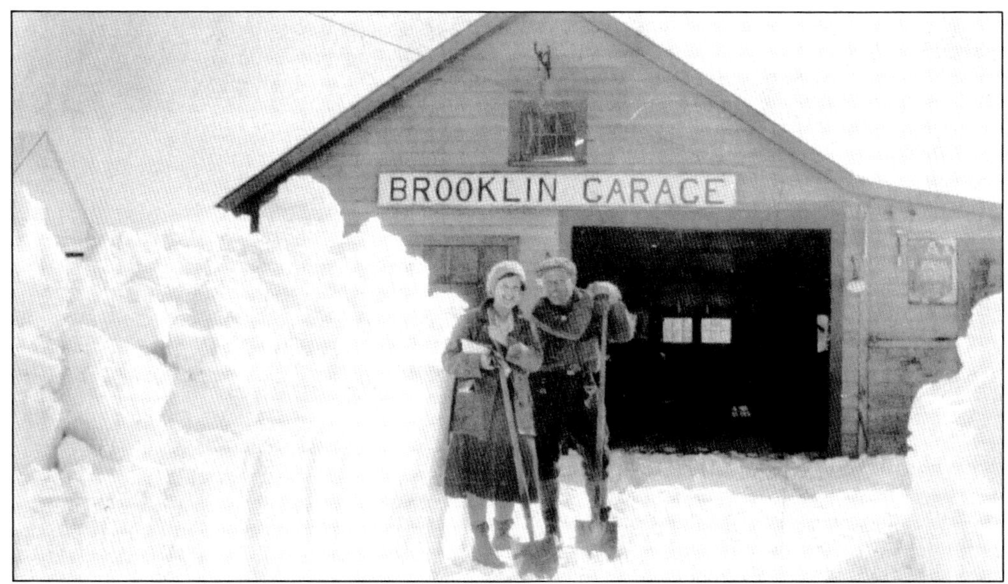

Alice and Tom Stanley are pictured in front of the Brooklin Garage, owned by Prin Allen Sr. It stood across from the house built by Alice's grandfather Arthur Herrick. This building later housed the Prin Allen Construction Company. Tom Stanley was the postmaster in Brooklin in the early 20th century and had a barbershop in town.

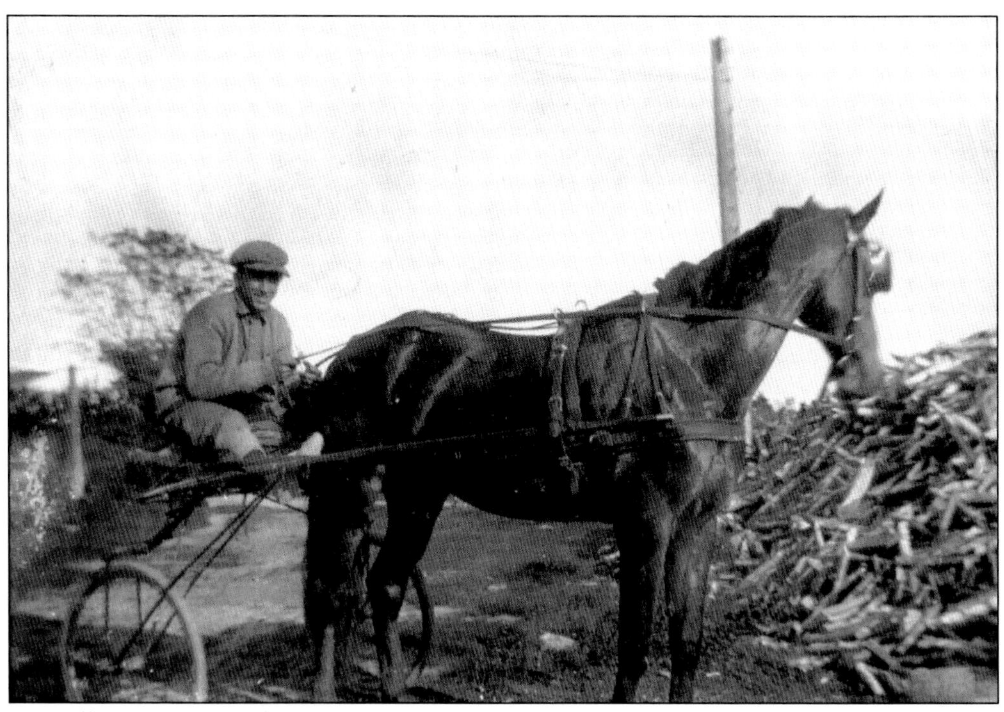

Prin Allen Sr. is pictured *c.* 1910 with his horse and buggy.

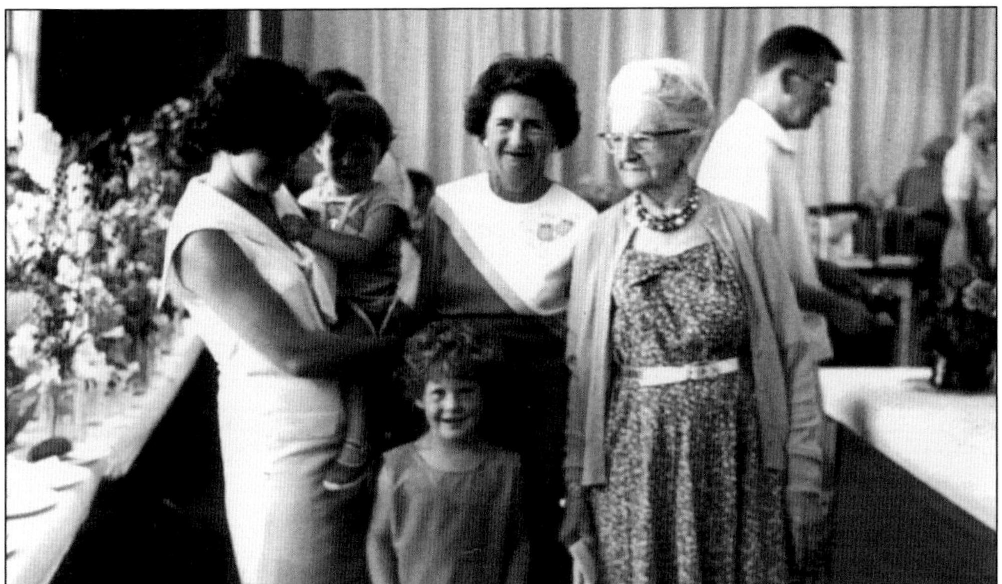

At the Brooklin Garden Club show in 1965, four generations of the Wilkins family are pictured. From left to right are Judy Fuller (holding Billy Fuller), Tracey Fuller (in front), Virginia Wilkins Fuller, and Ella McFarland Wilkins. The McFarlands lived on Old County Road.

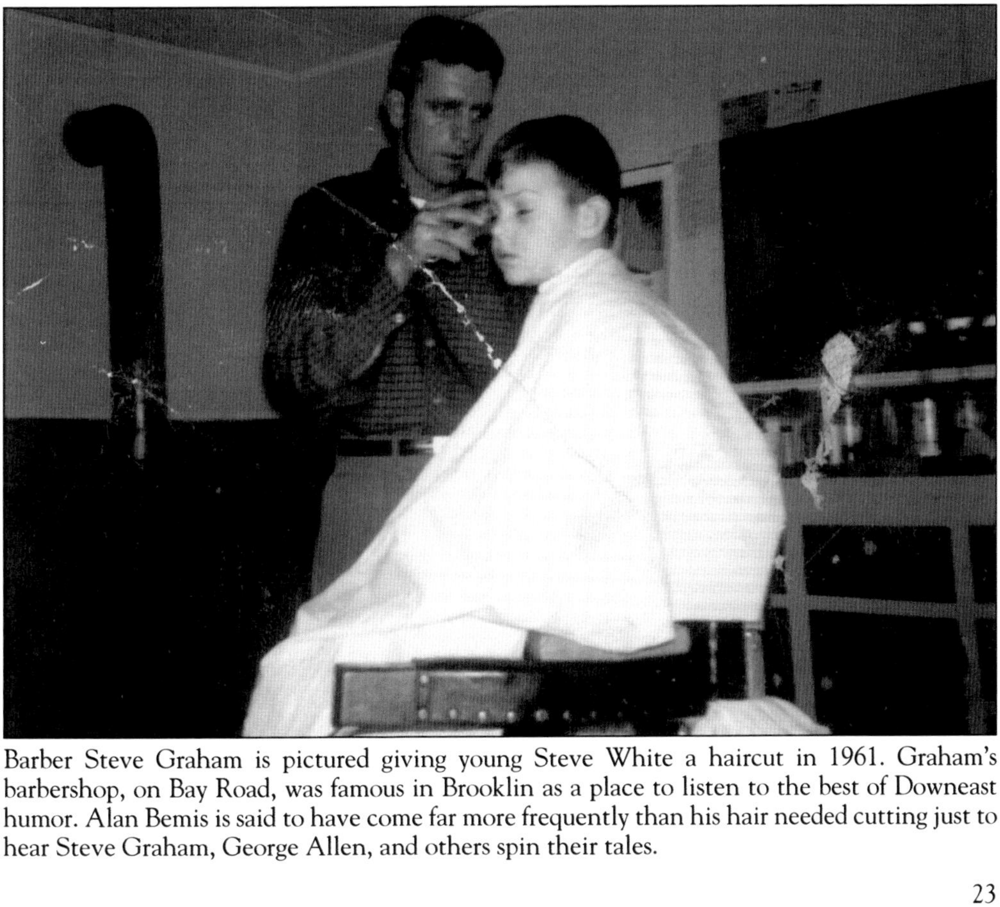

Barber Steve Graham is pictured giving young Steve White a haircut in 1961. Graham's barbershop, on Bay Road, was famous in Brooklin as a place to listen to the best of Downeast humor. Alan Bemis is said to have come far more frequently than his hair needed cutting just to hear Steve Graham, George Allen, and others spin their tales.

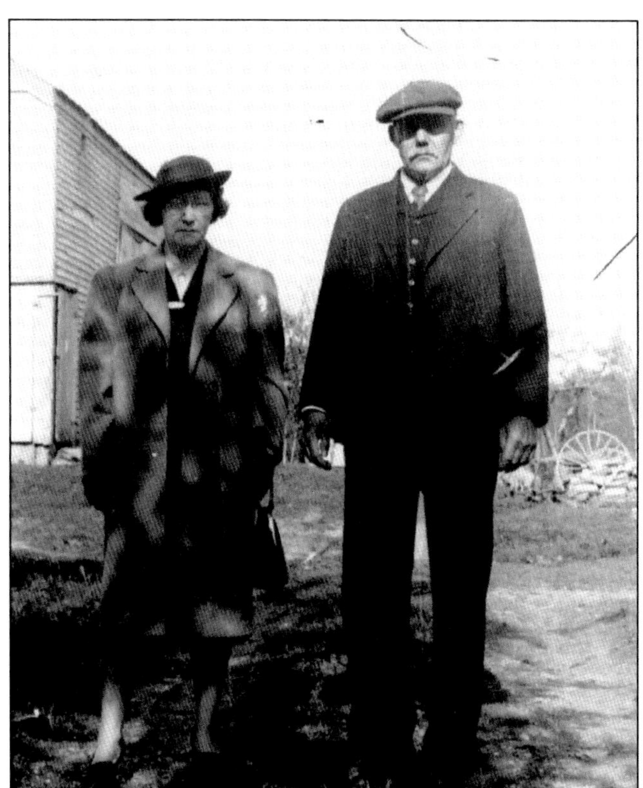

Wesley Cook Bartlett (1876–1948) and Evelyn M. Ober (d. 1974) lived on Old County Road, where they raised a family of nine children. After a devastating fire destroyed their home in 1945, they moved to North Brooklin near their daughter, Ruth Flye.

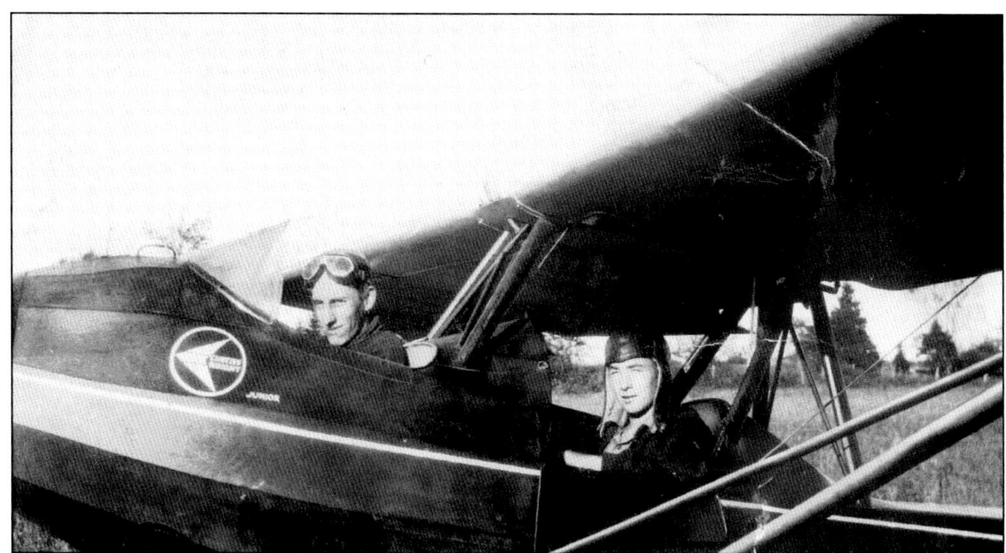

Reportedly, this is the first plane to land in Brooklin. Elmer Bent and Bill Allen are pictured in that plane in a field near the Bent home.

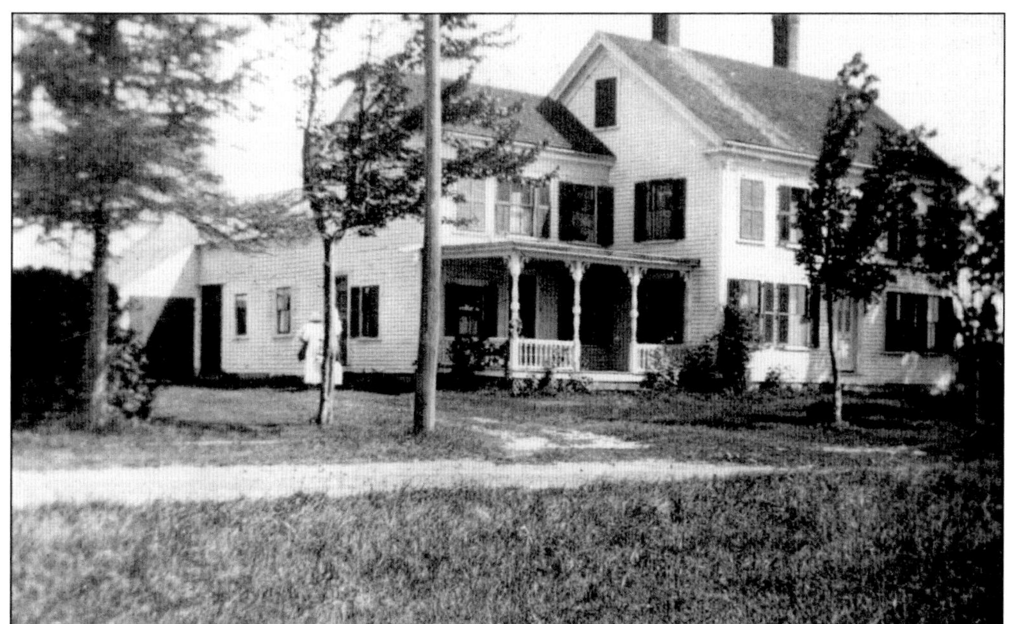

The Capt. Elijah Reed house was built *c.* 1850. On a trip to South America in 1856, Reed contracted yellow fever and had to turn the ship over to his mate. The ship was never heard from again. Reed then decided to become a merchant at Brooklin Corner with Nelson Herrick in 1865. In 1872, he moved his family to Virginia, where Reedsville is today. This house was later owned by the Reiss family.

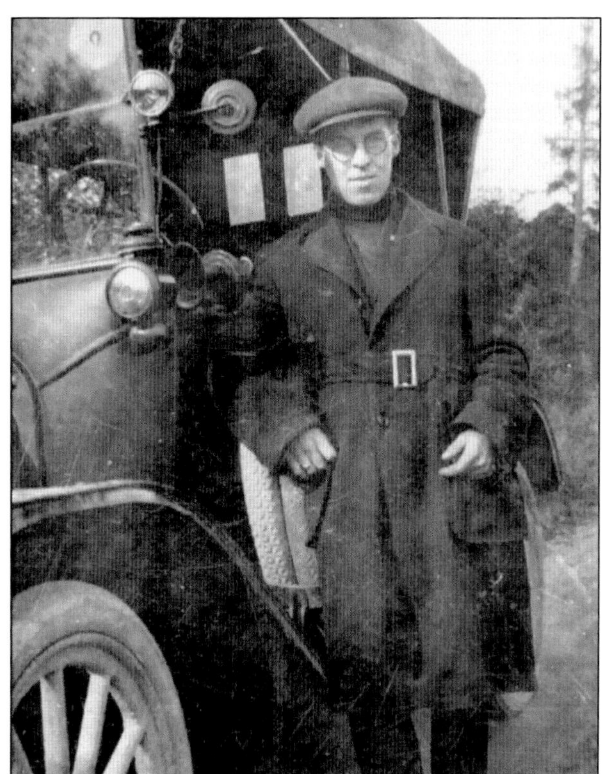

This is a picture of a proud Walter Gray in 1914 or 1915 with his first car, a Model T Ford. Gray was a carpenter who lived on the Naskeag Road in the house just before where the Barbett house is today. The father of Carlton and Belford Gray, he was also a bandleader and played the drums.

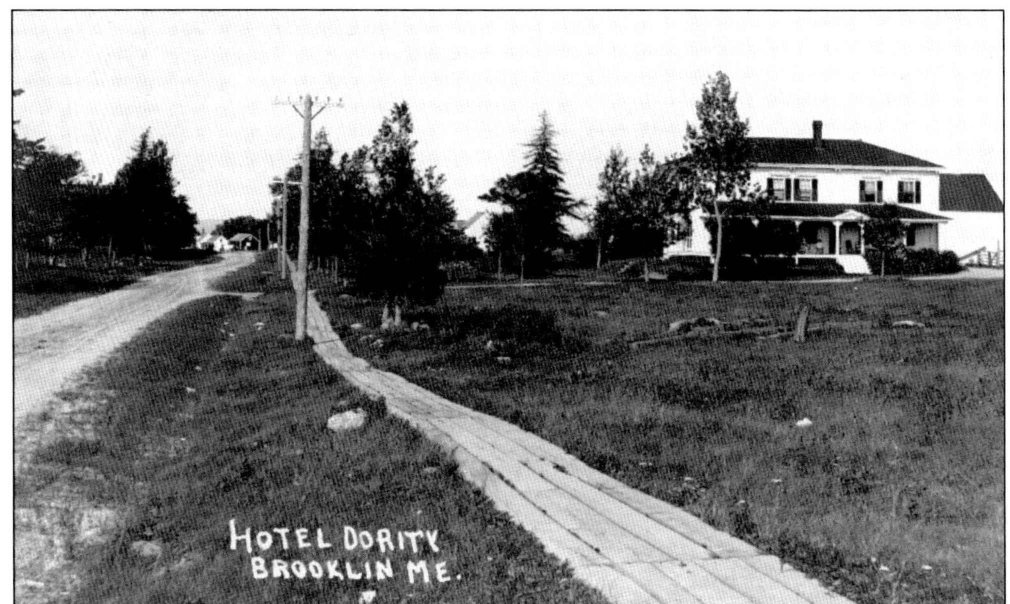

In 1890, the Hotel Dority, located next to the present town hall, was owned by George H. Dority and his wife, Johanna (Haskell) Dority. In the 1920s, it was purchased by Ernestine Tainter Crockett, who then ran it as the Crockett House. The wooden sidewalks, made of five planks across, are clearly seen in this postcard.

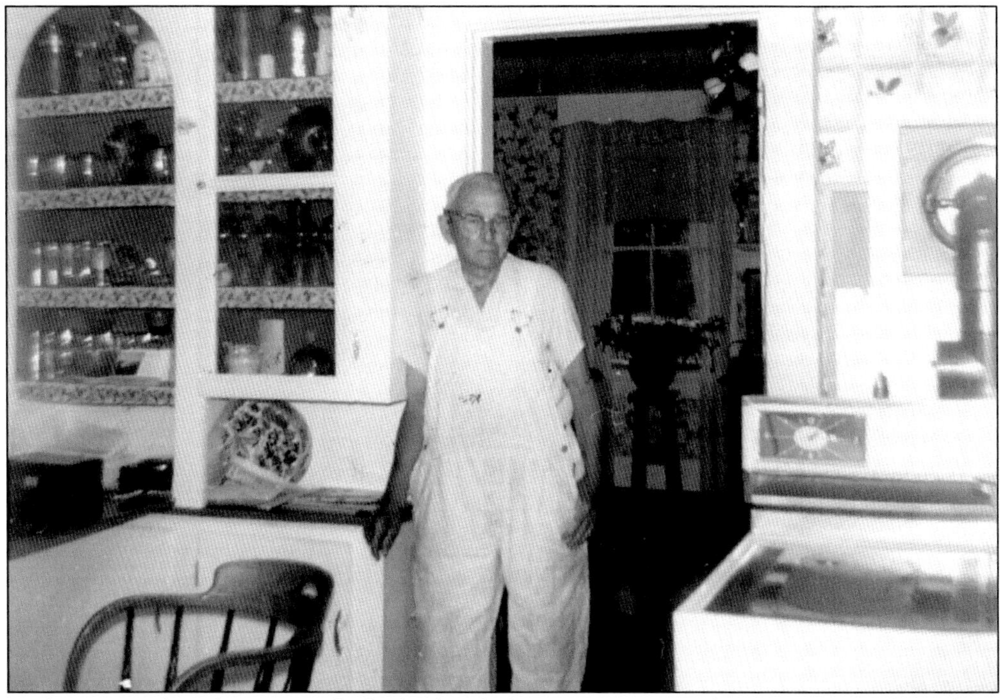

Walter S. Crockett (1881–1975), the husband of Ernestine Tainter (1884–1951), is shown here in the annex of the Crockett House. He was well known for his expert carpentry. Among his accomplishments are the Showles cottage in Center Harbor and the paneling in the J.R. Wiggins house in West Brooklin.

Two

Center Harbor

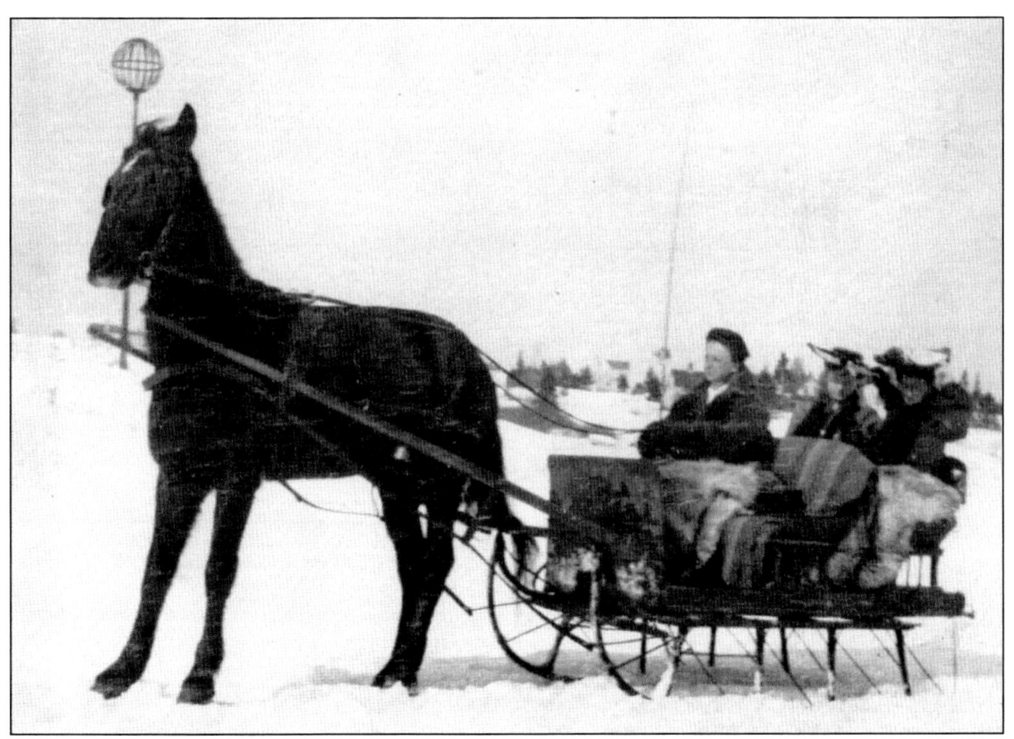

Annie Smith, driving Molly, is pictured taking some friends for a ride in her one-horse open sleigh in Center Harbor c. 1910.

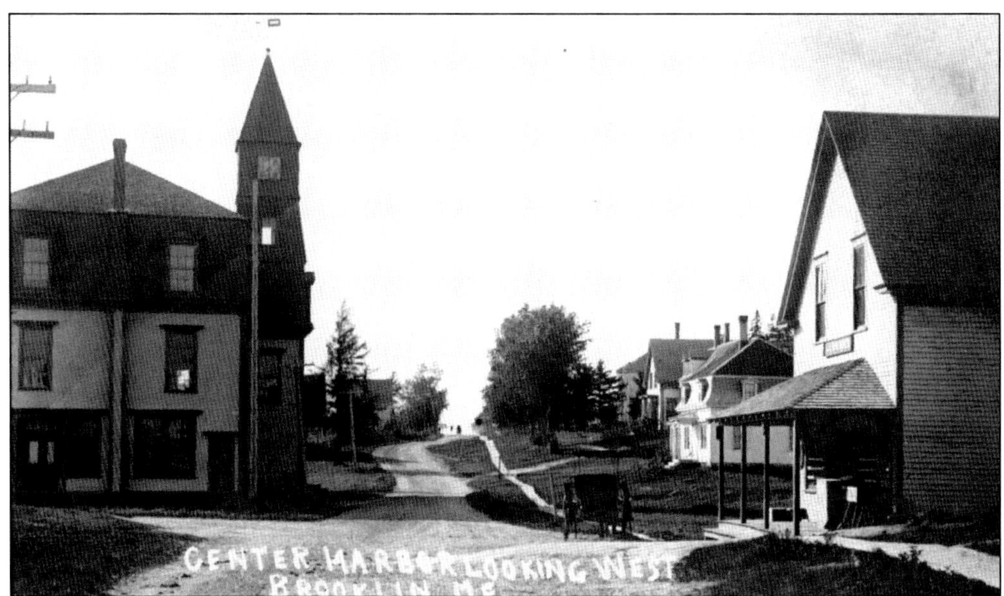

At the head of the Center Harbor Road, on the left, is the old Odd Fellows Hall. One half of the first floor was the store owned by Alfred Joyce and Leonell Flye. The other was Annie Dollard's notions and yard goods store. The second floor of the hall was used for many town events. Delia Tyler played the piano to accompany silent films there. The building across the street was at one time a custom house. Later, the Joyce and Flye store used it as an annex.

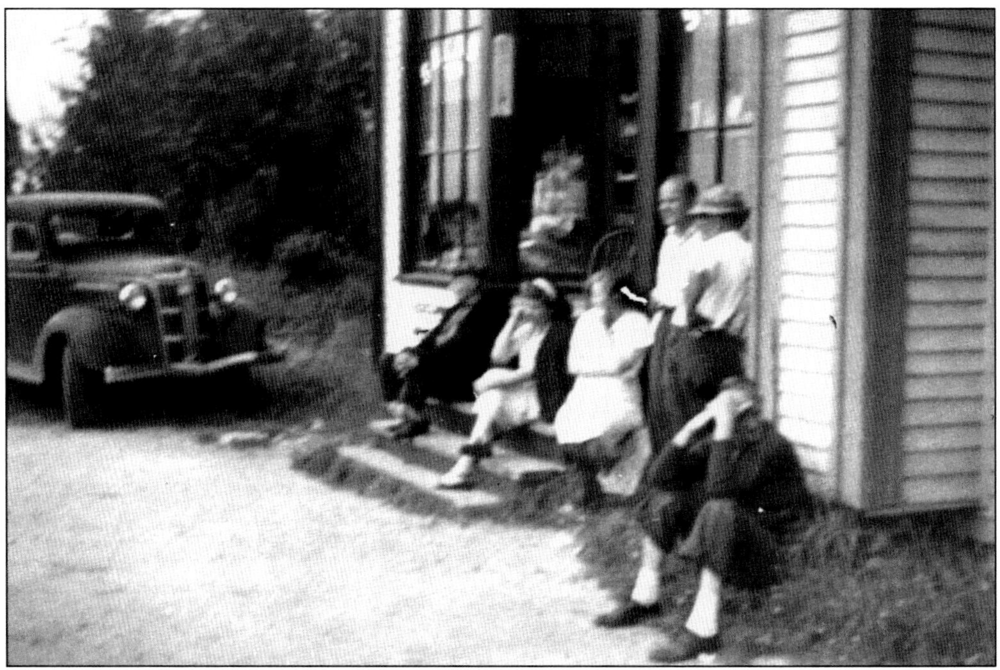

The Joyce and Flye store, in the first floor of the Odd Fellows Hall, was a favorite gathering place. This photograph shows a group on the steps outside the store.

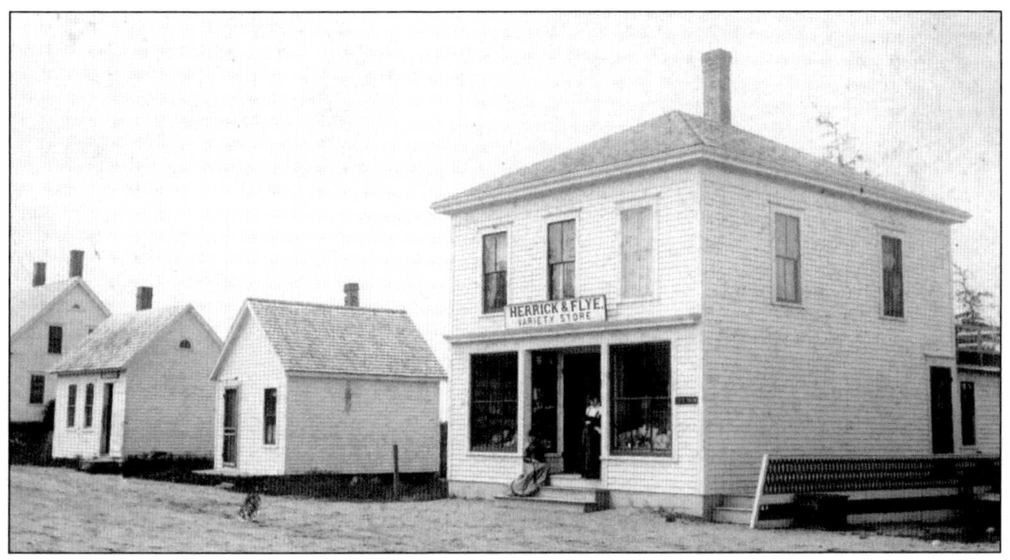

This building was the Herrick and Flye store. The little cottages are no longer there and are very similar to ones moved to the shore for housing the factory workers.

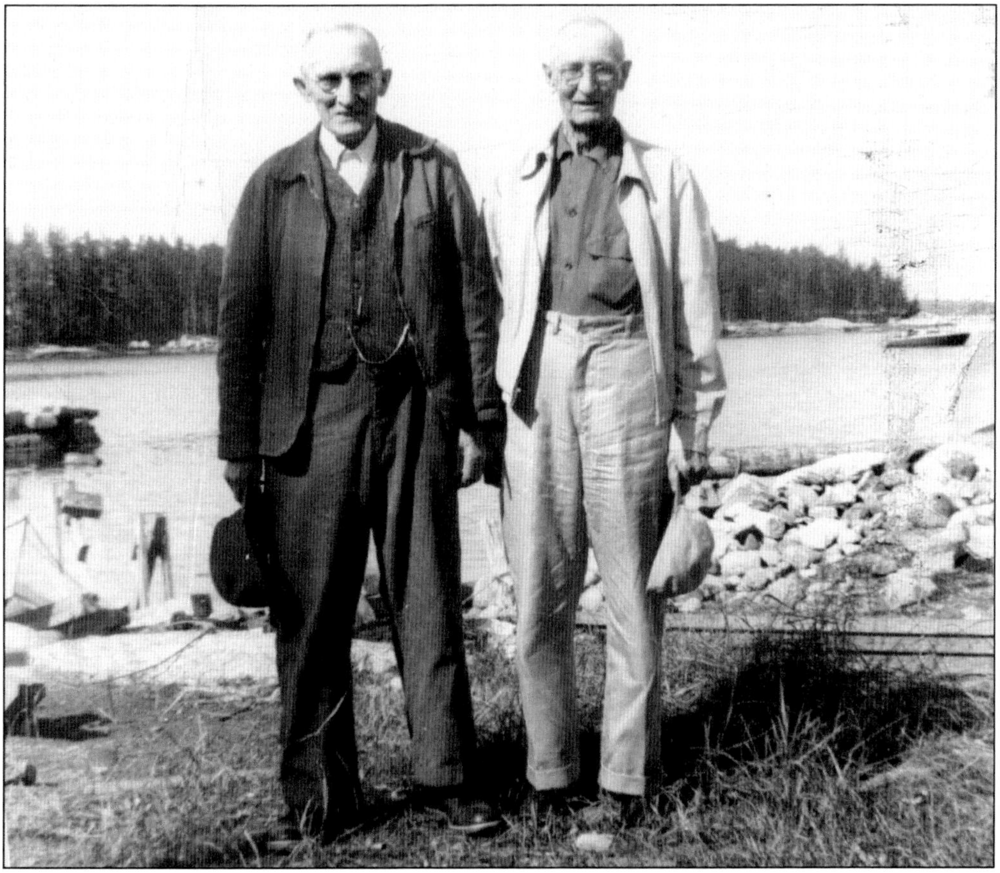

On the left is Alfred Joyce, owner of the Joyce and Flye store, and on the right is Roland Carter. Joyce's daughter Laura married Leonell Flye.

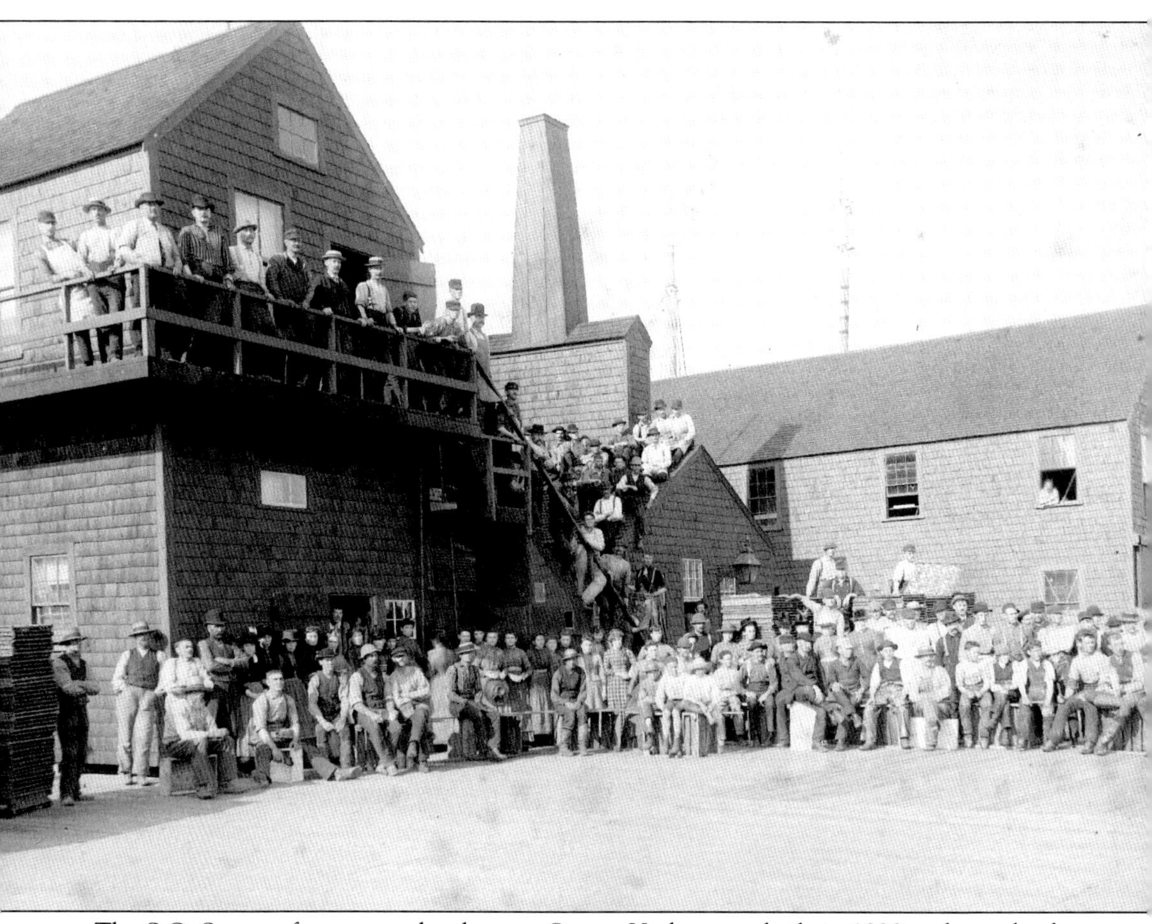

The S.G. Stevens factory, on the shore at Center Harbor, was built in 1890 and was the first factory to can sardines in Brooklin. As can be seen in this picture, the factory employed many workers. In 1902, A.E. Farnsworth bought the factory and added clams to the line of canned goods. Farnsworth also set up weirs at Flye Point.

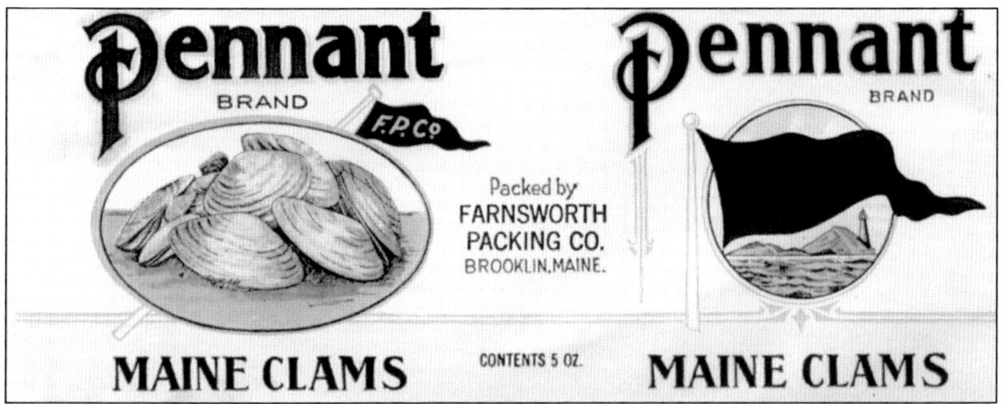

The Pennant label was used by the A.E. Farnsworth Packing Company, in operation from 1902 to 1923.

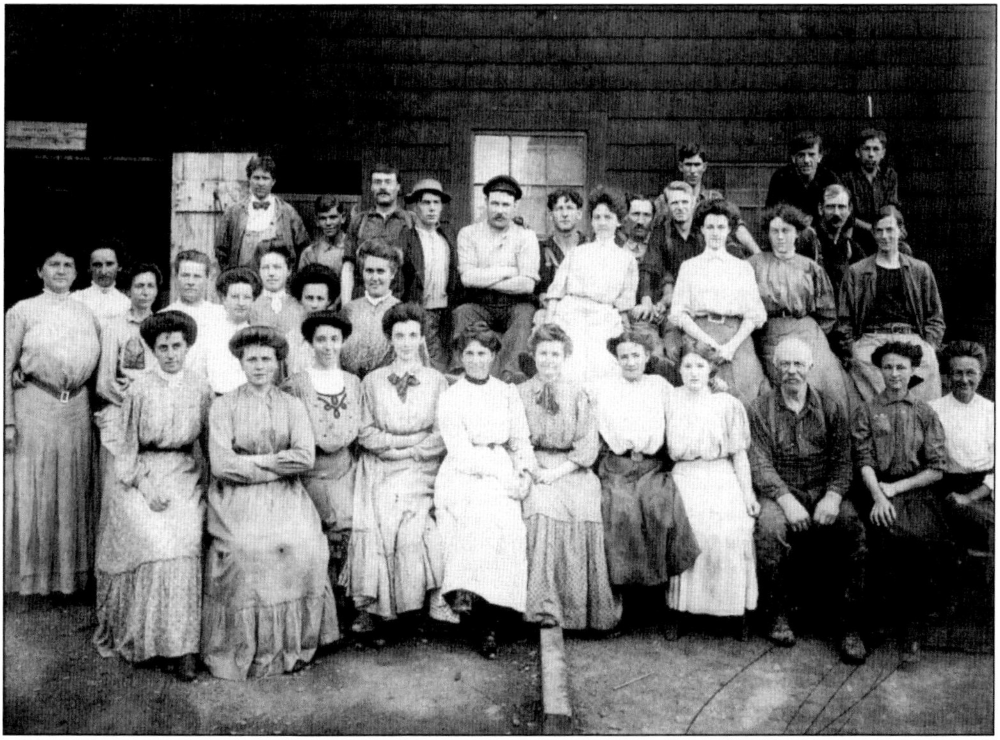

In the early 1900s, some of the A.E. Farnsworth workers included Charles Tyler (head of the packing room), William Cousins (in charge of the sealing room), and Horace Pease (director of labeling). The captains of the fishing boats were Herbert Tapley, Granville Phillips, and Fred Stewart. Howard Closson drove the truck that brought the workers. Melvin Sellers was the night watchman, and Victor Bridges was the head of cartoning.

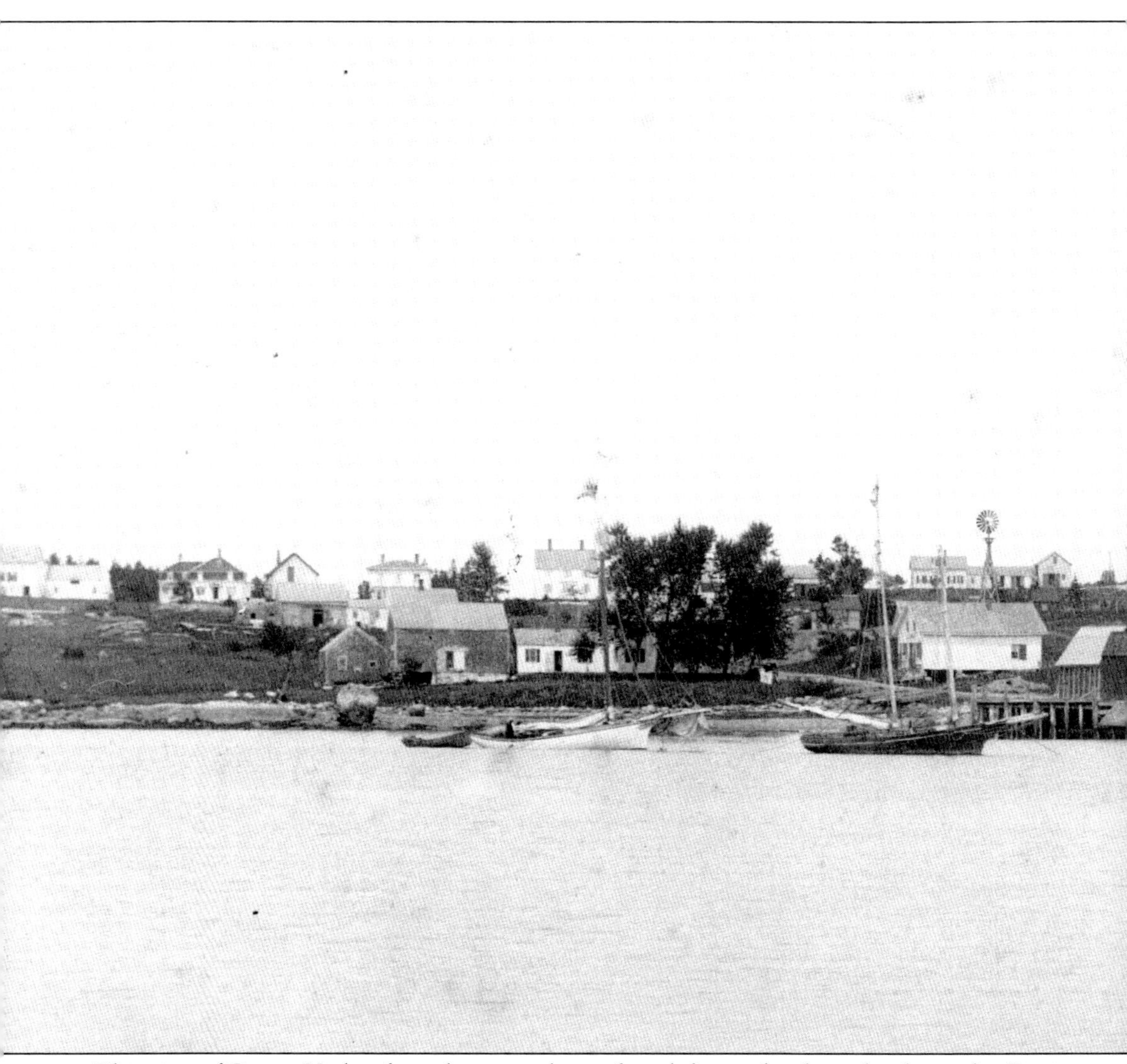

This view of Center Harbor from the water shows, from left to right along the shore, the Carrie and Melroy Flye house, the boatyard road, an unidentified white building, workers cottages, and the factory buildings. Along Reach Road above can be seen, from left to right, the Kane place, a place that burned, Bessie Allen's house, three unidentified structures, the John C. Tibbetts

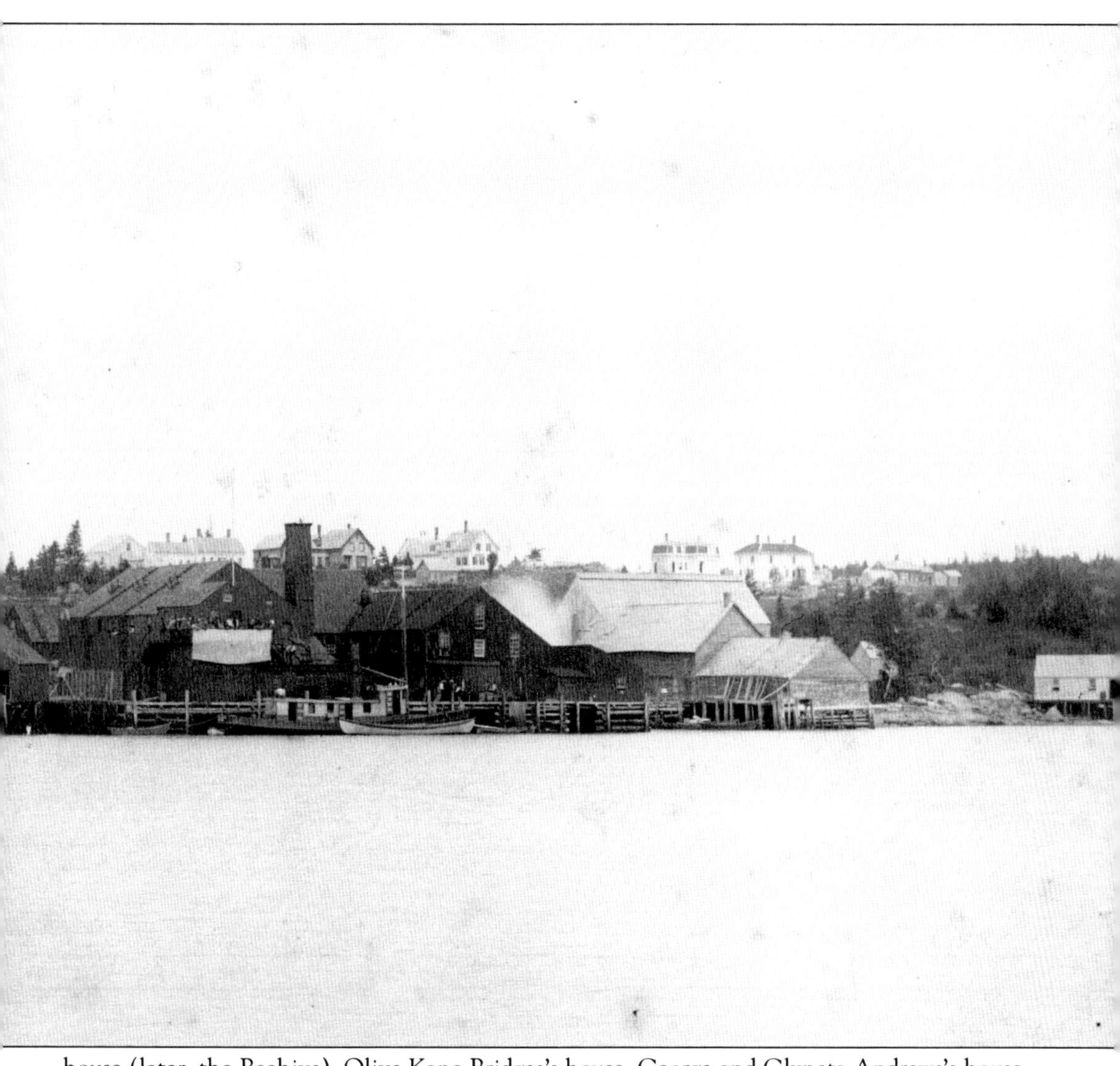

house (later, the Beehive), Olive Kane Bridges's house, George and Glyneta Andrews's house, two unidentified structures, B.O. Dollard's house, perhaps the Stewart house, the Oscar Ford house, and an unidentified house.

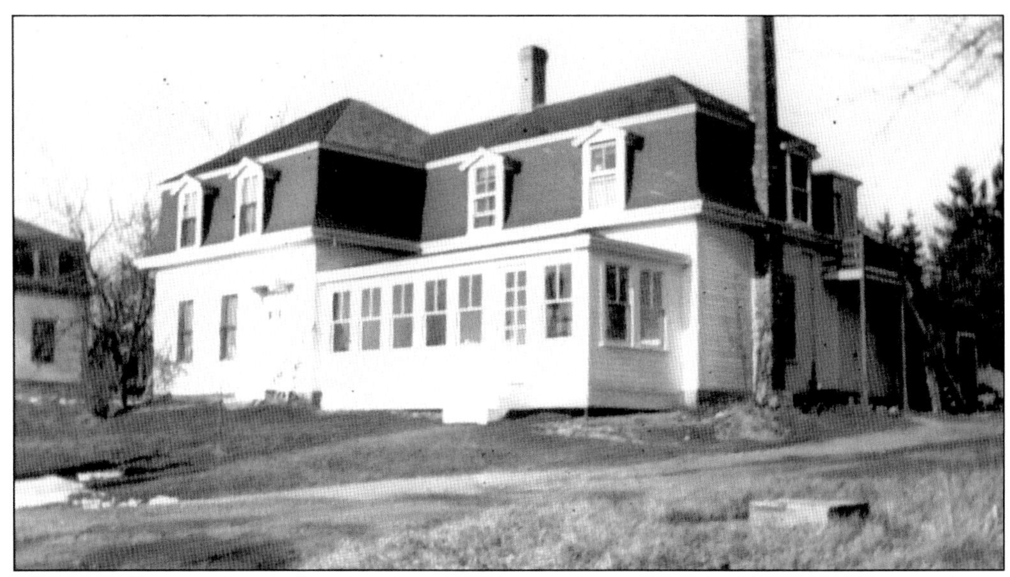

This is the Harry and Laurel Bridges house on Reach Road. Harry had a garage where, with the help of others, he built Brooklin's first fire truck. This is now the boatyard of Eric Dow.

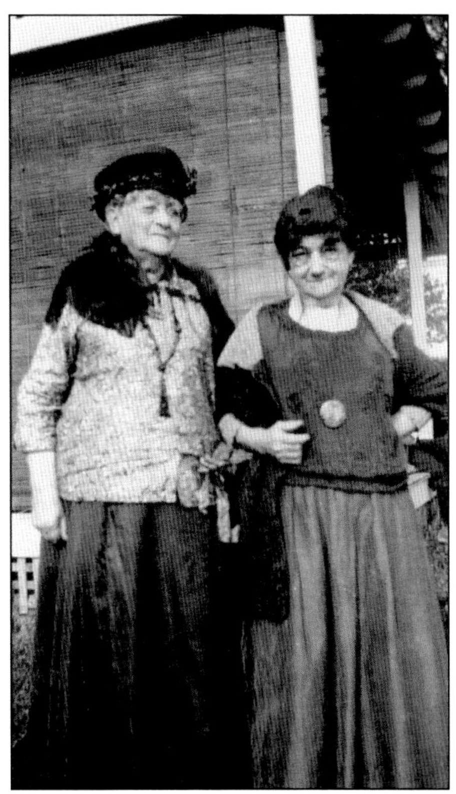

Pictured on the left is Annie Herrick Babson, the mother of Carrie Herrick Flye, on the right. When this picture was taken *c.* 1930, Babson was in her 90s. Flye, the wife of Melroy Flye, ran a hotel on the shore at Center Harbor.

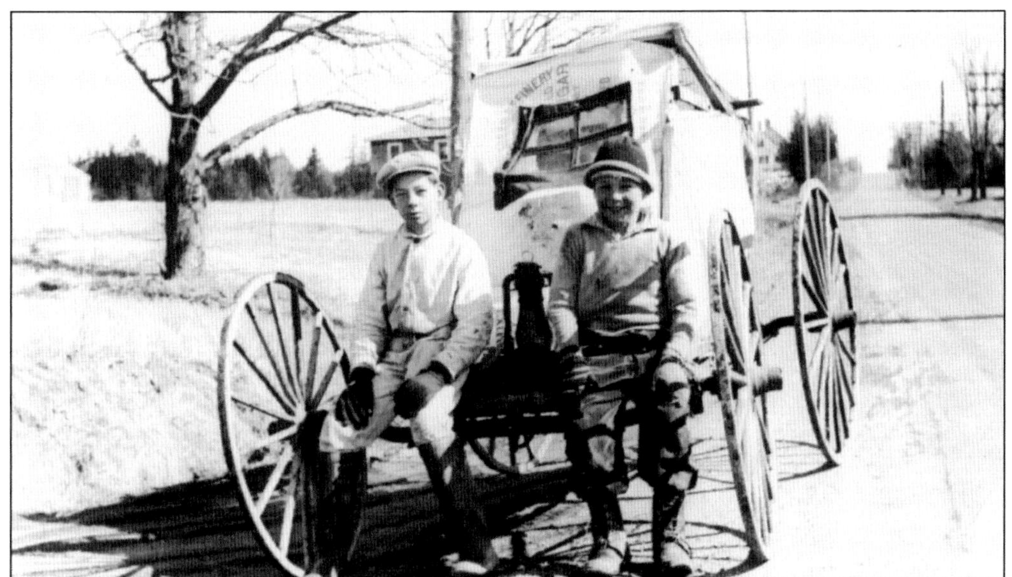

Young Royce Gray (left) and Avery Tyler are pictured sitting on the front of what appears to be a merchant's wagon. The wagon is located at the foot of York's Hill.

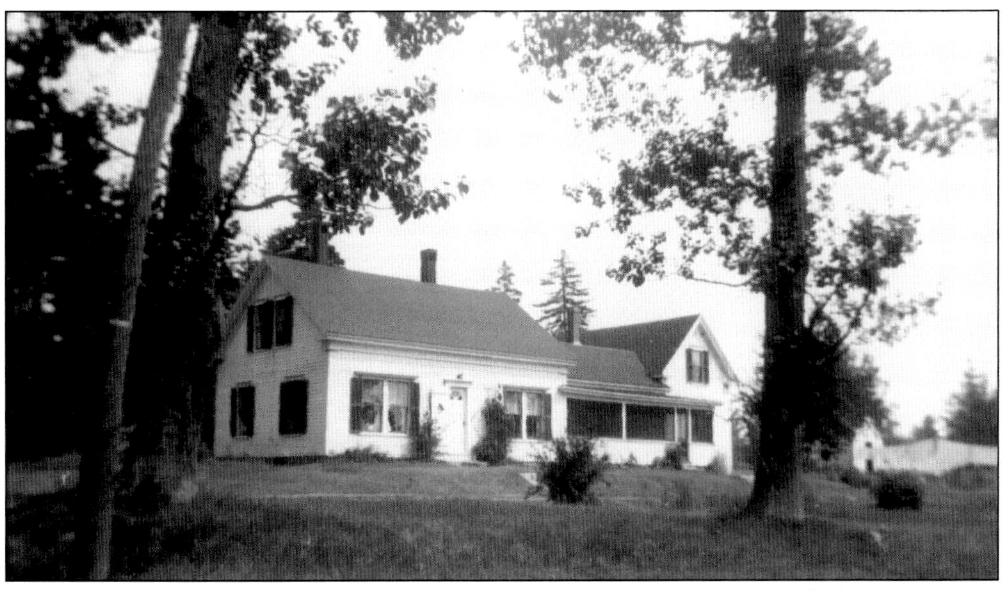

Formerly the home of Geneva Babson, this house belonged to Eldorus and Belle (Blake) Bridges. Later, it belonged to librarian Martha Tyler and her husband, Howard, and then to Jon Wilson.

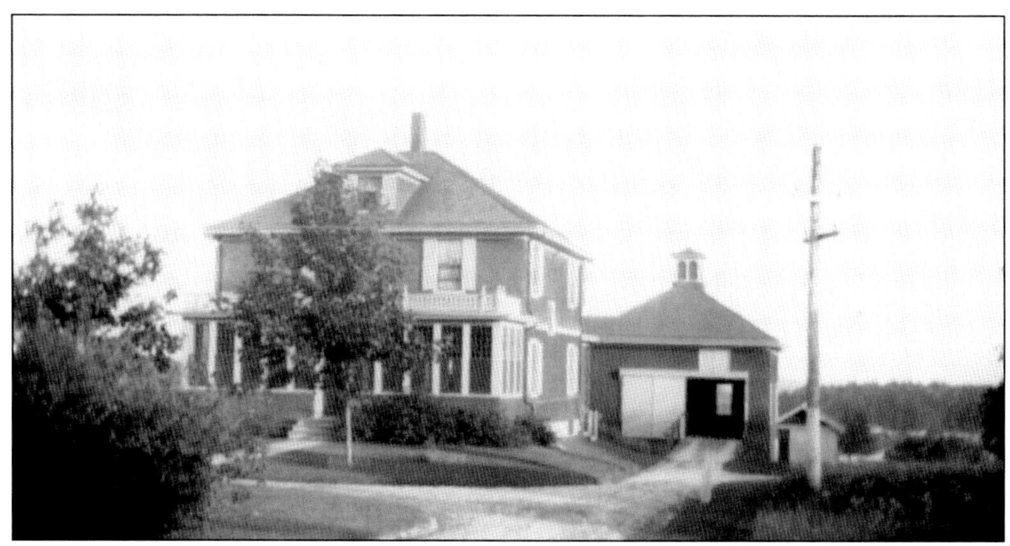
Between 1902 and 1923, this house belonged to sardine factory owner Alton E. Farnsworth and Edith (Mayo) Farnsworth. It is now the Emory Estate.

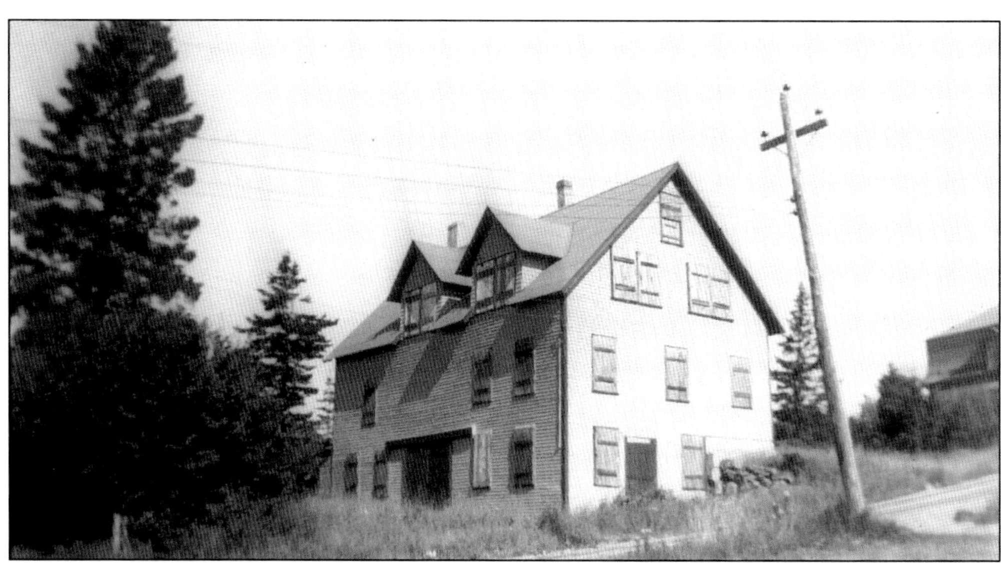
This building, located next to the Odd Fellows Hall, housed apartments and a blacksmith shop. Maynard Blaisdell did horseshoeing in the basement. Delia and Roy Tyler raised a large family in the upstairs apartment, and Louise and Rocky Rockwell had a restaurant there. In recent years, it was known as Stedman's Take-Out. The building has since been torn down.

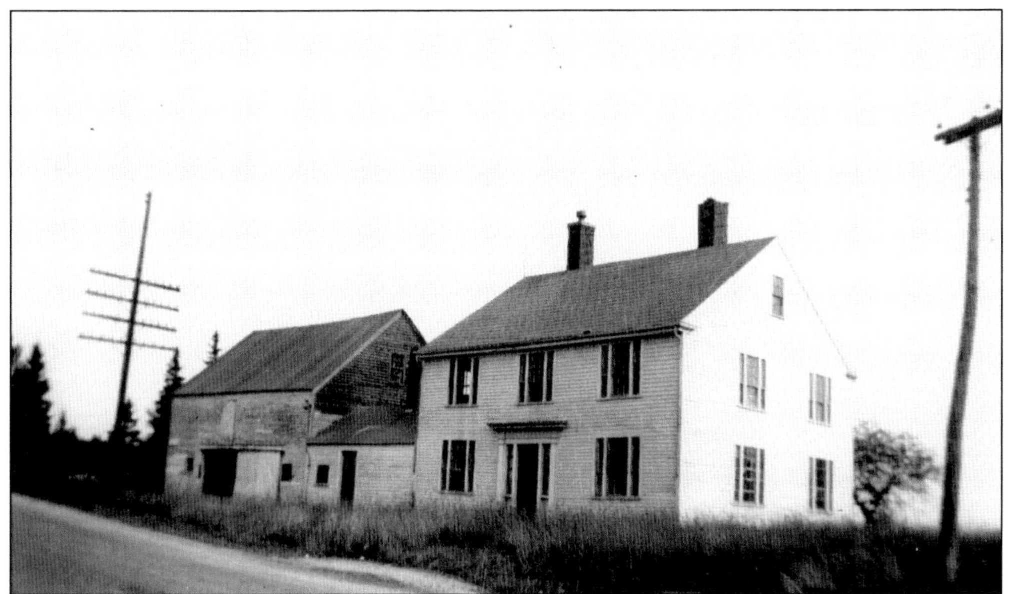

The Beehive, a boardinghouse in the early 20th century, was located across from the Odd Fellows Hall on land originally owned by A.J. Tibbets, master of the brig *Mary Means*. Capt. John C. Tibbetts, master of the schooner *Monitor* and the brig *Gulnare*, built the house *c.* 1830. John C. Tibbetts was the state legislator who fought for the town's separation from Sedgwick.

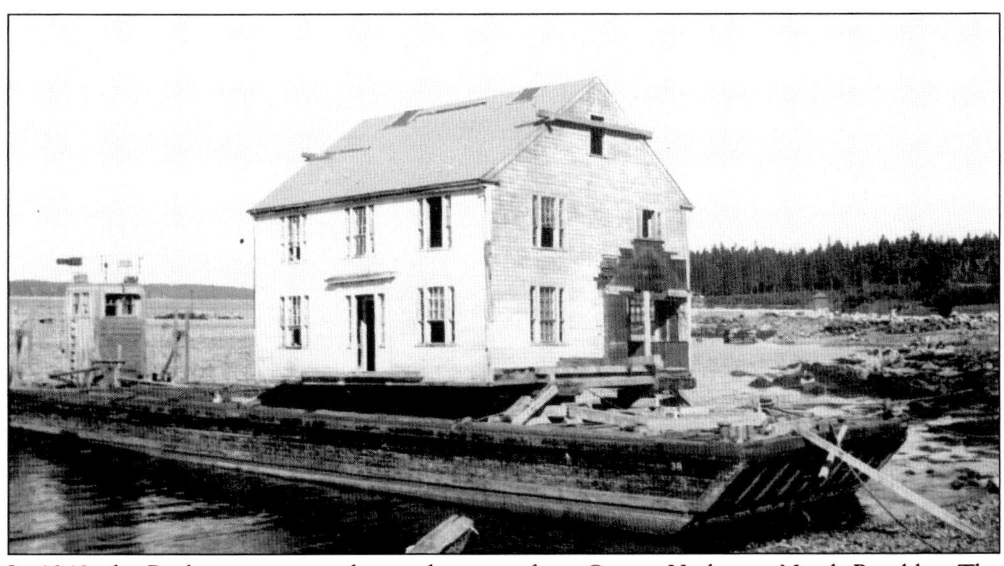

In 1948, the Beehive was moved over the water from Center Harbor to North Brooklin. The house is pictured here in 1948 on the 113-foot St. Regis Paper Company barge at the harbor shore. It was moved to the shore on two 40-foot-long, 12- by 12-inch timbers imported from the West. Captain Closson's tugboat *Ellen & Roy* pulled the barge for the 17-mile trip.

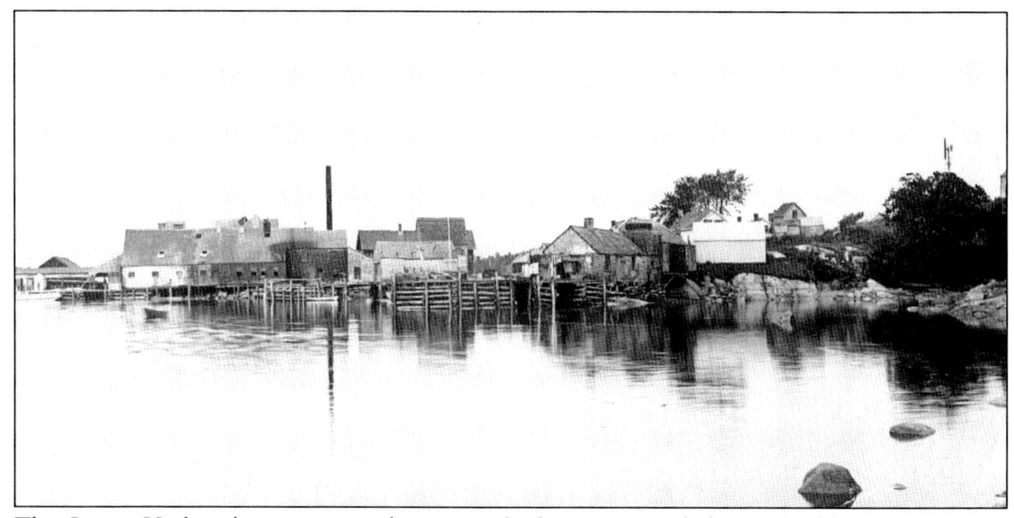

The Center Harbor shore is pictured in a view looking west, with factory buildings visible from another angle. In 1938, Frank Sylvester and Frank Day bought the Ramsdell sardine factory and started a boatyard. Arno Day, Frank Day's son, rented buildings there for the same purpose. Joel White joined Arno Day. In 1962, White bought the buildings and the land and established the Brooklin Boat Yard.

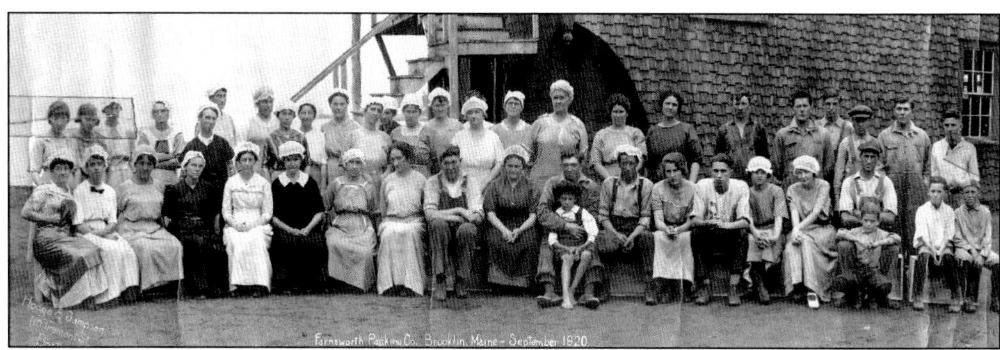

This 1920 photograph shows a group of workers at the A.E. Farnsworth Packing Company. Seated in the front row are, left to right, unidentified, Etta Bridges Sawyer, Eulalia Bridges, unidentified, Celestia or Mintie Seavey, Etta Kane, Mary Allen Freethey, three unidentified, Billy Young (holding small boy), two unidentified, Herbert or Fred Tyler, ? Freethey, Beulah Crockett, unidentified, and three unidentified boys. In the middle row, the only one identified is Ernestine Crockett, standing fifth from the left and wearing all white. In the back row are, from left to right, six unidentified, Eva Herrick Phillips, Anna Herrick, unidentified, Lizzy Duffy Staples, Cora May Bridges, Maude Hooper, Hattie Tyler, Maud Beatty, and two unidentified.

Three

Haven

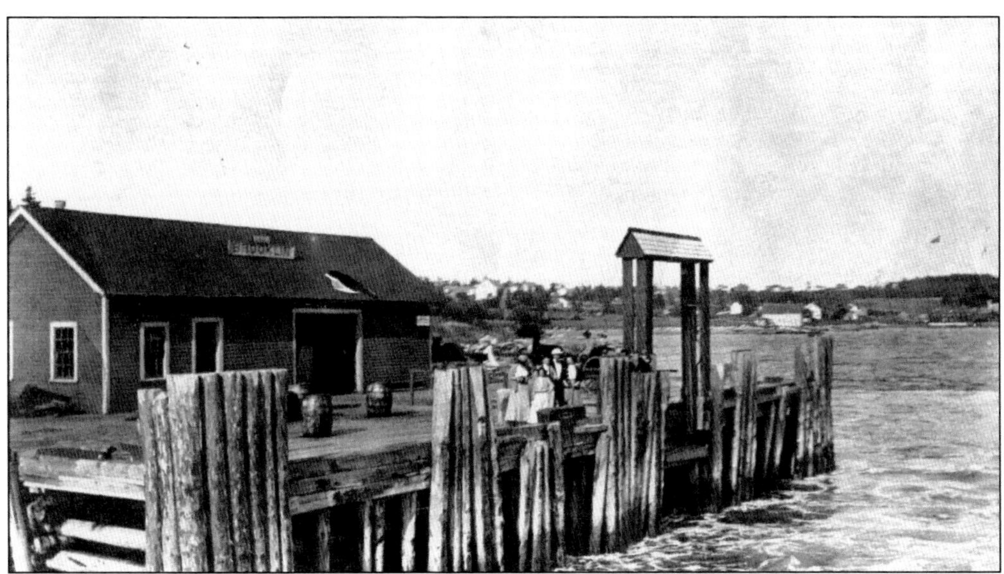

The Brooklin Steamboat Wharf in Haven made connections to Boston through Rockland. Steamboats also stopped at Deer Isle, North Brooklin, South Blue Hill, Surry, Bar Harbor, and Swan's Island. At one time, there were two arrivals and departures daily. Steamboats brought in mail, groceries, and supplies and steamed out with the products from the fish-packing factories nearby in Center Harbor.

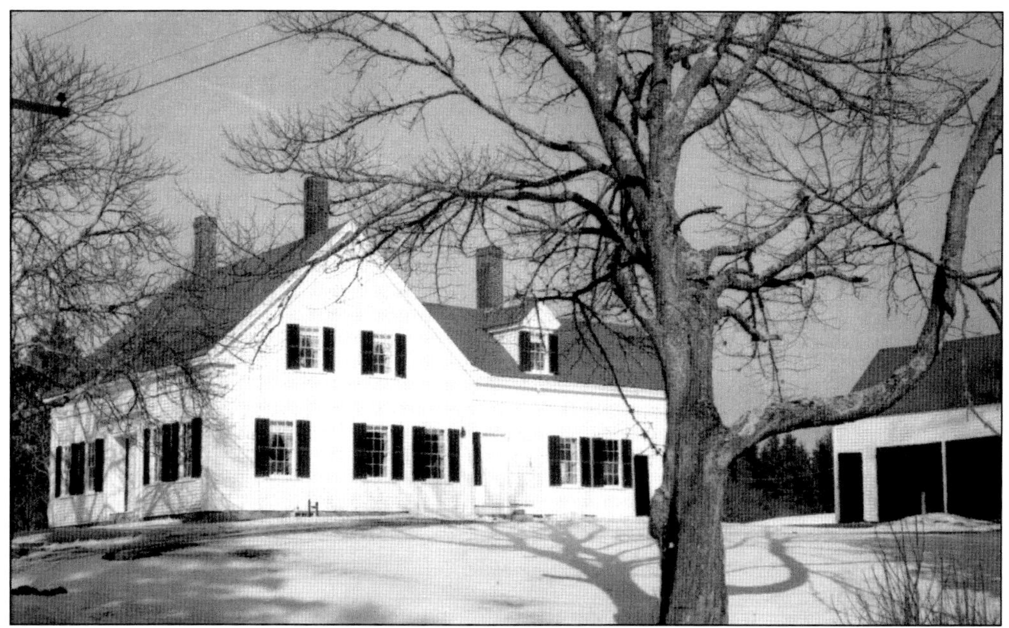

Known as Evergreen Farm, the Harvey and Emma Wells house in Haven was built by Harvey's grandfather Warren in 1851. Warren was the husband of Mary Ann Herrick.

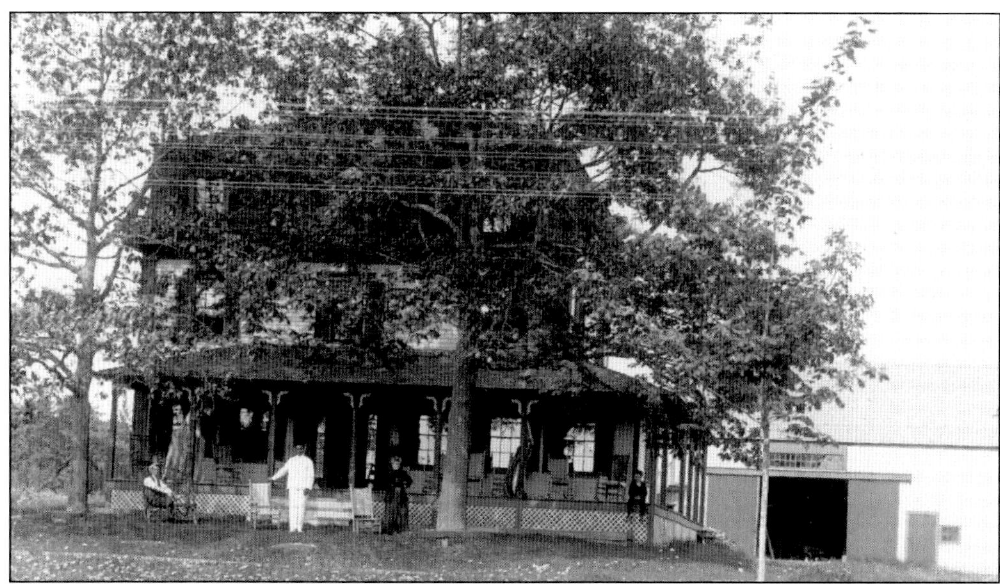

Pine Crest, an inn next to Evergreen Farm, was owned by J.L. Wells in the late 1890s. It served mostly the visitors at Haven Colony and, perhaps, the "drummers," who were salesmen who came to Brooklin to drum up their wares. A private residence occupies the site today.

Grace Mayo Wells was the wife of Rufus Wells and the mother of Irene Wells. Her home, built by Humprey Wells, was given to her daughter Irene and, most recently, belonged to the Gross family.

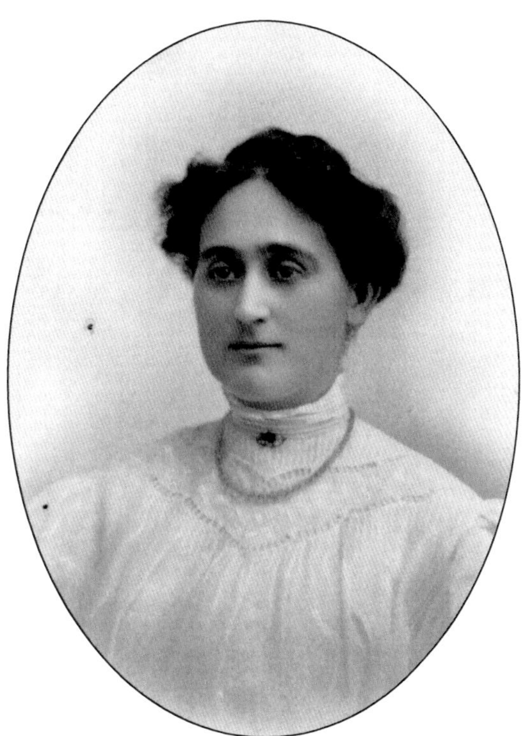

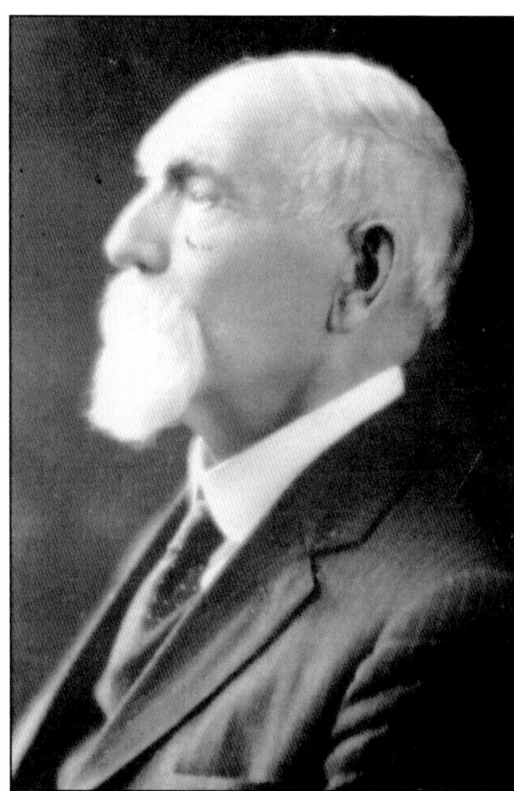

Capt. Rufus Wells was master of the schooner *Princton* (built at Wells Cove) and spent his life on the sea. He lived west of Evergreen Farm, on the opposite side of Reach Road, in the house his father, Capt. Humphrey Wells, built in 1840. The Rufus Wells papers are in the Sedgwick-Brooklin Historical Society. Wells left his house to his only child, Irene.

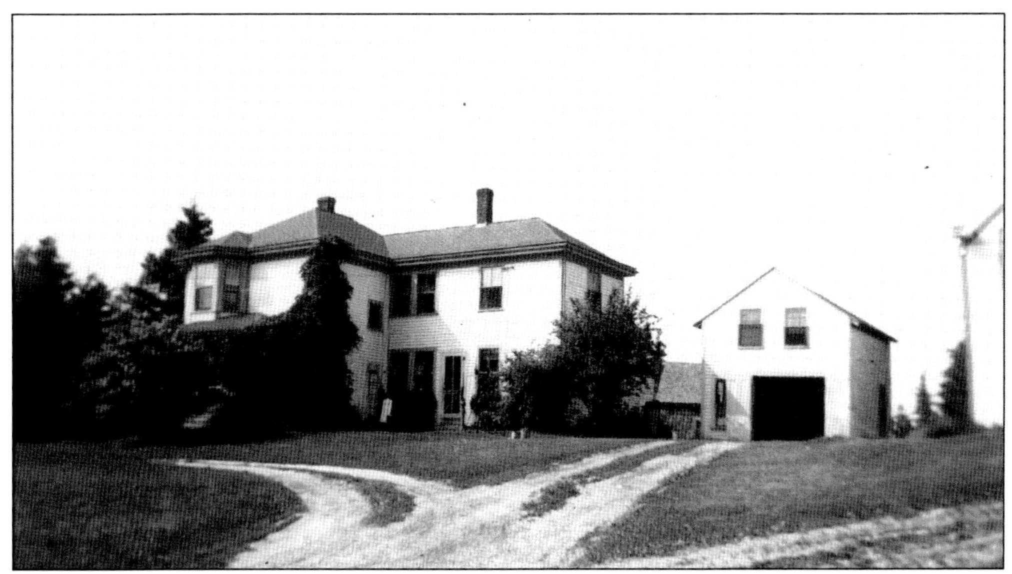

Pictured here is the house of Victor C. and Millie Bridges *c.* 1930. Victor was tax collector in Brooklin from 1935 to his death in 1962, when Millie took over the position. They lived next door to the old Haven schoolhouse, where she later had an antique shop.

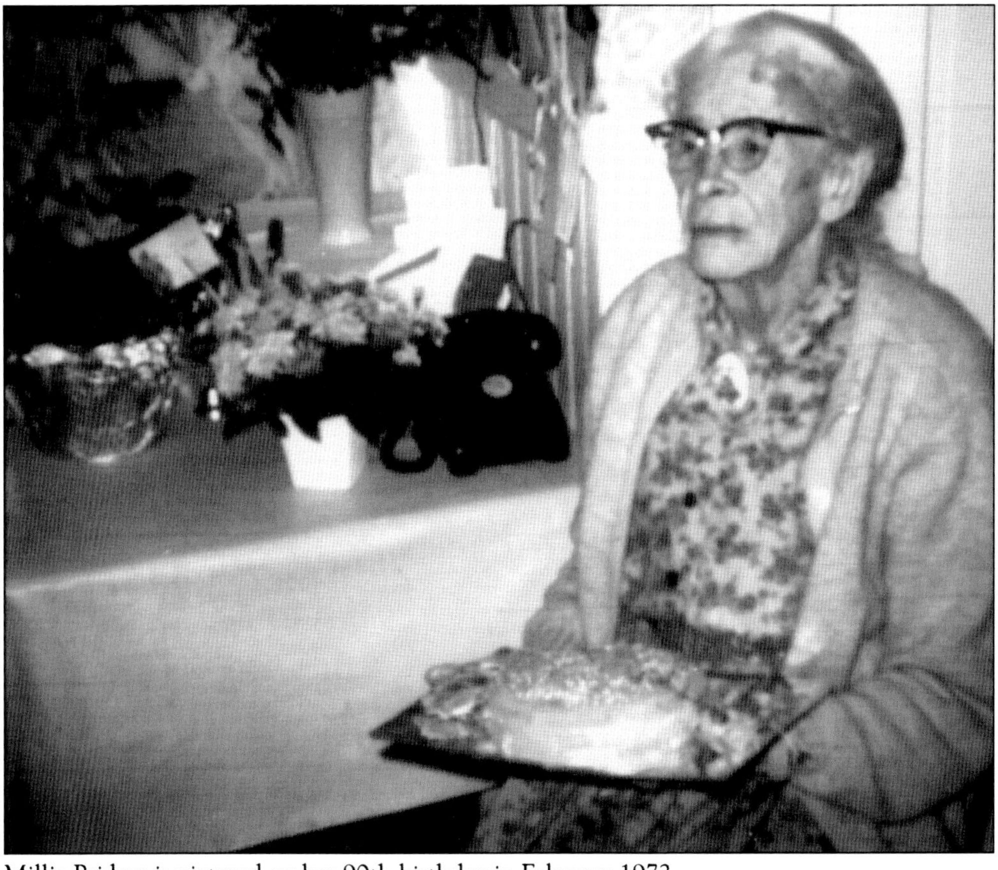

Millie Bridges is pictured on her 90th birthday in February 1972.

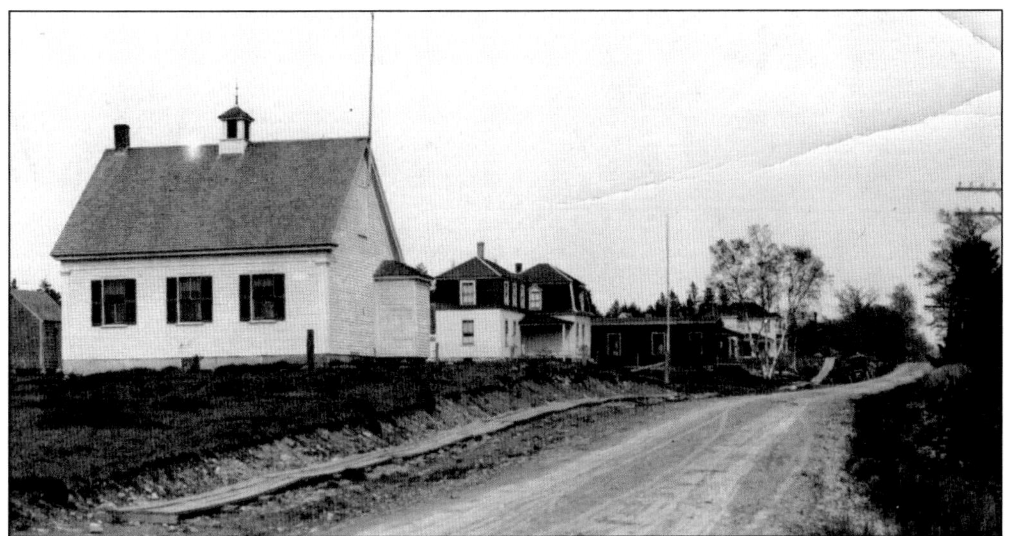

This is the Haven schoolhouse No. 2, which still stands today. In the early 1900s, Emma Tibbetts, a daughter of Noah Tibbetts, ran the White Schoolhouse Gift Shop here. Later, the building housed Millie Bridges's and then Kay Rodgers's antique shops. Today, it is a private home and guest cottage. Behind the school, the house of Rufus and Octavia Bridges is visible. It is no longer there.

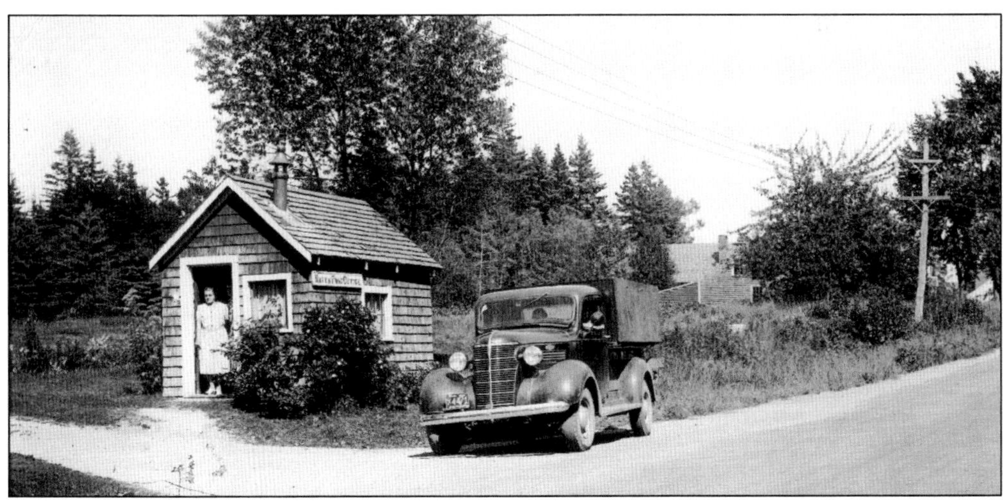

The post office in Haven was reported to be the smallest post office in Maine. Susie Grindle, shown in the doorway c. 1928, was postmaster there for many years. Serving in that position before her at another location were Etta Carter, Nancy Mayo, and Harvey Wells.

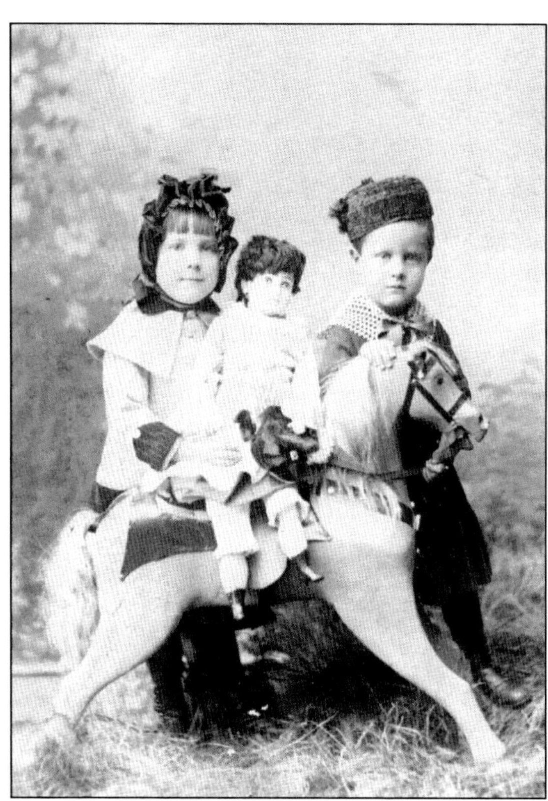

Shown here in 1879 are Milton and Emma Tibbetts, children of Noah and Ida Tibbetts. Noah Tibbetts founded Haven Colony c. 1890 after he bought land on the Haven shore and divided it into 54 lots under the name Castle View Cottage Lots.

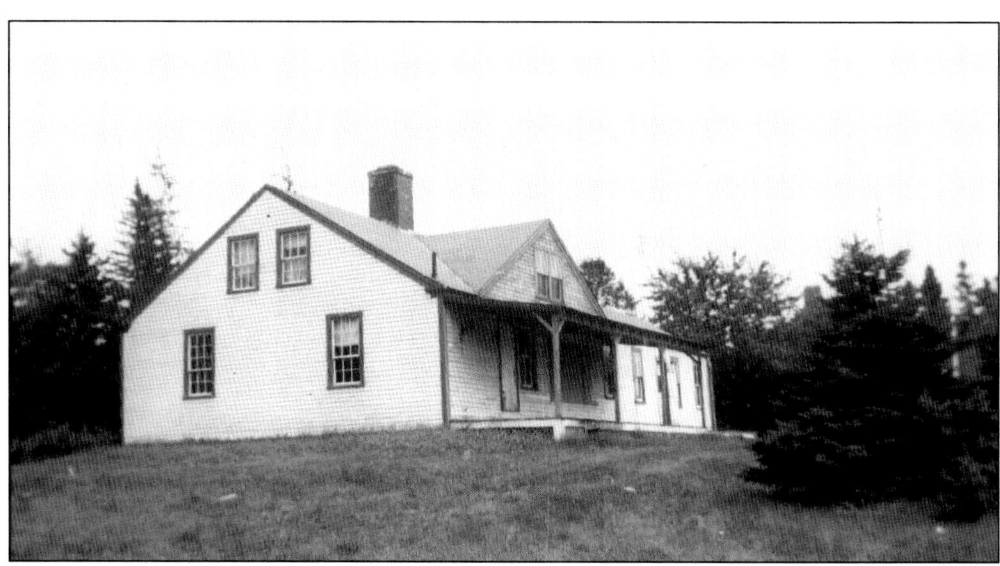

The summer home of Noah Tibbetts (1851–1942) was known as the Old Homestead. It is on land that was part of the Watson Farm, which Tibbetts purchased in 1883. He was born in Brooksville and spent most of his life in Washington, D.C., where he worked in the U.S. Pension Bureau.

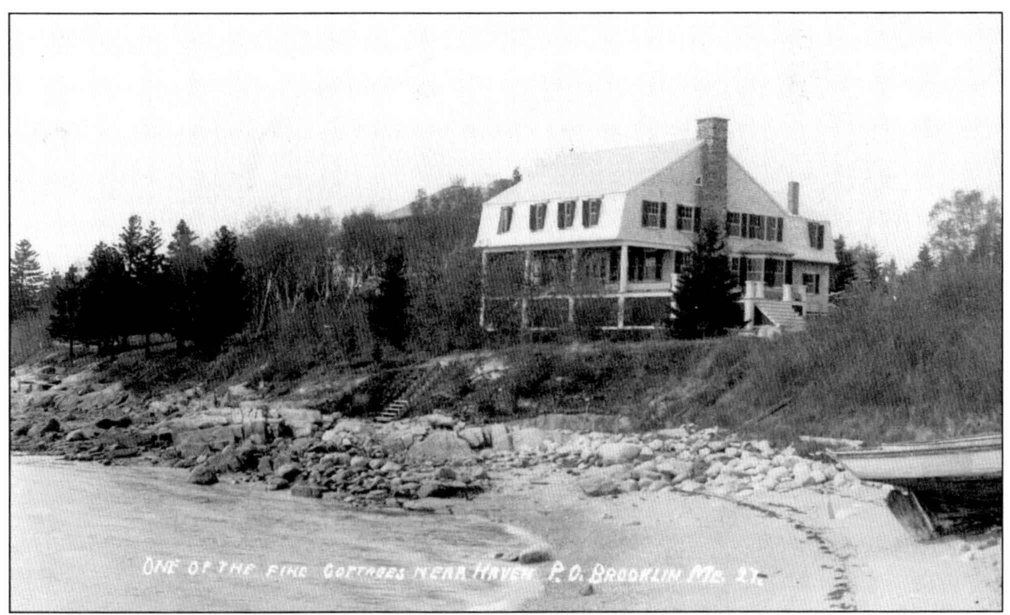

The George and Katherine Parson cottage near Haven is pictured here in Haven Colony. It is now owned by Sally Lupfer.

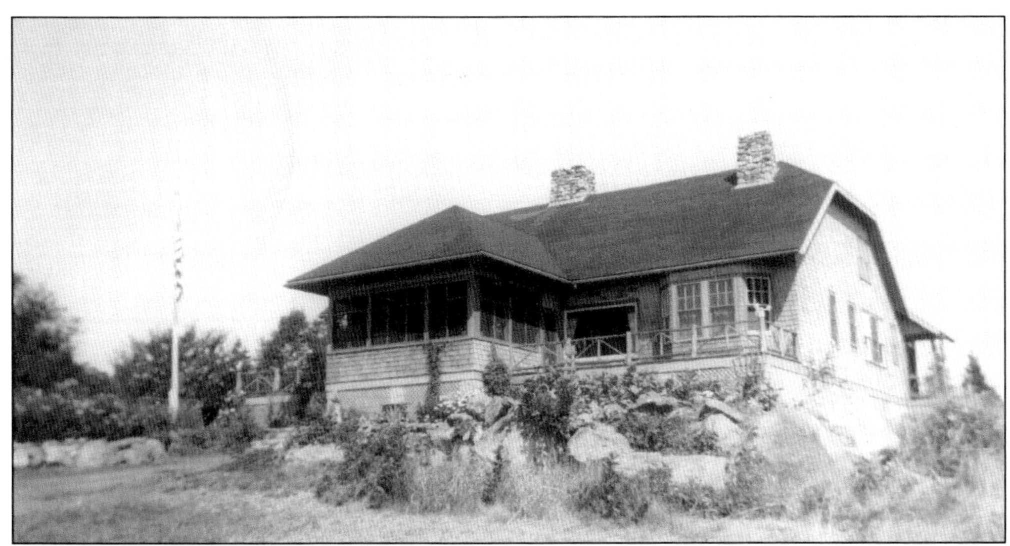

This house was built by master craftsman Walter Crockett of Brooklin for the Showles family.

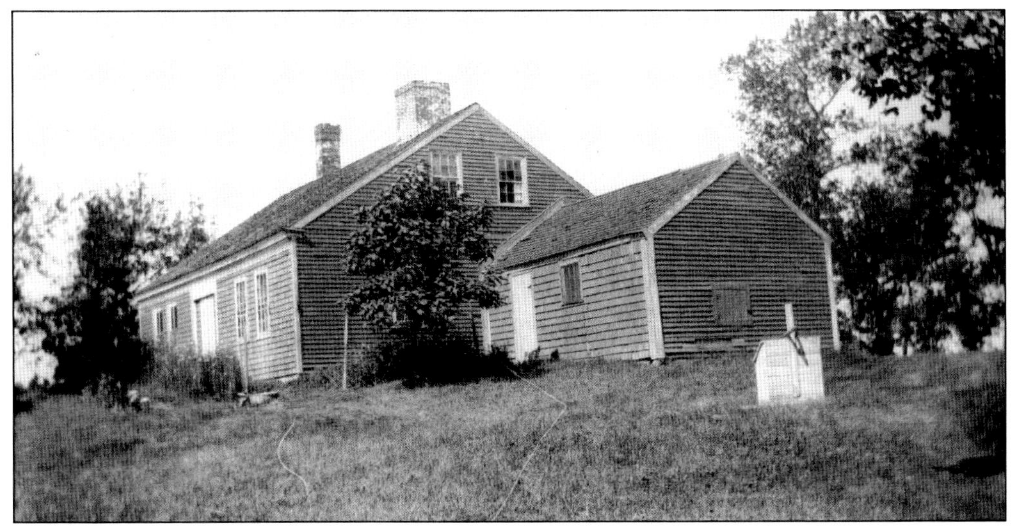

The home of Peleg Curtis (1839–1925) is pictured as it looked in 1927. Curtis was a cooper and barrel maker. His house was located on land now owned by German Emory descendants.

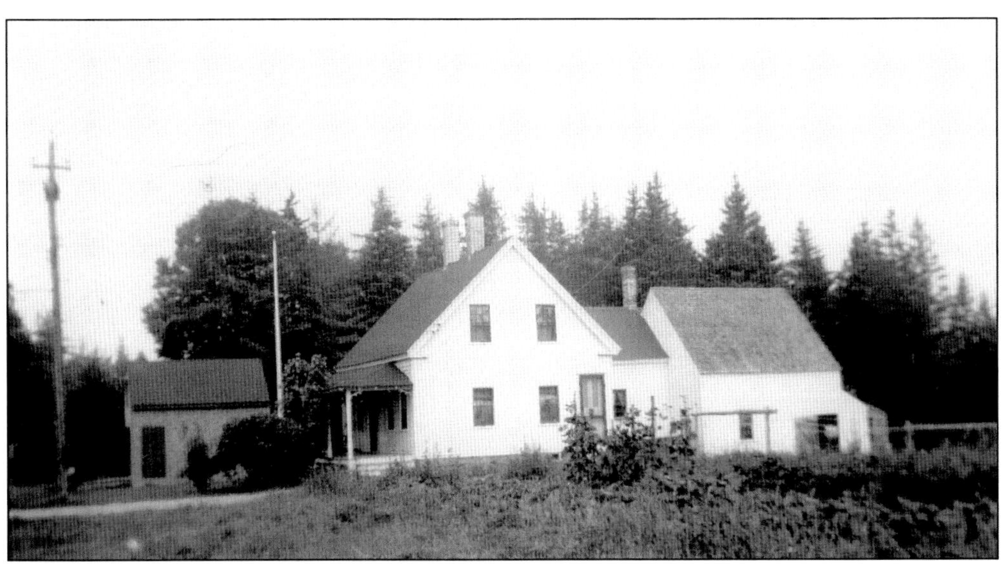

Willard Gott's home in Haven is pictured here *c.* 1930. Later, the house was owned by the Dennisons and, later, by Vivian and Robert Smith.

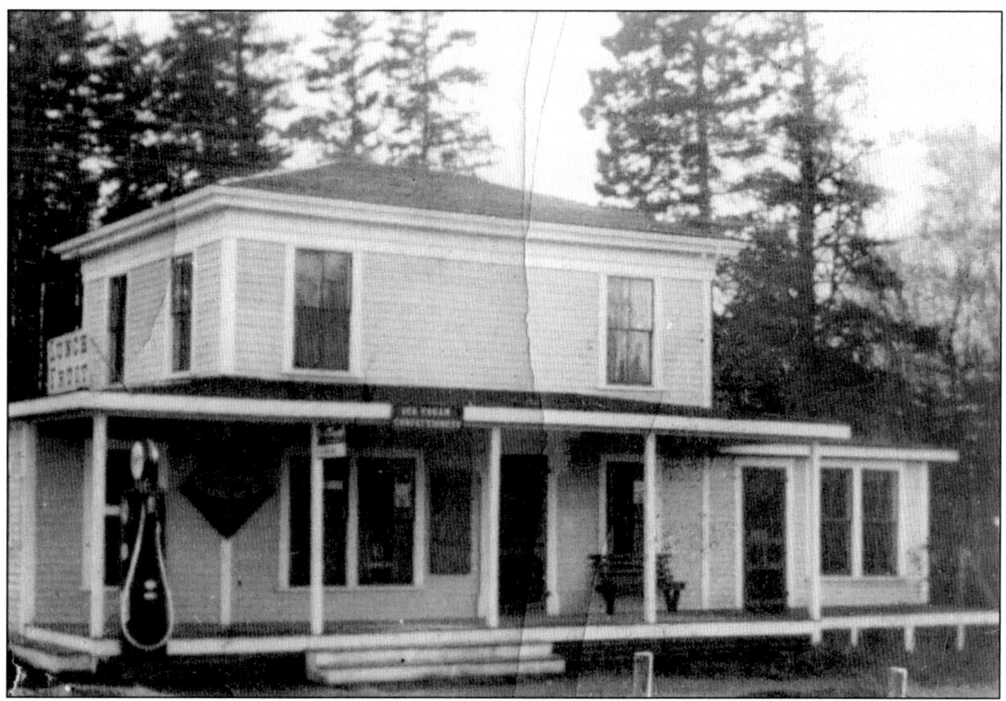

This lunch room and ice-cream parlor at Haven is fondly remembered as a gathering place in the 1930s. At various times, it was owned by the Sawyers, the Kimballs, Lee Sullivan and Brooksie Kane, the Blodgetts, and Victor and Millie Bridges.

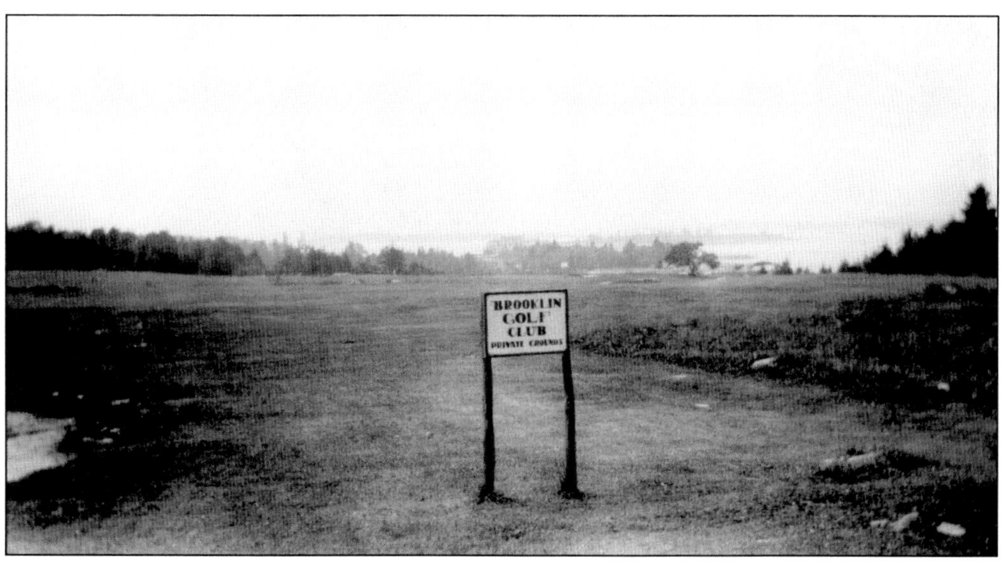

The Brooklin Golf Course was built in the 1930s on a field off Reach Road, across from where Eric Dow's boatyard is today. It closed during World War II and was afterward used as a baseball field.

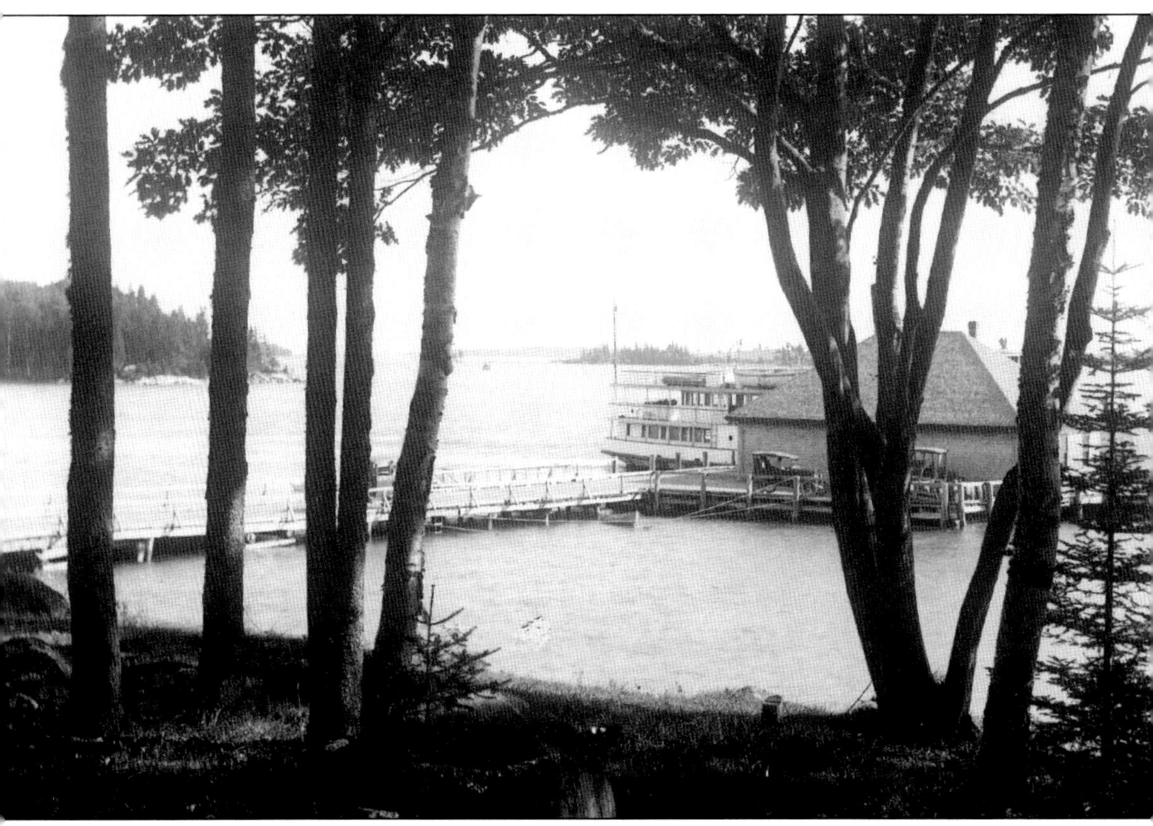

The Eastern Steamship Company wharf and freight shed is pictured c. 1920–1930 at Brooklin Landing in Haven. This is the second shed notable for the gabled roof. The landing and the road area above it, known as the "West End," were the centers of activity in Brooklin at that time. There was a livery stable and several stores on the road above the wharf.

Four

West Brooklin

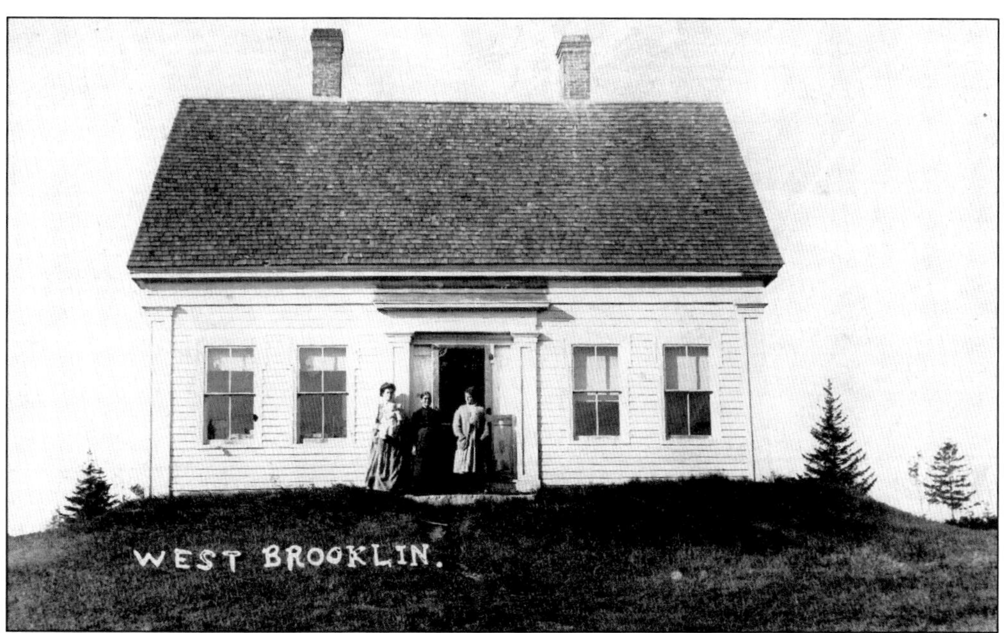

The Bridges-Tapley house was moved with 20 teams of oxen from near the Eaton Shore, over pastures, and then across Reach Road, to the hill on which it now sits about a half-mile to the west.

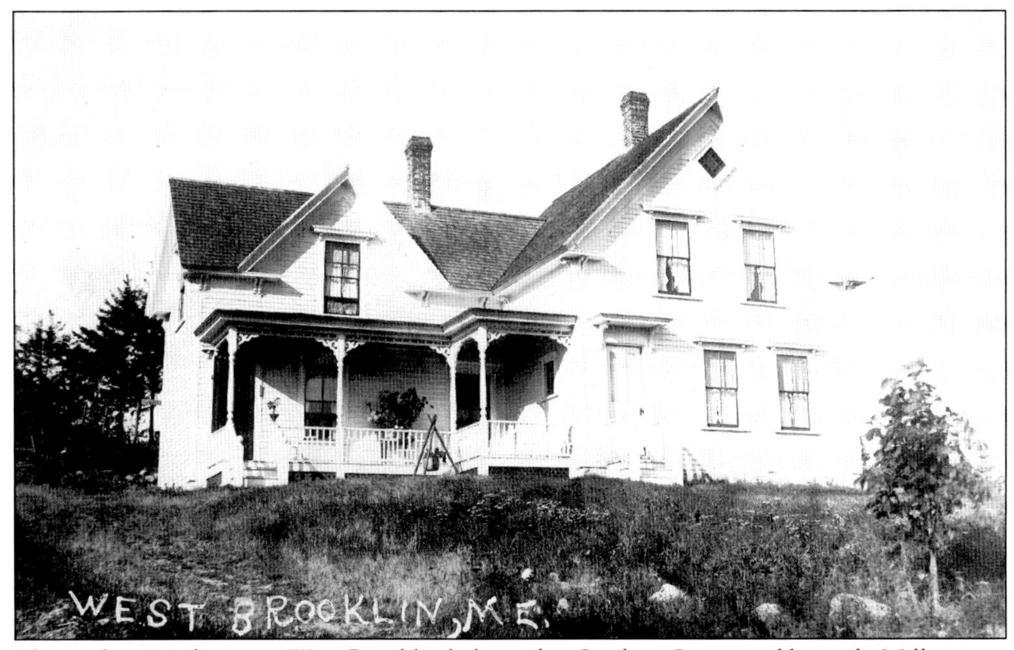

This early-1900s house in West Brooklin belonged to Sterling Carter and his wife, Millie.

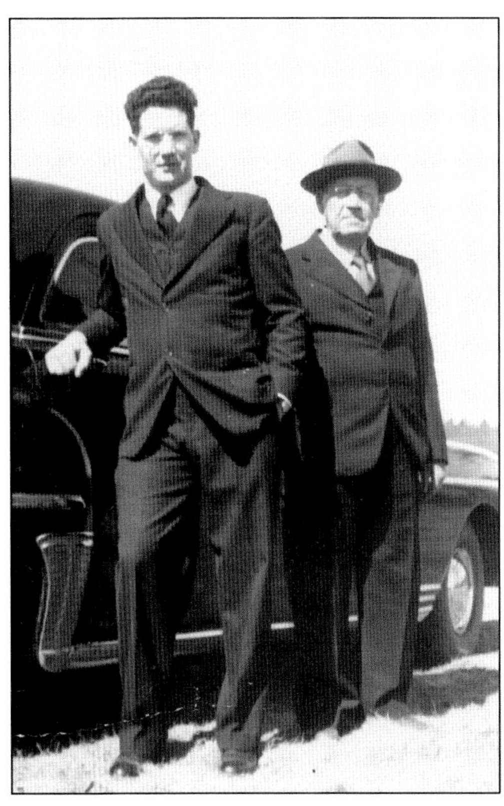

Shown here are Basil Friend (left) and Sterling Carter in 1952 on the day of Millie Carter's funeral.

This photograph of Gleason Friend was taken on July 3, 1943, when he was home on leave from the army. On November 28, 1944, he was killed in action while serving in France during World War II. He was the only Brooklin casualty of the war.

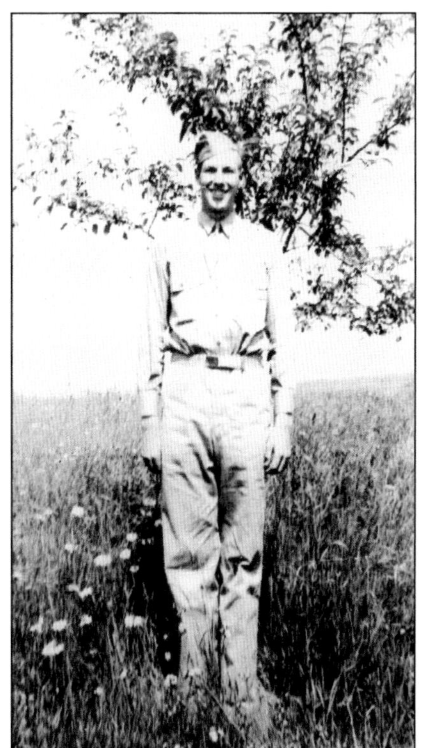

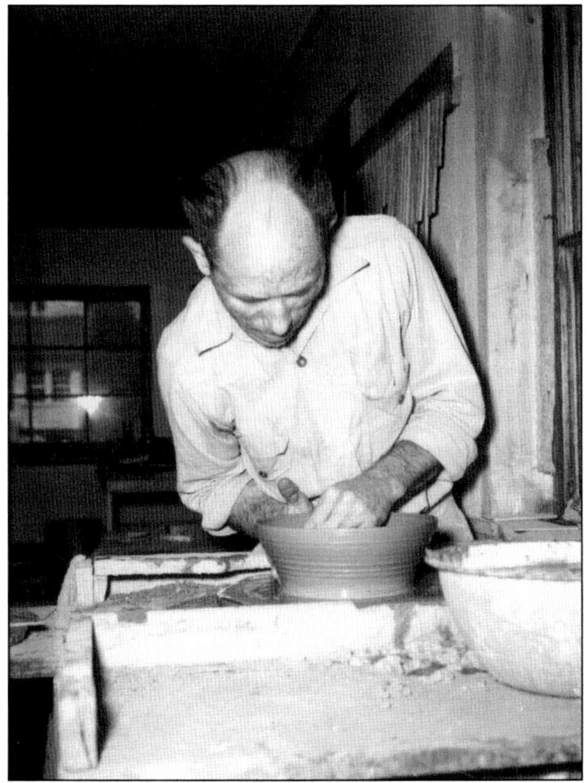

John Laughlin first worked as a potter with Frank Day at South Blue Hill Pottery. There, he met and married Celia Bridges and started his own pottery in West Brooklin. Under the "Brooklin Pottery" mark, Laughlin dug his own clay in Oakum Bay and produced complete dinner sets as well as yacht club racing trophies, wedding plates, and memory jugs.

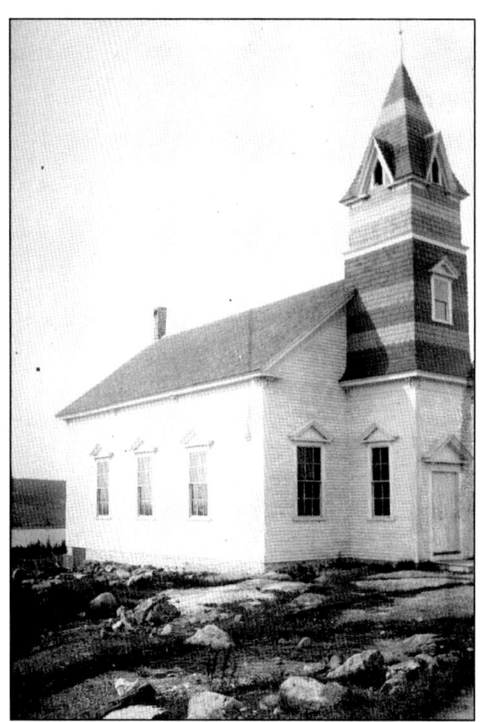

The Rock Bound Chapel was completed in 1902. According to the original charter, it was to be used as "a union building and shall be open for religious services of any denomination." The first officers were Lelia Bridges, Mary Fogg, Mary J. Bridges, and Lucius Bridges. Roy Blake and, later, Louisa Goodyear organized hymn sings, with piano music provided by Myrtle Tapley, Harriet Becker, and Alice Egland. The chimes were donated by Austin Goodyear in memory of his father.

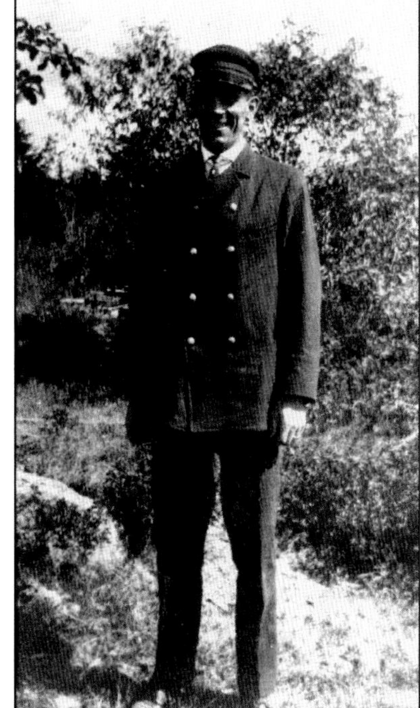

Ahira W. Bridges (1881–1960) of West Brooklin is shown here in uniform. He served in the navy during World War I and spent most of his life in steamboat service.

David and Abbie Sophronia Bridges, pictured in the late 1800s, raised 17 children in their home in West Brooklin. Their children were Edward, Roscoe, Arthur, Osmand, Eldorus, Groves, Victor, Lutie, Nina, John, Kate, Francis, Percy, David, Lillian, Ahira, and Rufus.

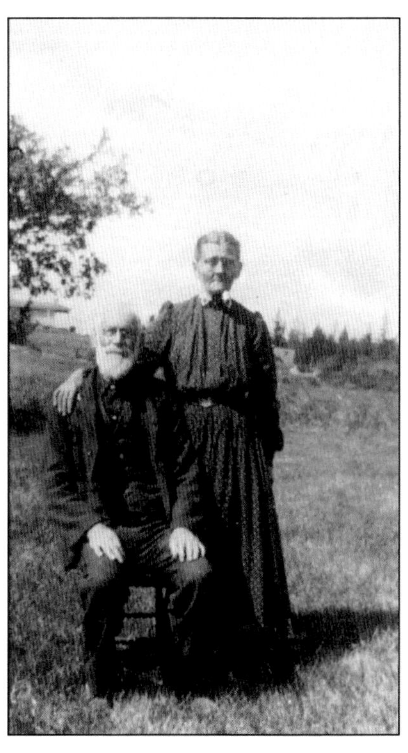

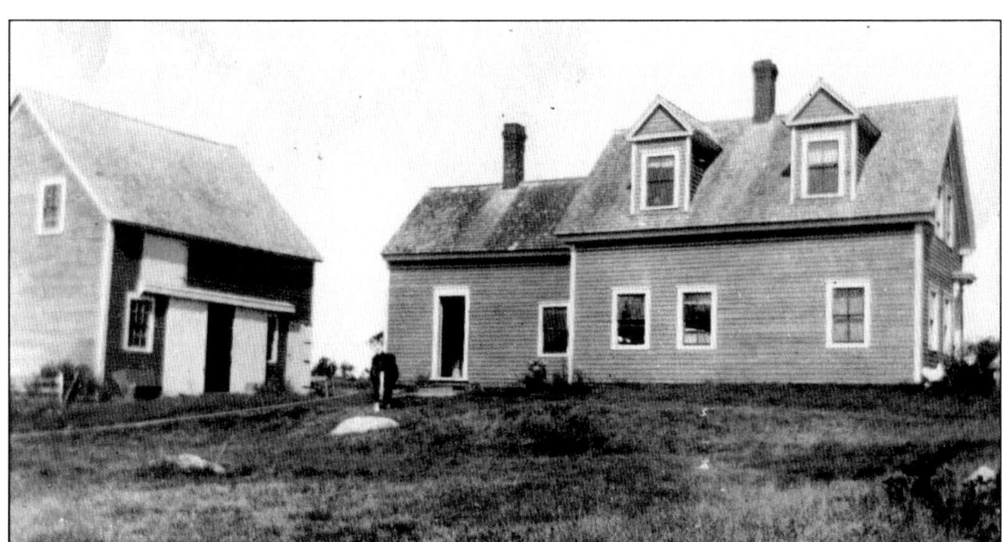

The home of David and Abbie Sophronia Bridges was located on Reach Road in West Brooklin. It later belonged to Irving Hatch.

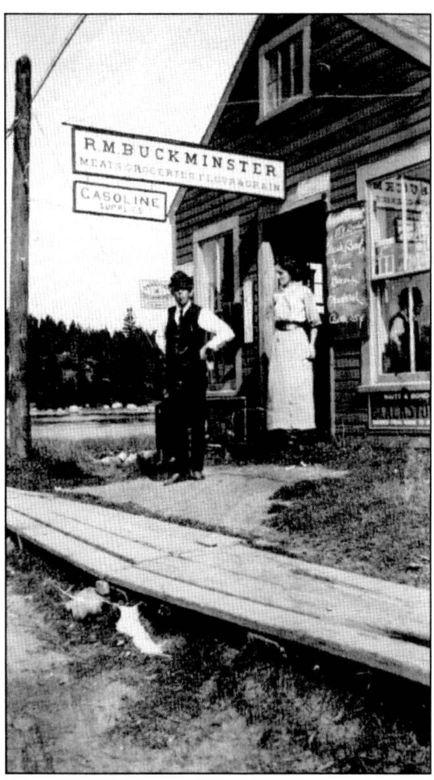

The R.M. Buckminster store was next to the Benjamin River Bridge near where the old Dick Howard garage is today. Ralph "Buck" was a minister who came from Deer Isle and ran a clam factory near this site at one time. Later, Irving Candage ran the store. Alice Herrick, Frank Herrick's wife, who ran a boardinghouse across the bridge, is shown in the doorway.

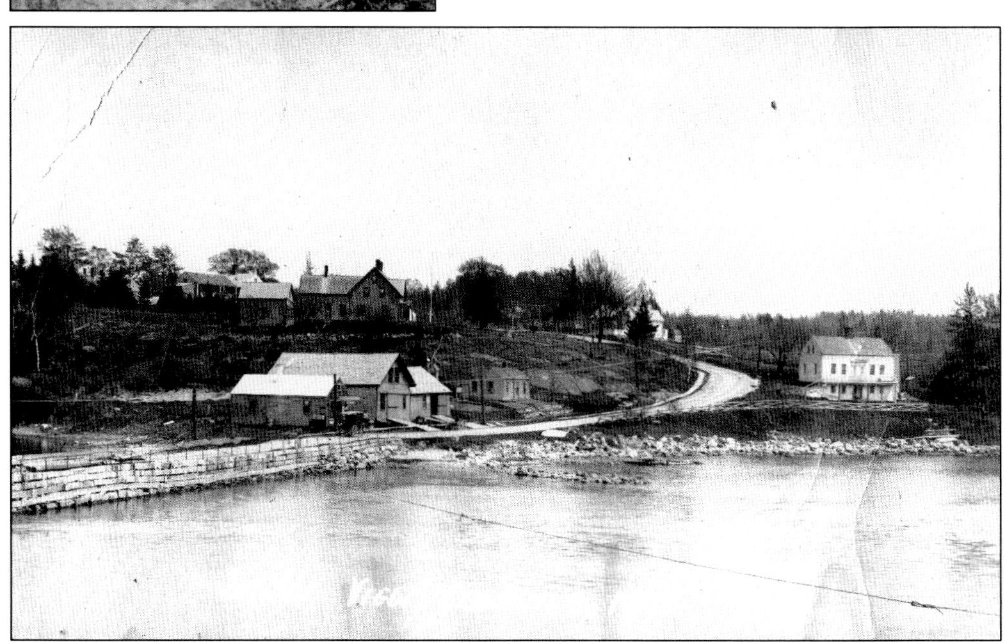

Viewed from the Sedgwick side of the Benjamin River is an old panorama of West Brooklin. On one side is a livery stable, Clapp Hooper's house, and the Buckminster store. Up the hill, on the left, is a big yellow house owned by Capt. Sheldon Torrey, which later burned. Eugene Day's house is just behind Torrey's. To the right of the road, on the shore, is the house owned by Sam Hazen at the start of Hazen's Hill.

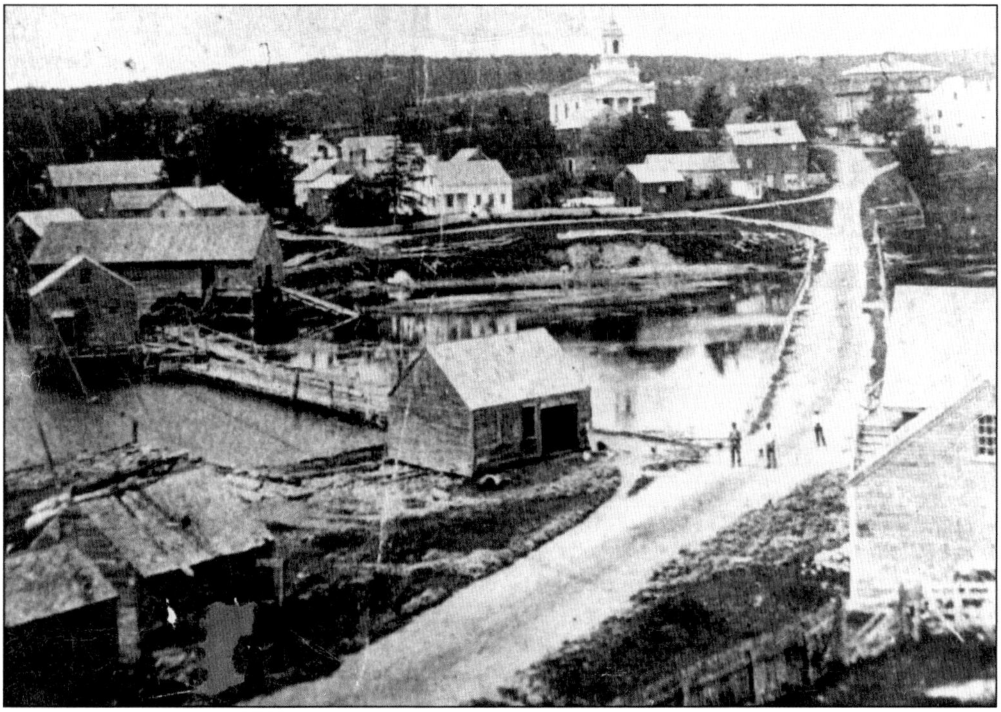

In this early view of the Benjamin River area, we can see a floating dock and several buildings extending out into Carlton Cove. Here, in 1818, Rowland Carlton built the *Rowland & John* with John Means. Carlton also built the schooners *Scio* (1824) and *Cyprus* (1826) and the bark *F.A. Everett* (1848). One of these buildings housed a sawmill, and Eugene Day's motorboat was often seen up on the dock.

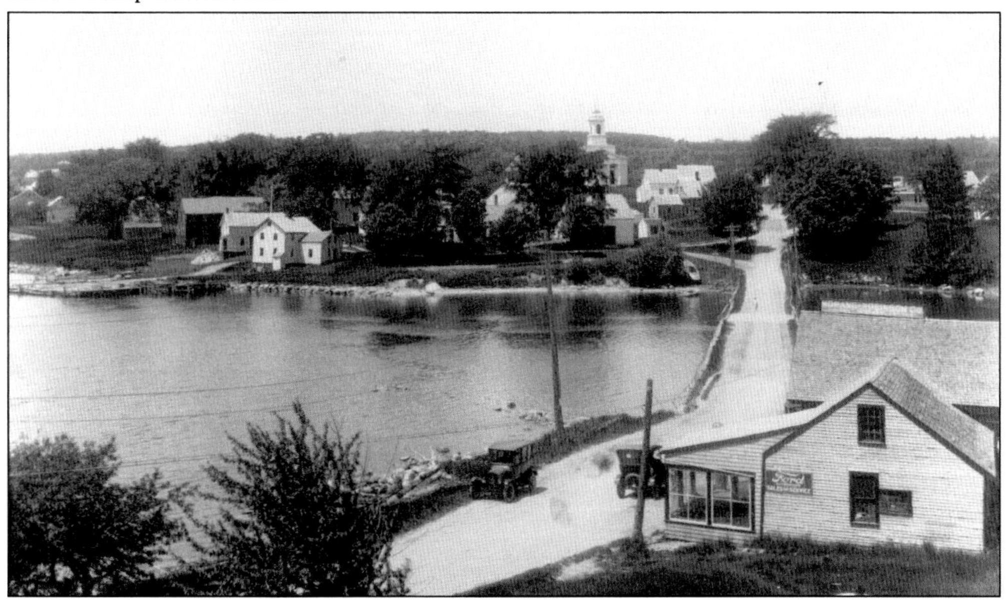

This view of the same area in the early 1900s shows that most of the buildings in Carlton Cove are gone. The building on the right is the Ford dealership where Cleaves Clapp was a salesman. Later, this was Howard's Garage, and Lynn Leighton once had a bakery there.

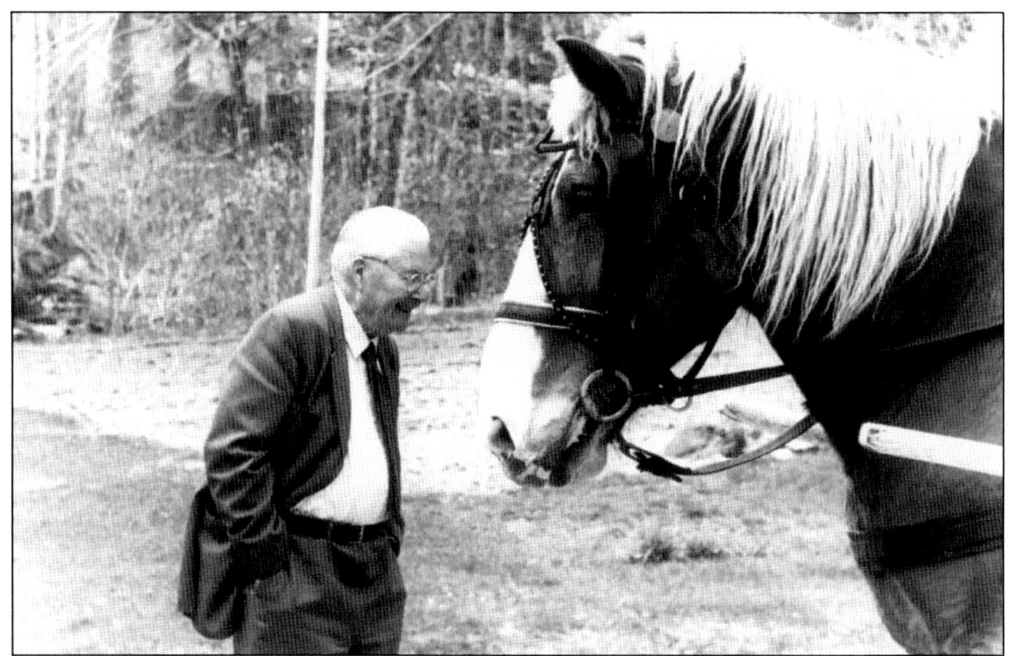

James Russell Wiggins (1903–2000) was an author, journalist, *Washington Post* editor, U.S. ambassador to the United Nations, and editor of the the *Ellsworth American*. He bought the Carlton Cove Farm in Brooklin in 1961. This photograph shows him having genial conversation with his horse, Chub, who is now the resident farm horse and still living at the Wiggins Farm.

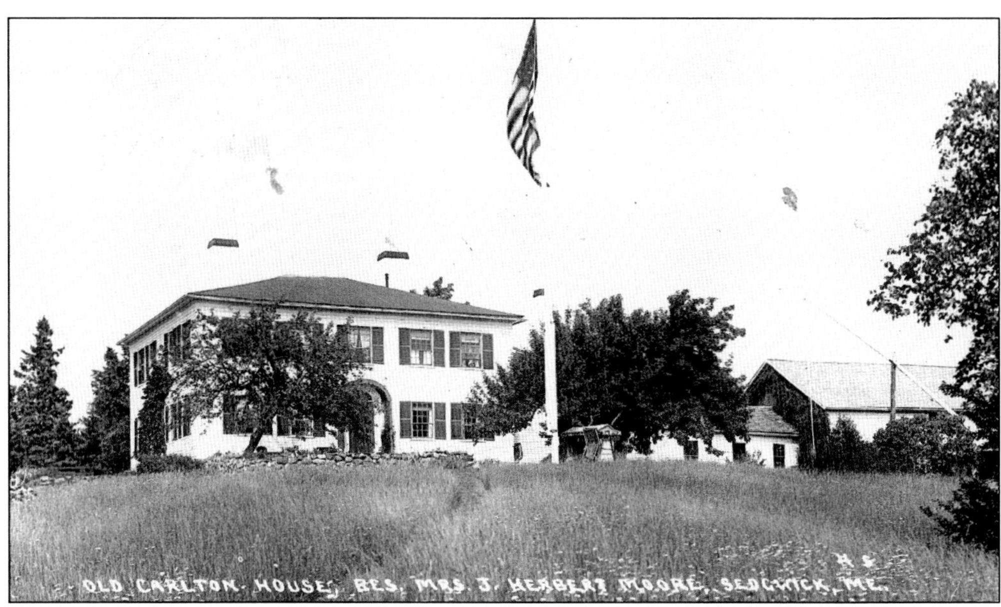

Rowland Carlton built this house (once known as the Willows) in 1802, and the Carlton family lived there until 1906. In the 1950s, John Ellsworth opened up the old brick oven fireplace, one of nine in the house. Wiggins had paneling made by Walter Crockett of Brooklin to surround the fireplace. Today, it is still run as a farm by J.R. Wiggins's granddaughter, Jennifer Schroth, and her husband, Jon Ellsworth.

Five

NASKEAG

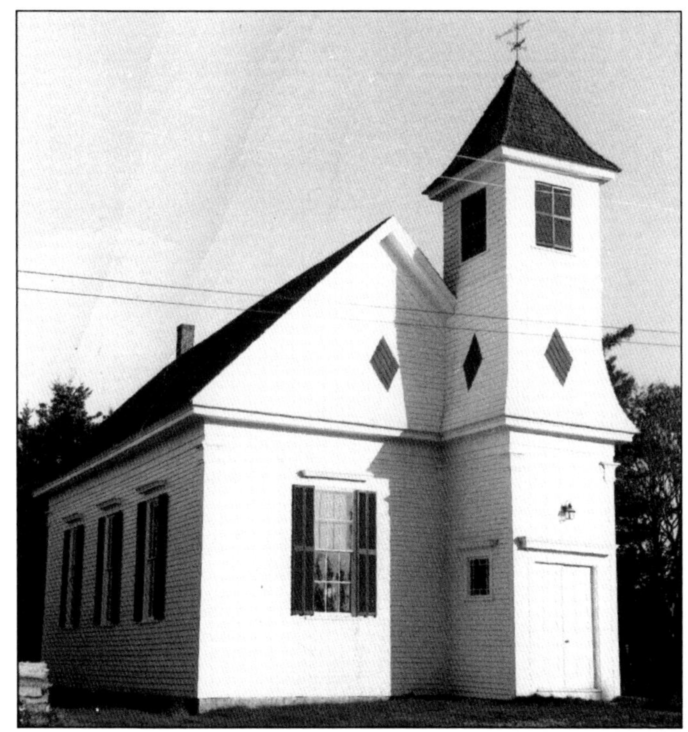

Beth Eden Chapel, named in 2001 to the National Register of Historic Places, was dedicated in 1900 as "a house for the worship of God favoring no one denomination," according to the minutes of the dedication ceremony. In the 1960s and 1970s, many Naskeag residents donated time and money for the upkeep and refurbishing of the building. The chapel stands near the end of Naskeag Point across the road from a cemetery in which are buried many of Brooklin's earliest settlers.

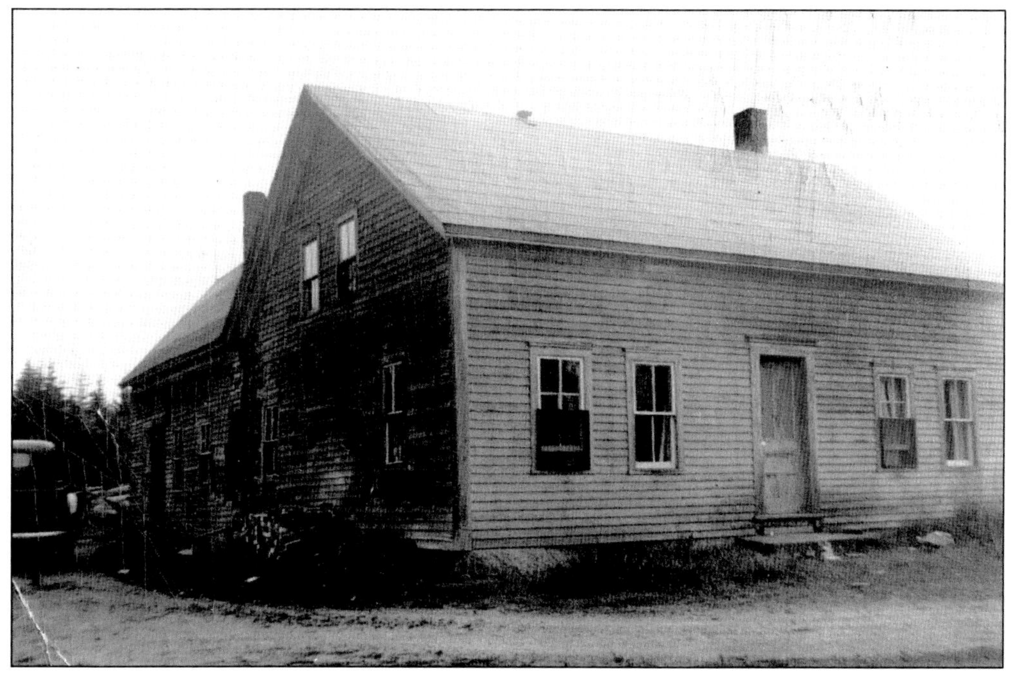

This is the home of Rocky and Louise Rockwell as it looked in 1946. The house was brought up from the shore to its present location on the Naskeag Road. The Rockwells were still living in the house by 2001, when they were given the Alumni Citizen Award for their service and generosity to the town.

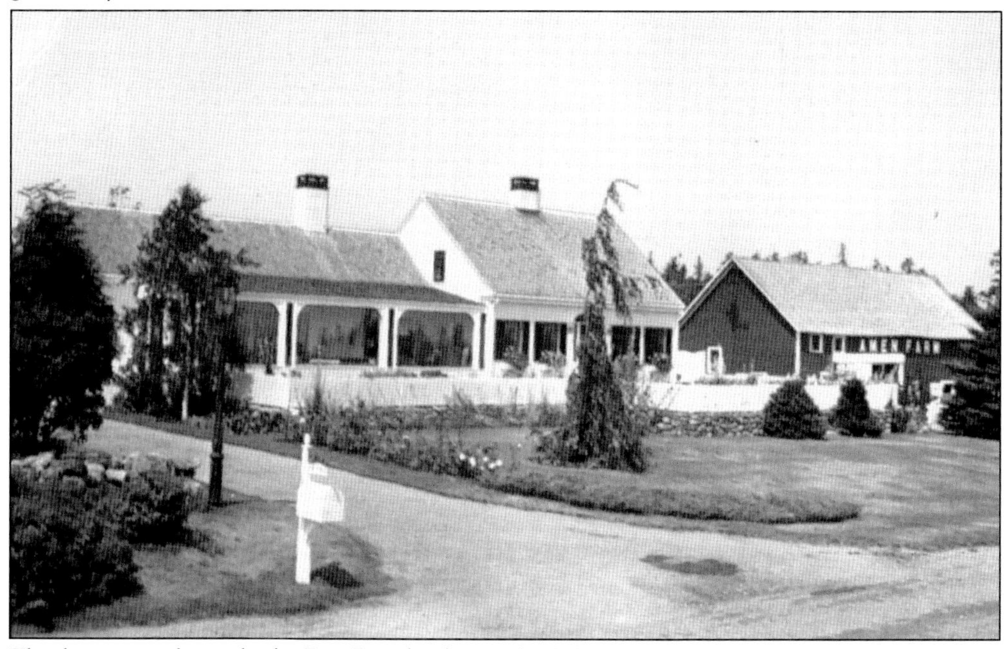

This house was formerly the Roy Bowden house, built by Arthur Wood. J. Roy Barrette and his wife, Helen, came here in 1958 to "retire." Subsequently, Roy wrote three books and the weekly "Retired Gard'ner" column for the *Ellsworth American*. The Barrettes named the property Amen Farm, which was known for beautiful gardens and landscaping.

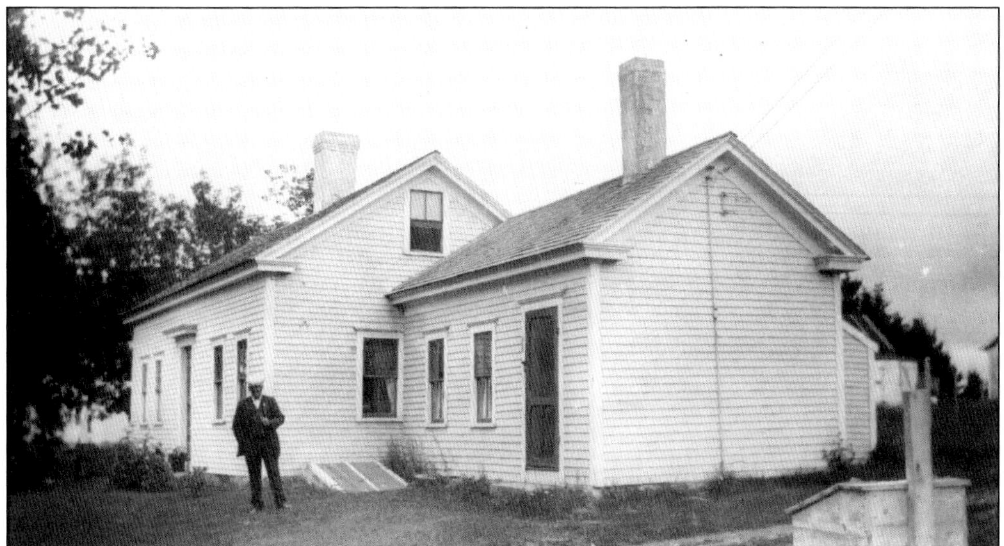

Frank Herrick is shown outside his home *c.* 1920. This house is opposite the Edna Cutliff place and was later owned by Wallace and Claribelle (Herrick) (Staples) Tainter. Catherine and Henry Allen also lived there at one time.

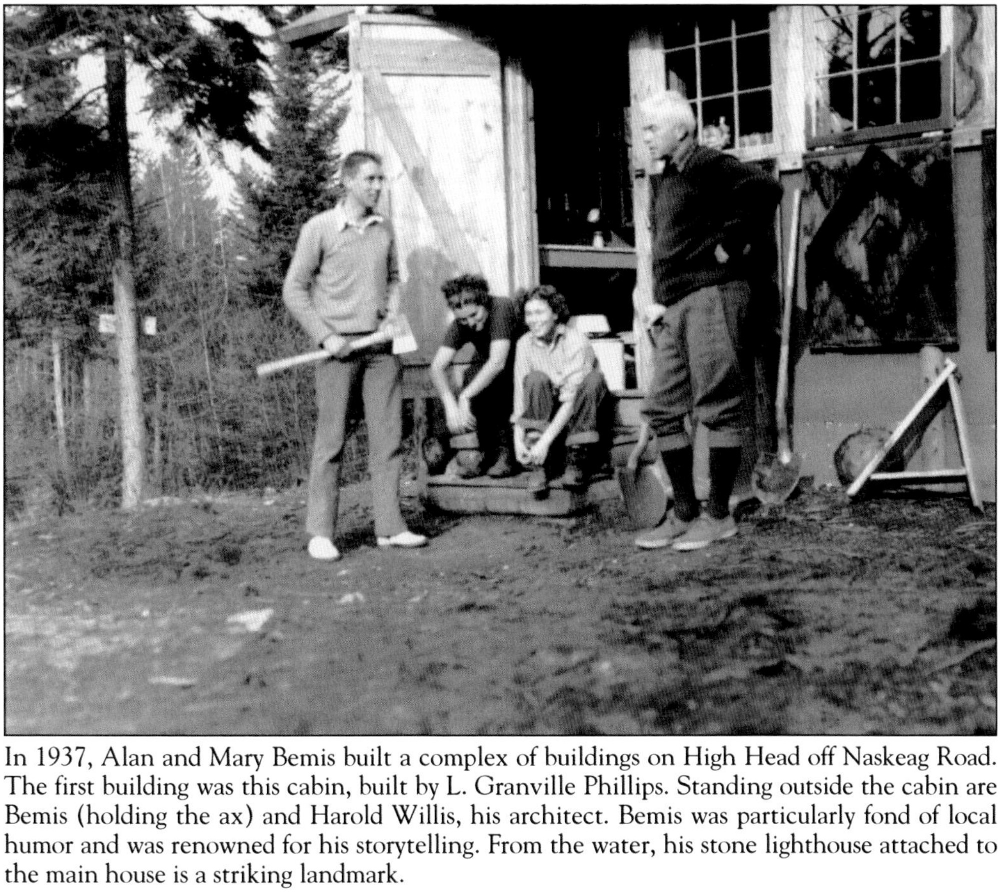

In 1937, Alan and Mary Bemis built a complex of buildings on High Head off Naskeag Road. The first building was this cabin, built by L. Granville Phillips. Standing outside the cabin are Bemis (holding the ax) and Harold Willis, his architect. Bemis was particularly fond of local humor and was renowned for his storytelling. From the water, his stone lighthouse attached to the main house is a striking landmark.

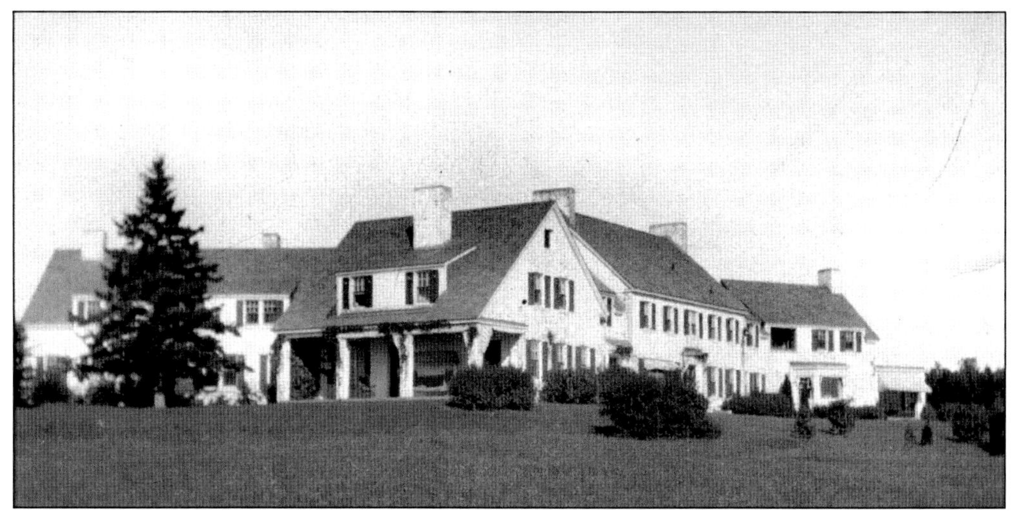

This house, now the WoodenBoat Publishing headquarters, is shown as it looked in 1920, four years after it was built by Alexander S. Porter Jr. Located on Great Cove, the estate contained a boathouse, a farmhouse, an office, and a fireproof, heated, electrified stable. The house, designed by James Hopkins, was built under a heated airplane hangar during the winter at a cost of about $200,000.

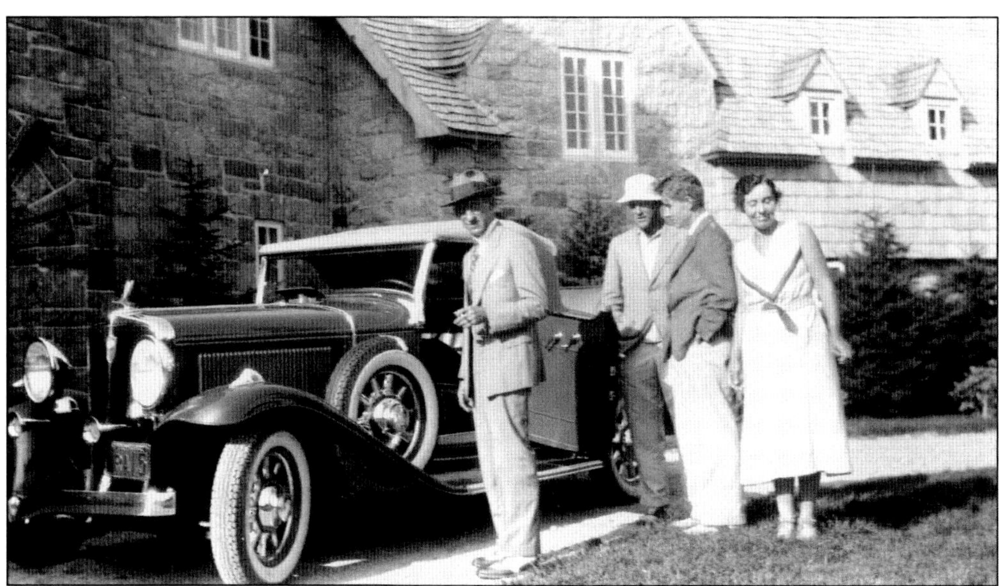

What is now known as the Hunt House was built earlier by Donald Parson Sr. Pictured here in front of the house and ready for a trip in their touring car are, from left to right, Donald Parson Sr., sons John and Donald Parson Jr., and wife Frances Parson. The car is probably a Duesenburg or Auburn.

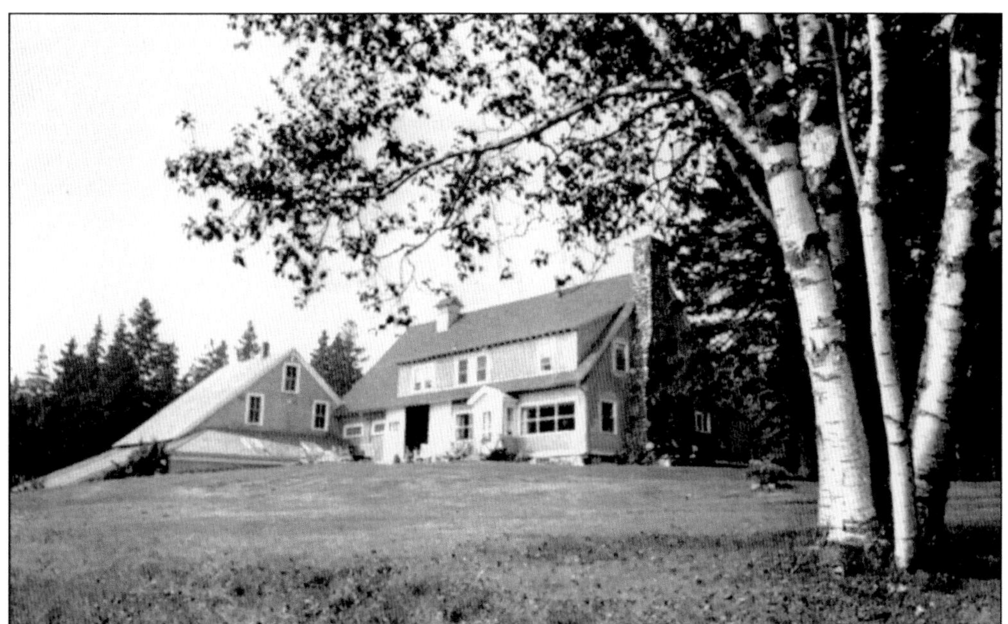

Morrill Goddard found his Naskeag Point property while sailing in the area *c.* 1902. This property became world famous when it was revealed that an 11th-century Norse coin had been found here in 1957. The Maine State Museum archeological investigations, under Steven L. Cox, revealed that the site had artifacts from all the prehistoric cultures known in Maine.

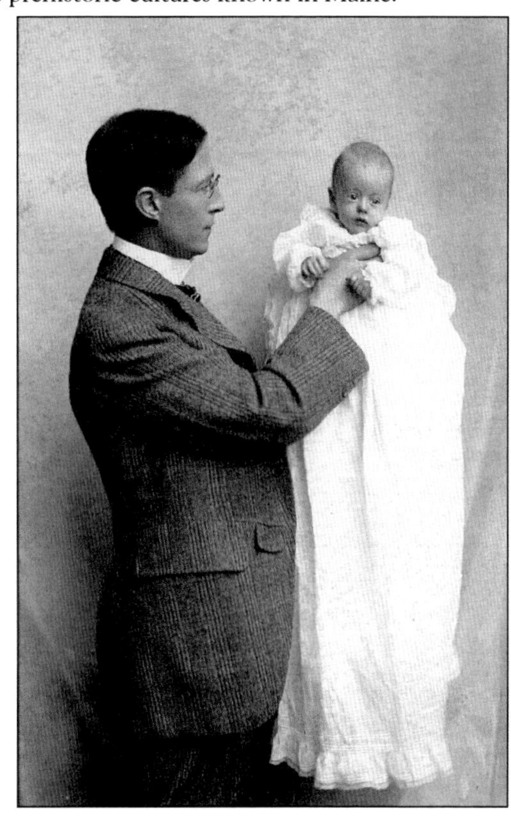

Pictured are Morrill Goddard, editor of Hearst publisher's Sunday magazine, the *American Weekly*, and his son, Morrill Goddard Jr., in 1902. Goddard and his wife, Jessamine, built their house on the end of Naskeag *c.* 1906. Their other children were Dewitt, Mary, Jessamine, and Rowena.

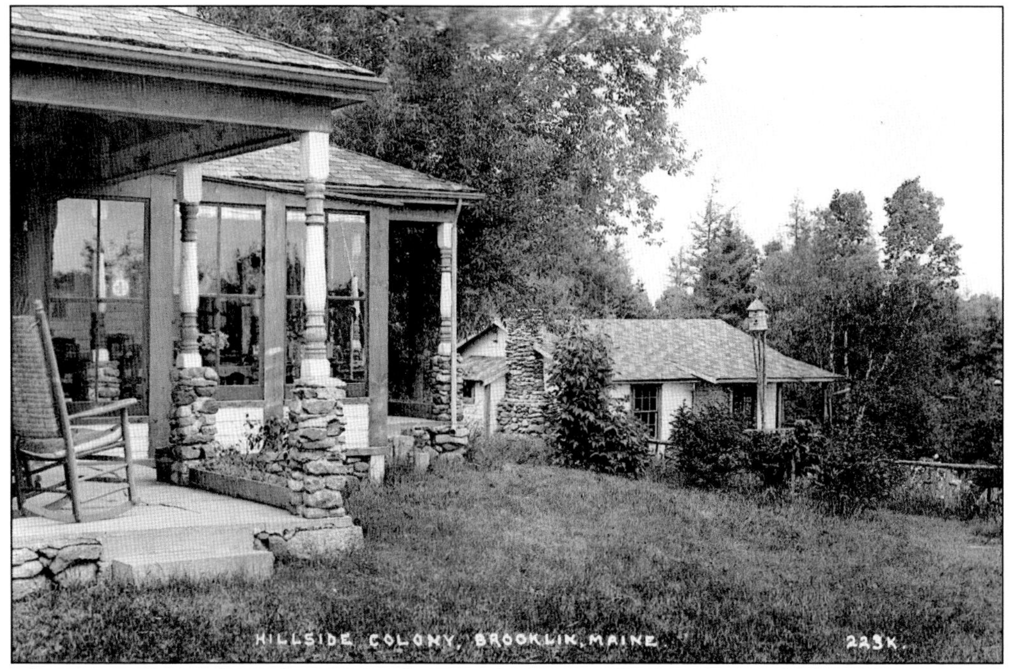

This picture shows the rock posts for the main house at Hillside Colony. The house was built by Eben Allen, the father of Essva Idella Allen Hill (1853–1944). By 1926, her daughter, Idella, and her husband, George Love, were running Hillside as a summer colony. In 1946, it was sold to the Ballards. It then passed to Sally Sypher and then to the Hammonds. In 1978, Roxanne (Twitchell) Sly, a lifelong visitor to Hillside, and her husband, Richard, purchased the house.

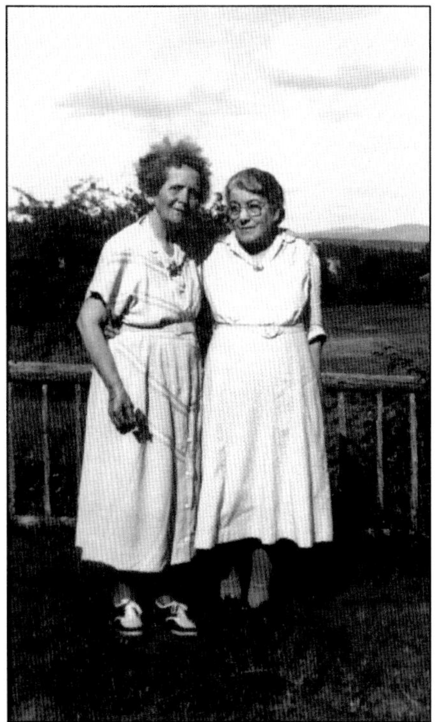

Idella (Hill) Love, owner of Hillside, is shown here on the right with Violet Pierson. Hillside sits overlooking Herrick's Bay with views of the lighthouse on Green's Island across to the mountains on Mount Dessert. Summer visitors took their noon meals in the dining room and enjoyed sailing, swimming, and lobster bakes on nearby islands.

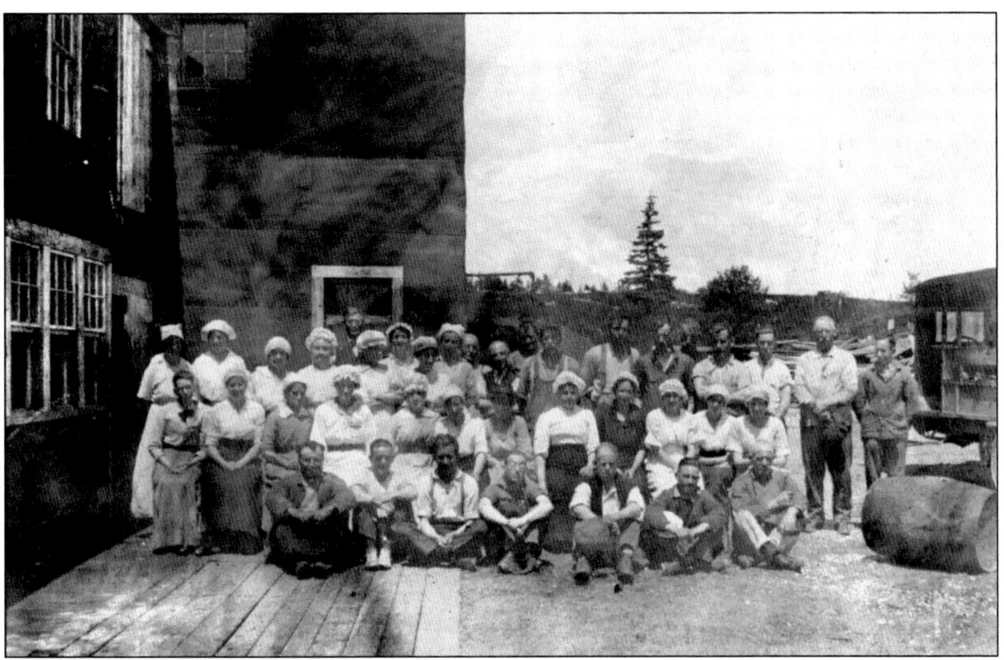

Here, the workers of the Alanson H. Mayo (1864–1929) clam factory on Naskeag are gathered for a photograph. This first clam factory, built *c.* 1902, was located near the end of Naskeag Point, where piling remnants can still be seen. Mayo was the husband of Lizzie P. Mayo (1865–1941).

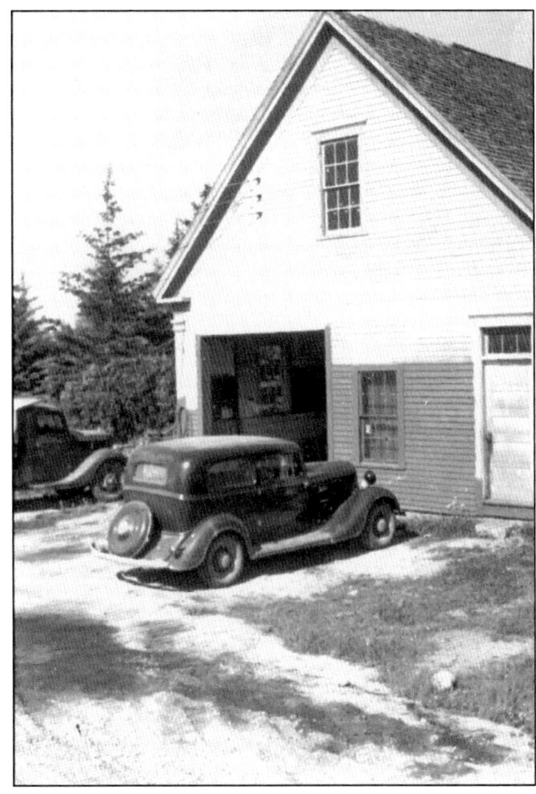

Arthur Smith's garage was located near the end of the Naskeag Road next to Beth Eden Chapel. Both Arthur and his wife, Arlene, worked as mechanics there. Arlene was also Brooklin's town treasurer for many years. Originally, this building was the Naskeag schoolhouse No. 1, which closed in 1937.

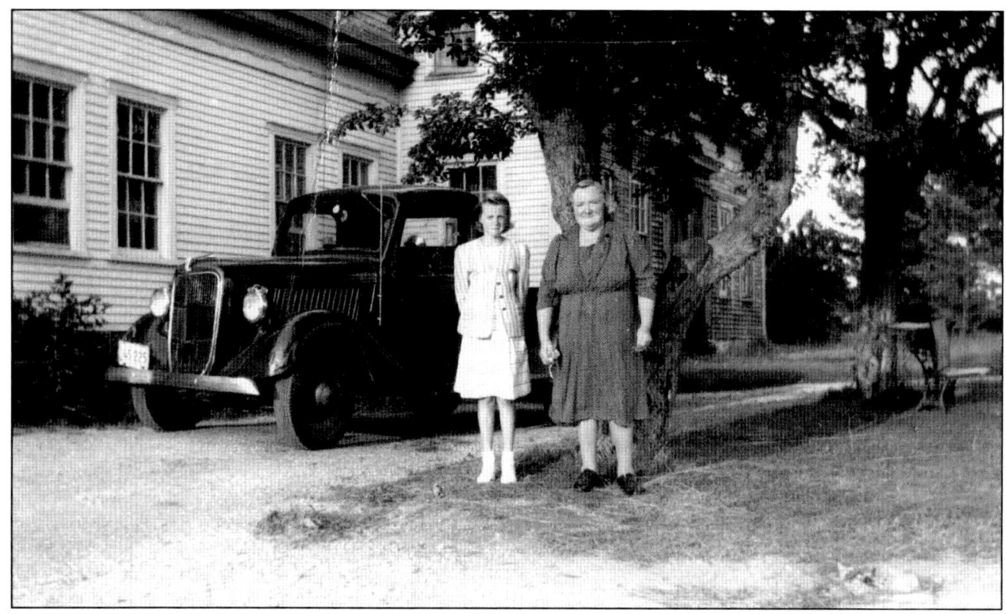

Bessie (Allen) Smith and her granddaughter Melba Smith are shown in front of the family homestead on Back Road on Naskeag Point. Hilda Smith Bryant was the fifth generation of Smiths to live in this house.

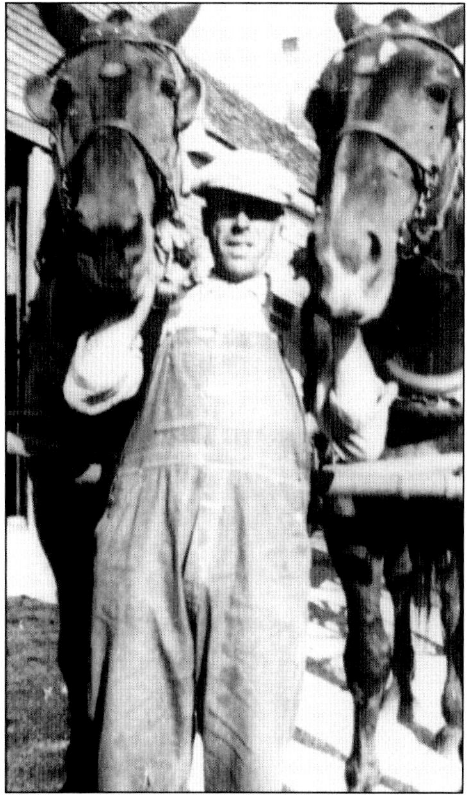

Henry Smith, pictured with his horses, was a farmer, a caretaker for the Nichols property, and an employee of the town. He and his wife, Bessie, were the parents of Gordon, Robert, Norton, Arthur, Cecil, Russell, Roger, and Hilda Bryant.

Six

Flye Point

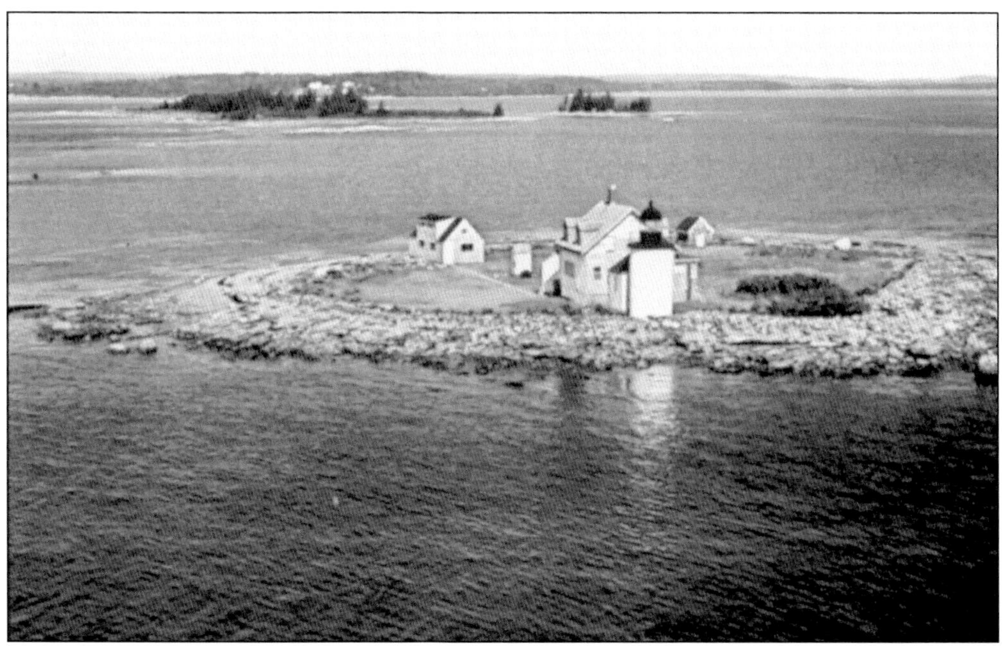

Green Island Light (sometimes called Flye Point or Blue Hill Bay Light) sits at the end of a string of ledges and islands extending out from Flye Point at the junction of Blue Hill Bay and Jericho Bay. Today, the light is automated and the buildings are privately owned. In the background, on the left, is Flye Island, with Goose Island on the right. In the far distance, the Lookout Inn and cottages can be seen.

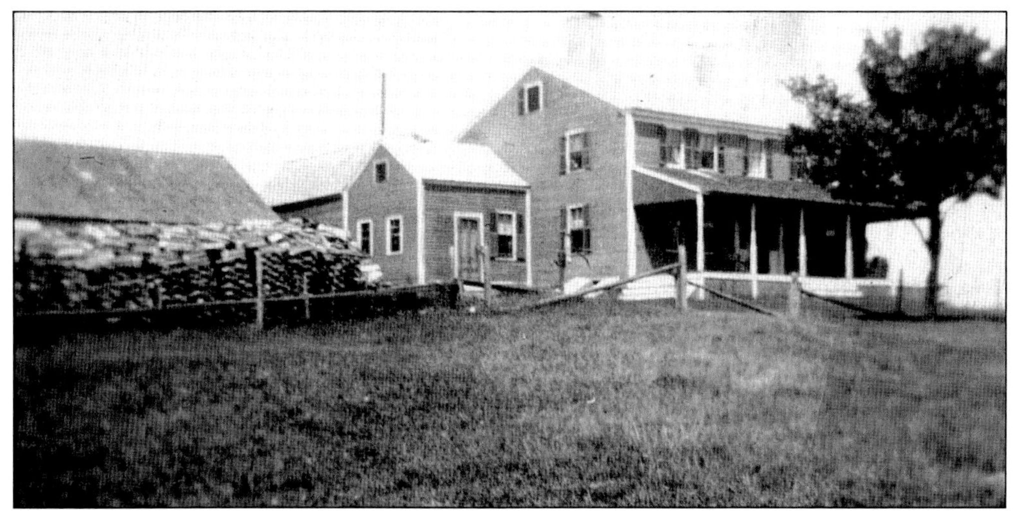

The Phillips House was situated on the Flye Point Road at the top of the hill. It belonged to Benjamin L. (1835–1895) and Edith Parker (1855–1919) Phillips and was run as an inn from the late 1800s to *c.* 1920. After that time, it was owned by Orville N. Purdy, who had it as a summer place until the early 1930s.

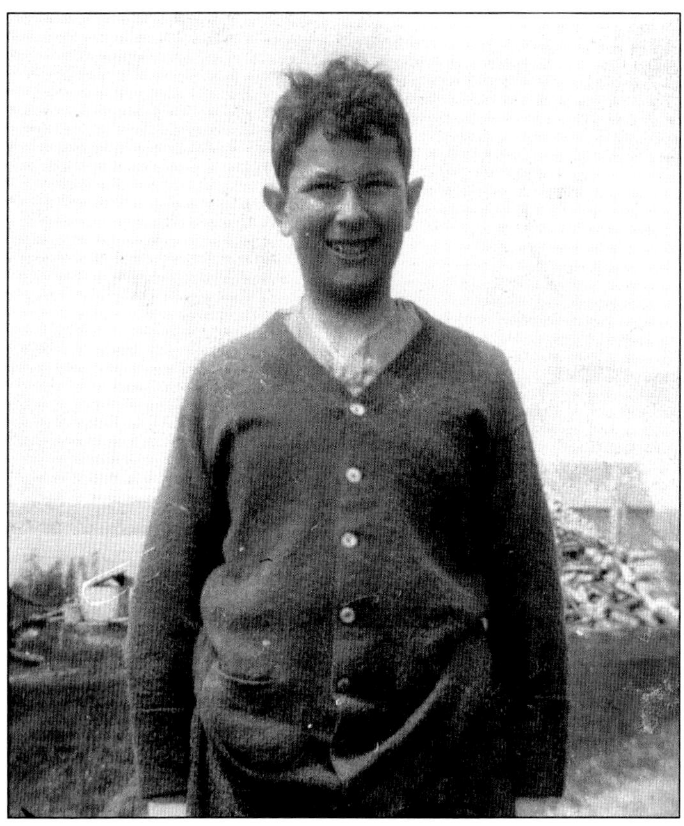

Charles Purdy is pictured at the Phillips House. In the 1910 register, Mr. and Mrs. Charles Purdy of Brookline, Massachusetts, are listed with Augustus, Charles, and Orville Purdy as summer residents on Flye Point. Also listed are C. Phillips Purdy, Mrs. M.A. Phillips, Daniel Jackson Jr., and Alice Hof. Later, the Purdys owned the Phillips House, and it was known as the Purdy Place. The barn burned, and the house was torn down sometime after 1930.

Pictured at the Phillips House are Eva Herrick Phillips, the wife of L. Granville, and Jennie Young, the sister of Foster and Leslie Young.

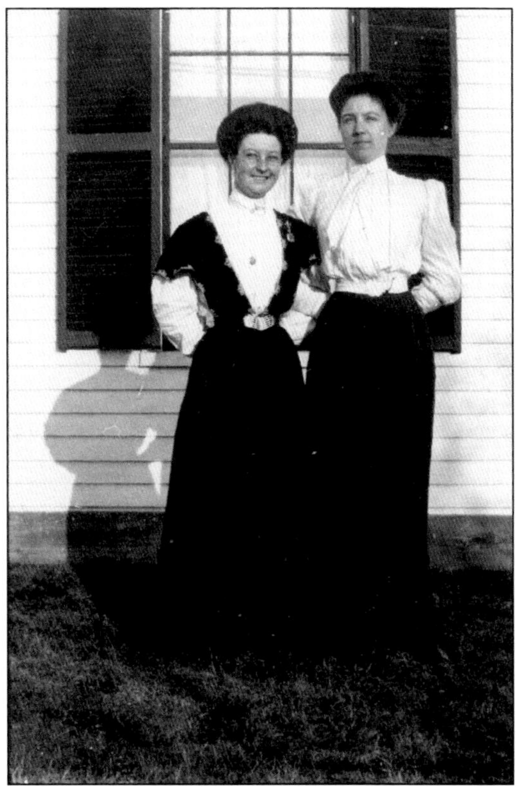

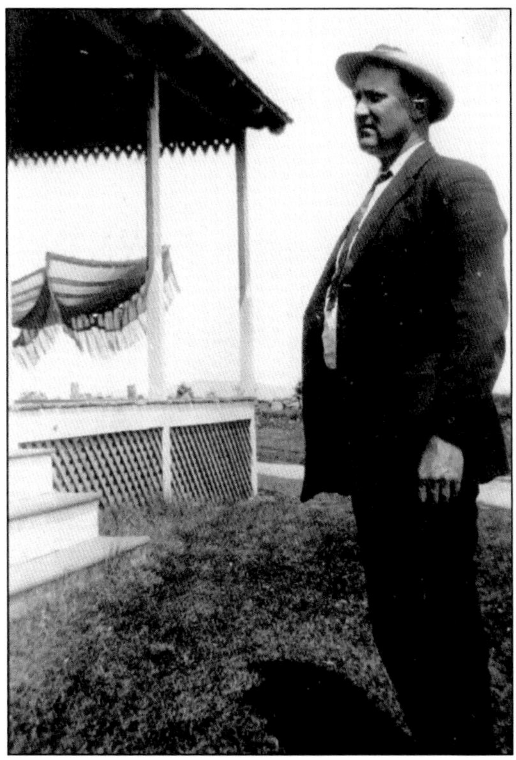

Capt. L. Granville Phillips, the son of Benjamin and Edith Phillips, is shown next to the porch of the Phillips House. Phillips was a sailing master and builder. He and his wife, Eva Herrick, lived at Brooklin Corner next to the general store in the home of Eva's parents, William and Annie Herrick. Eva and Granville had one daughter, Annie Marguerite, who married Philip Bartlett.

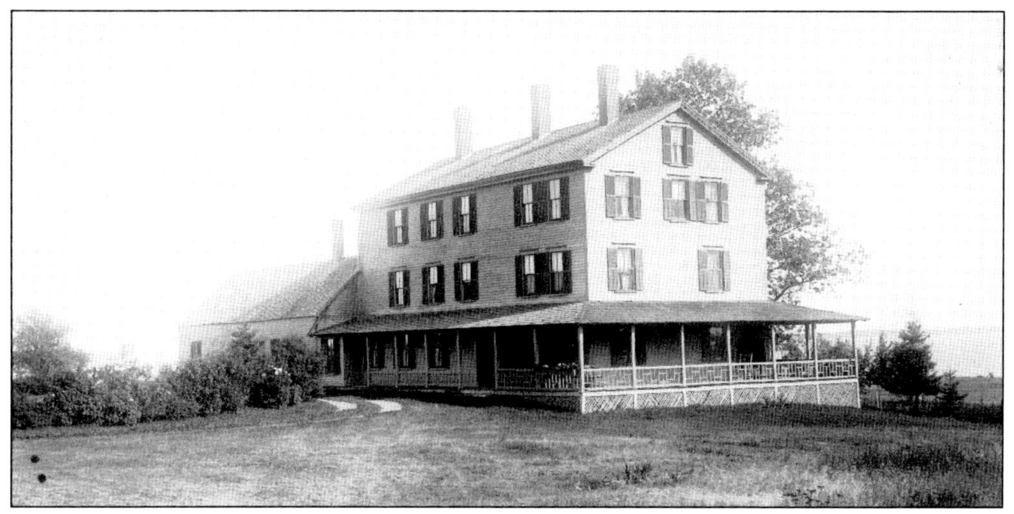

The Lookout Inn was built in the late 1800s by adding a third floor and a west wing on the original Flye Colonial-style house. The land has been in the Flye family since William Flye had the original land grant from the king of England. The early Flyes were boatbuilders and built schooners on the shore here. In 1817, John Flye built the *Hannah* and, in 1837, the *Sailor's Delight*. In 1828, Abraham Flye built the *Monitor*, and in 1853, Gilman Flye built the *Graduate*.

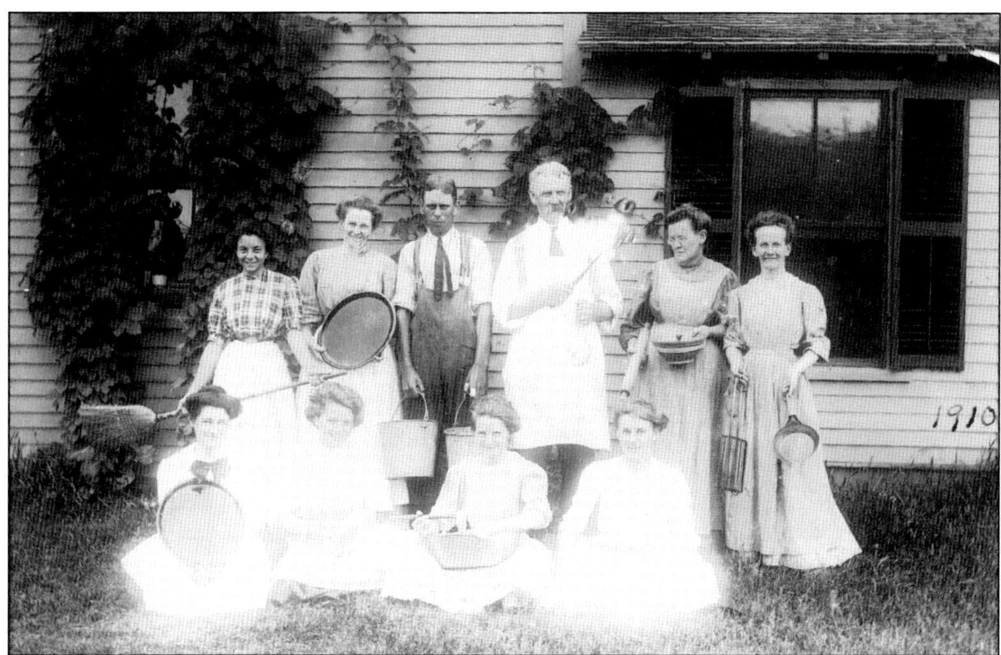

Staff members of the Lookout Inn are pictured here in 1910 with their trays and cooking implements. Standing fourth from the left is Owen Flye, founder of the inn, and seated to the far right is his niece Lettie Flye. Over the years, many Brooklin folks worked here. In 1910, Helen McFarland and her sisters Adele and Alline were employed and are most likely in this picture.

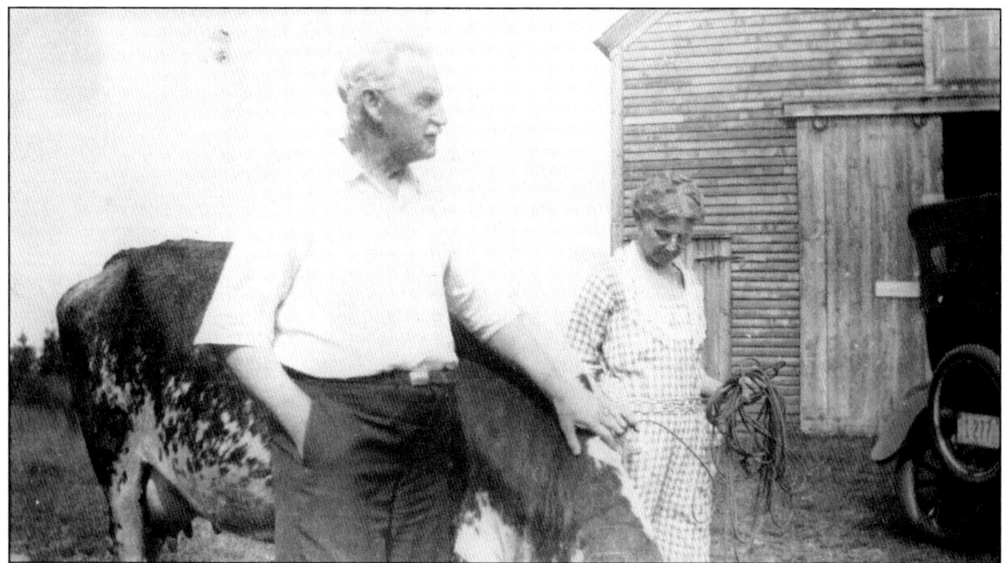

Owen Flye and his sister Clara are pictured near the barn with a cow named Ida. In the door of the barn is Owen Flye's Model T. Clara and her husband, Henry Flye, were the parents of Lettie Flye. Owen was a teacher and superintendent of schools in Brooklin. A man of many talents, he belonged to the town band and was a cook at the inn, an accomplished weaver, and a developer of Flye Point as a summer colony.

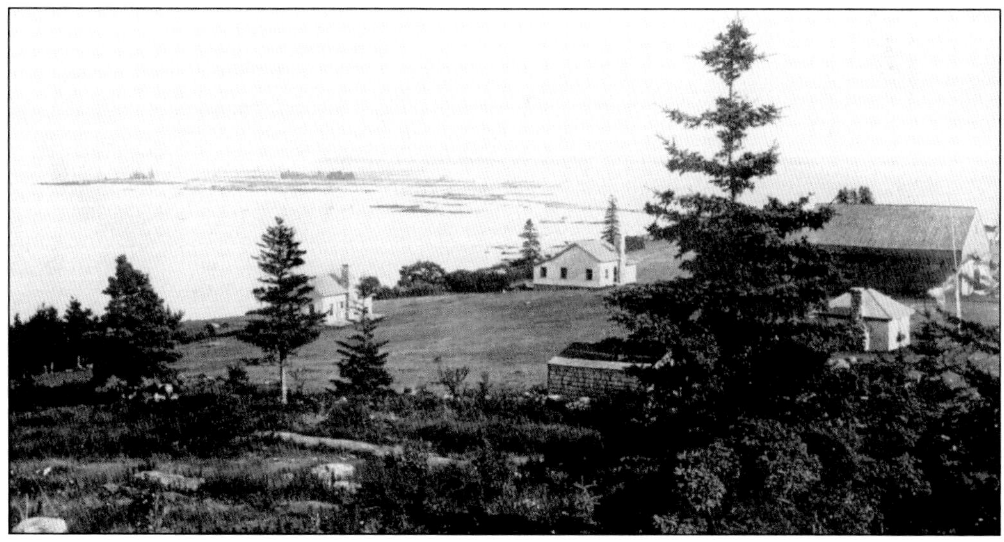

The cottages at Flye Point are seen in this view from the hill. To the far left is Denhilde, built by Wesley Gott in 1910 and owned by the Hildebrand family. The Boulders and the small cottage Owenta, in the front right, are still used as summer rentals. The old barn was later torn down.

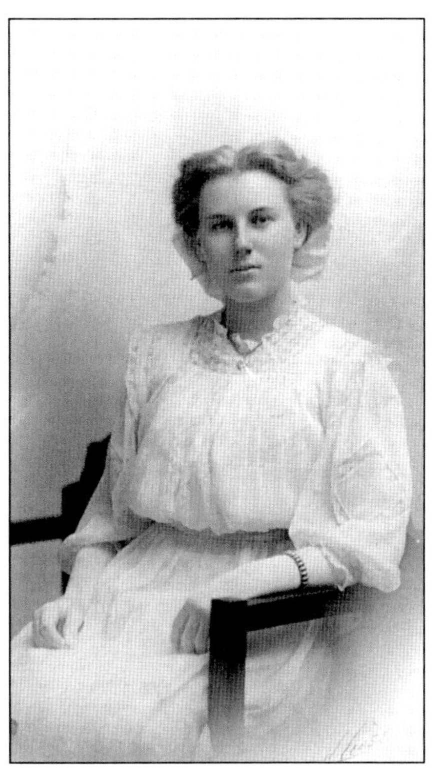

Lettie Beryl Flye was the second owner of the Lookout Inn and cottages. She was the only child of Henry and Clara Flye and part of the long line of Flye descendants who resided on Flye Point since the time of the original land grant. After her graduation from Brooklin High School in 1905, she went to Burdett Business College, married R. Lewis Smith, and raised four children.

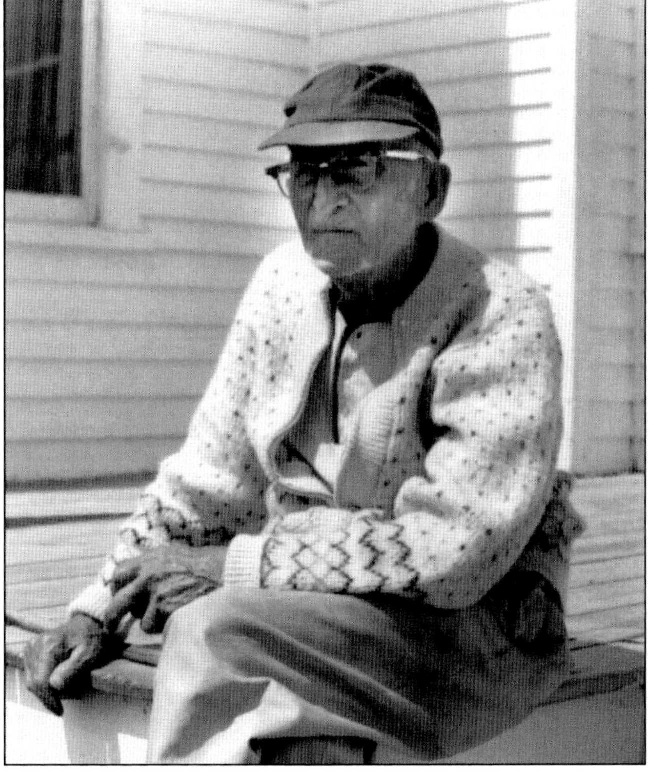

Rodney Lewis Smith was known best in Brooklin as the agent for the Eastern Steamship Company. For 30 years, he worked on the wharf and knew all the comings and goings in Brooklin. Later, he was a selectman for the town until he retired and spent his last years at Flye Point. He was the son of Rodney and Jennie H. Smith.

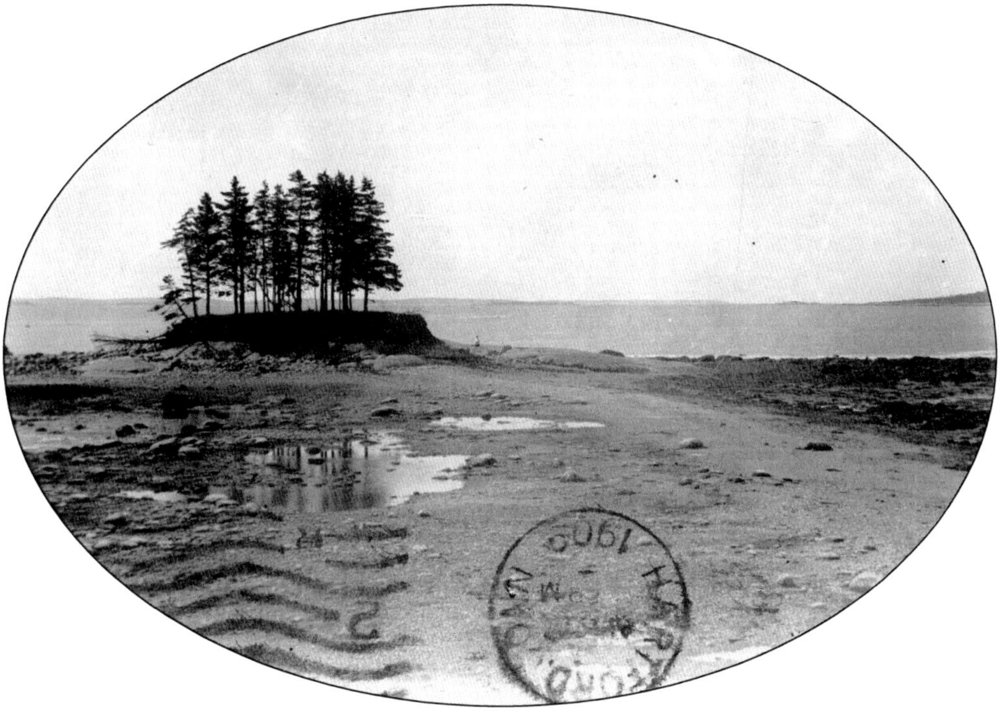

The Hub, off the end of Flye Point, had many tall trees and soil to hold them c. 1910. Today, there is just one little tree on top of large granite rocks.

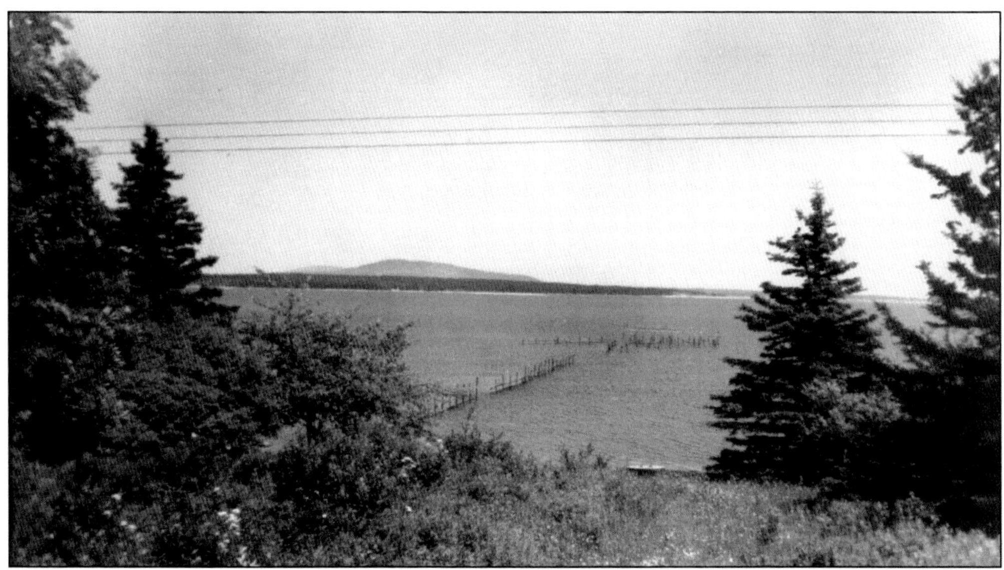

The fish weir off Flye Point belonged to Kenneth Dow, whose son Wade Dow remembers building the weir out of sticks and brush when he was a boy.

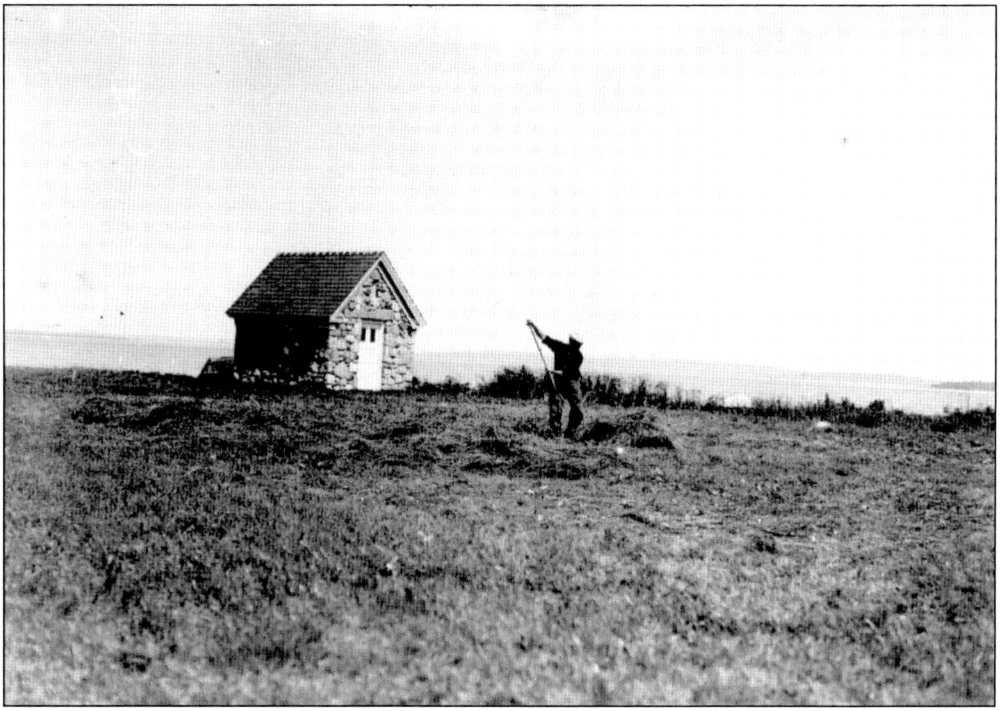

Keeper Rosco Chandler is shown haying on Green Island Light.

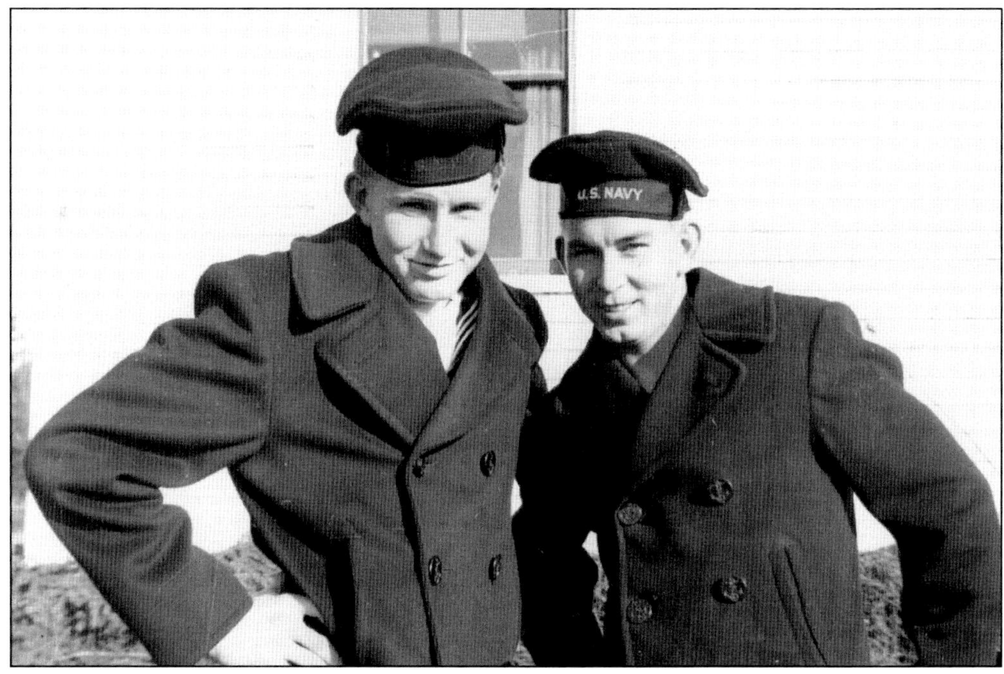

Brothers Linwood (right) and Ken Carter are pictured in their navy uniforms. Linwood served from 1950 to 1954, married Elizabeth Gray, and became a lobsterman. Ken was a navy career man, married Betty Carter, and later became a lobsterman.

Seven

North Brooklin

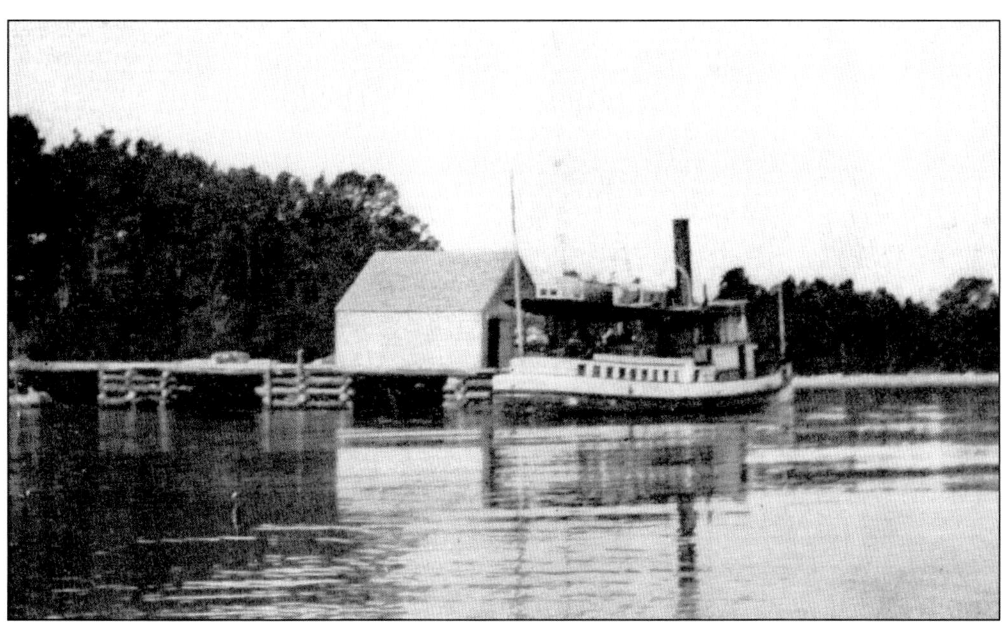

Known as Dodge's Wharf, the Eastern Steamship Company wharf at North Brooklin was on the shore near the Murfey house. Steamers such as the *Percy V.*, pictured here, made regular stops on the way to Surry and Blue Hill.

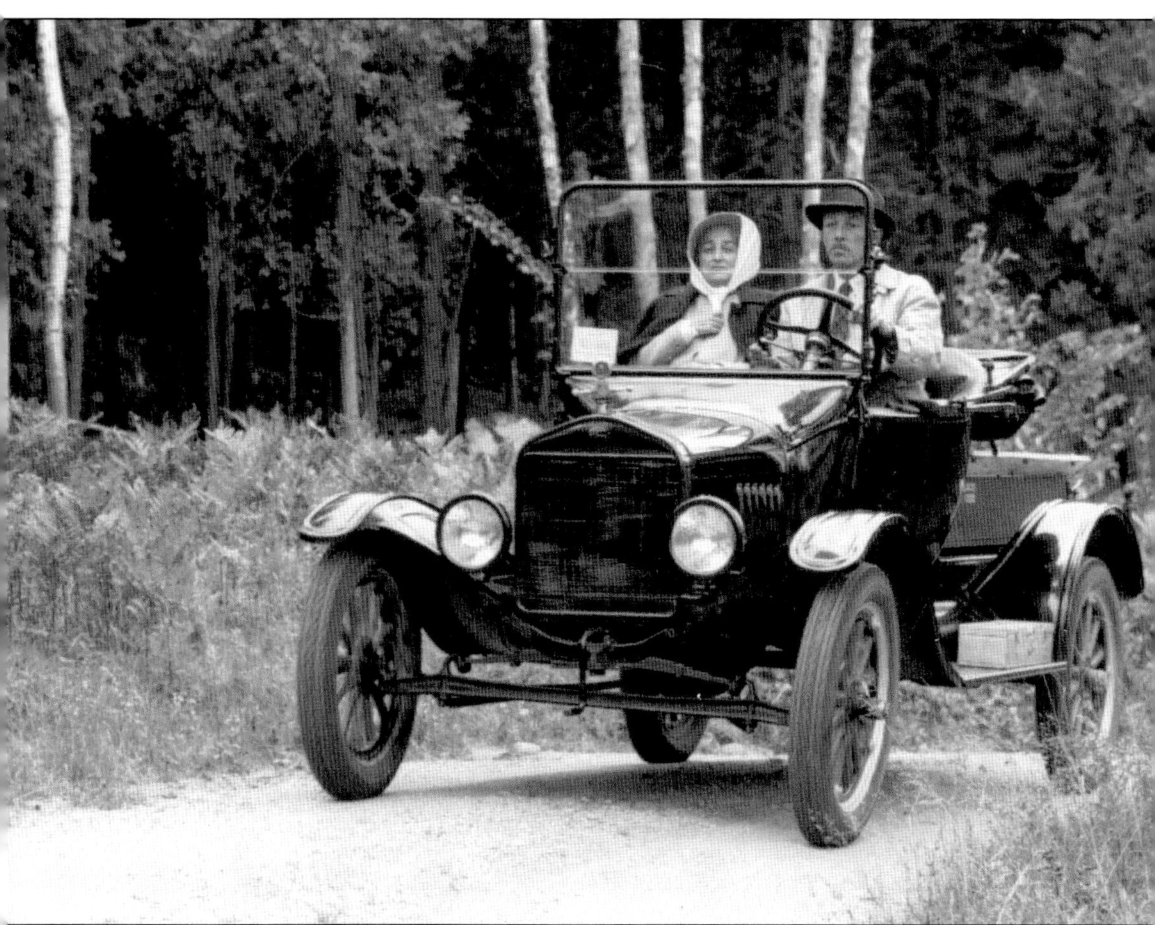

Katharine and E.B. White are shown on an outing in Brooklin in his beloved Model T. The Whites had been coming to Brooklin for many years before they moved permanently to their farm in North Brooklin in 1958. In that barn lived the spider and pig that were the inspiration for the characters in *Charlotte's Web*. Both Whites continued their writing careers from Brooklin and were instrumental in revitalizing the Friend Memorial Public Library in town.

On the porch of the E.B. White house are longtime employees Arlene Freethey and Claribel (Herrick) (Staples) Tainter. Arlene, the wife of Minard, was known for her fine cooking skills. Claribel, the wife of Wallace, kept the household running in good order.

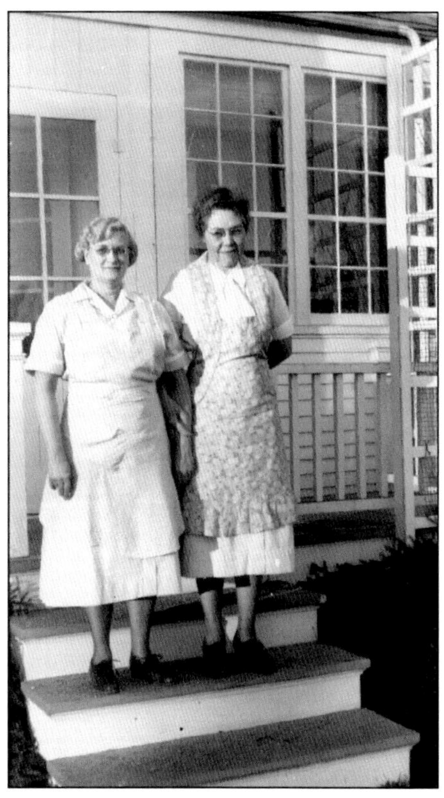

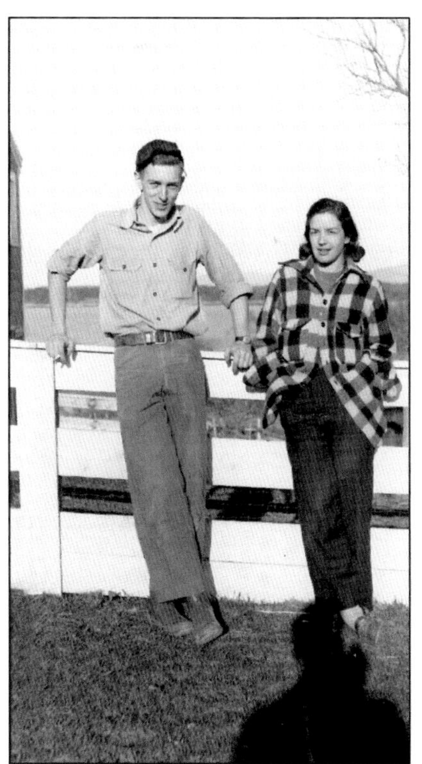

Katharine and E.B. White's son Joel and his wife, Allene, are shown in Brooklin in 1953. Joel, owner of the Brooklin Boat Yard in Center Harbor, designed 55 boats during his life, from the Center Harbor 12½-foot to the 76-foot W-class racing sloops. Allene writes a cooking column called "Mutual Benefit" in the *Ellsworth American*.

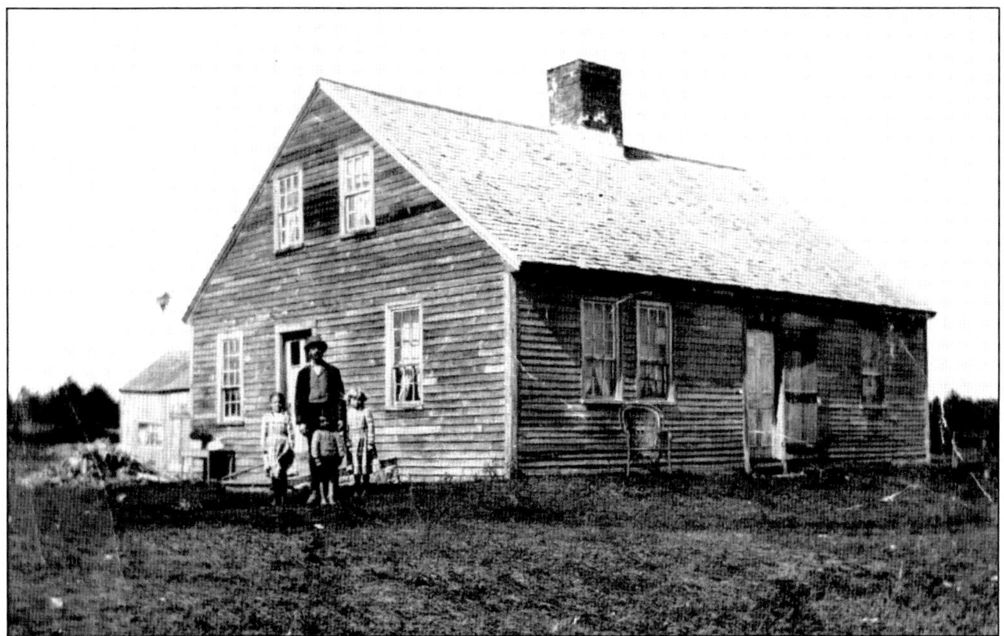

Capt. John Allen's old home, in North Brooklin, is across from the E.B. White farm. In front of the house, Bessie Allen Smith and Lucy Allen Choate are pictured standing with their father. Today, the house at that site belongs to Captain Allen's son George and George's wife, Georgene, and is known as Creeping Thyme Farm.

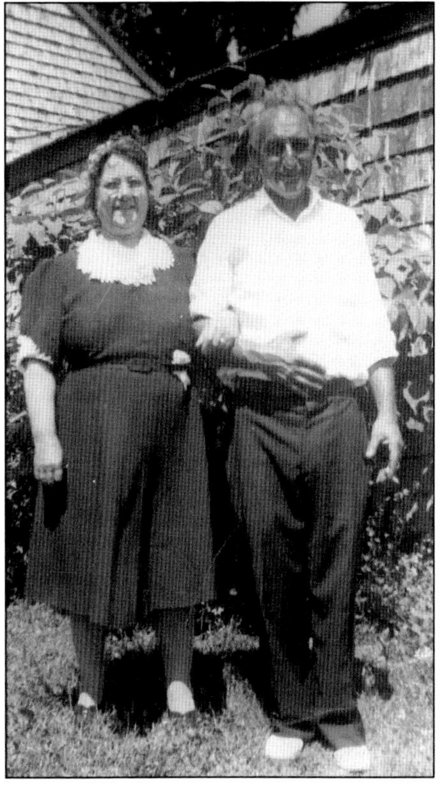

Pictured here are Capt. John Allen and his wife, Effie Ryan. Their children were Rachel, John, Stanley, George, and Louise.

Capt. Charles Sherman founded the Grovehurst Inn with his wife, Eldora Mary Allen. They had three children—Eugene M., Louis A., and Mabel A. (Sherman) Davis—and lived in the Means house on High Street before moving to the farmhouse across from the inn. Mabel Sherman Davis later ran Grovehurst, and in the 1940s, Bertha (Shepherd) Sherman became the third hostess.

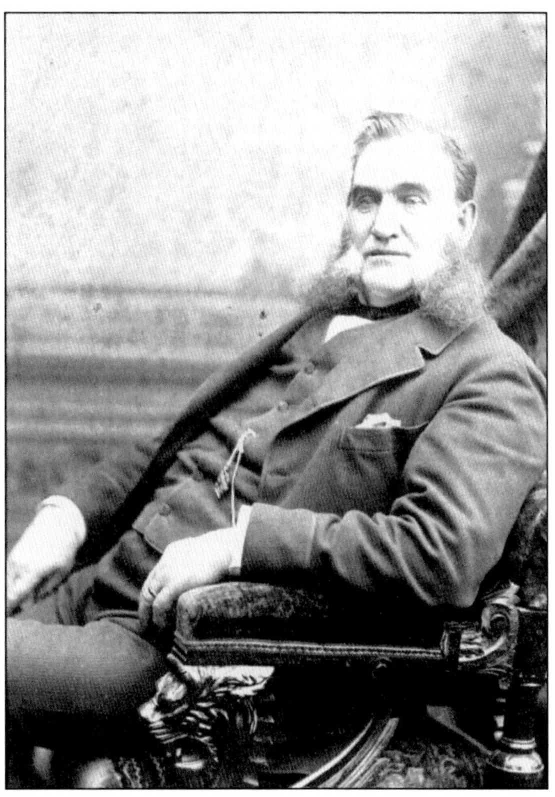

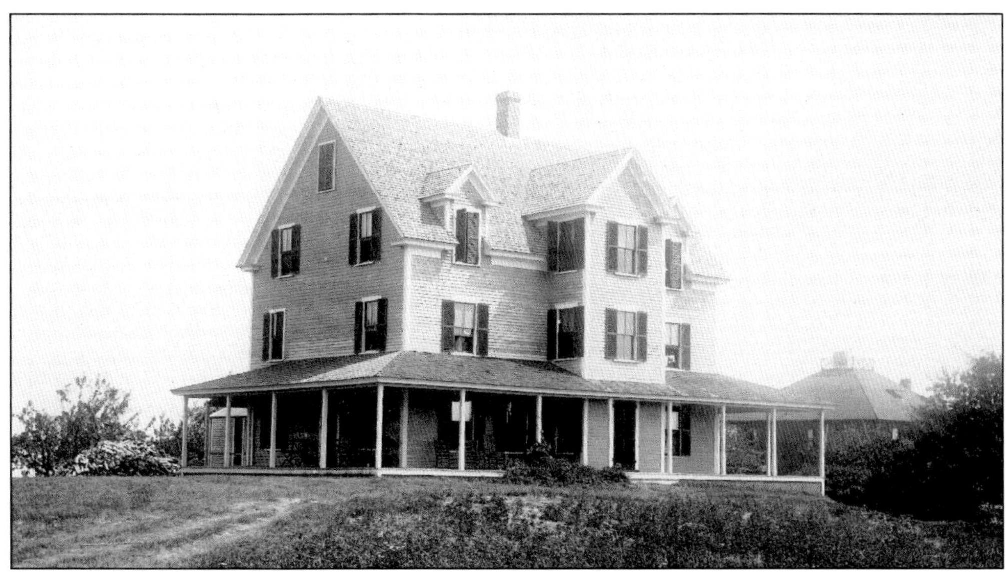

The Grovehurst Inn, in North Brooklin, is pictured in 1897. It was built by adding two floors to Nehemiah Allen's 1700s homestead on the knoll overlooking Allen's Cove. A guest, Charles Bragg, recalls the trips to Gott's and Tinker's Islands on the *Rodera* and the visits to Allen Cole's boat shop in the nearby cove as a few of the pleasures of his visits to Grovehurst. The Grovehurst Inn was taken down in 1954.

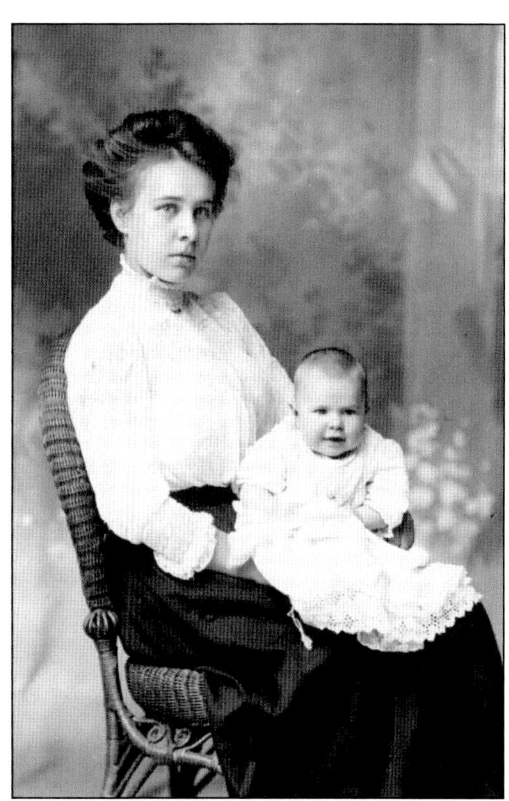

Laura (Cole) Sherman is pictured with her daughter Gertrude. Laura and her husband, Lawrence, lived in what is now known as the Godfrey house in North Brooklin.

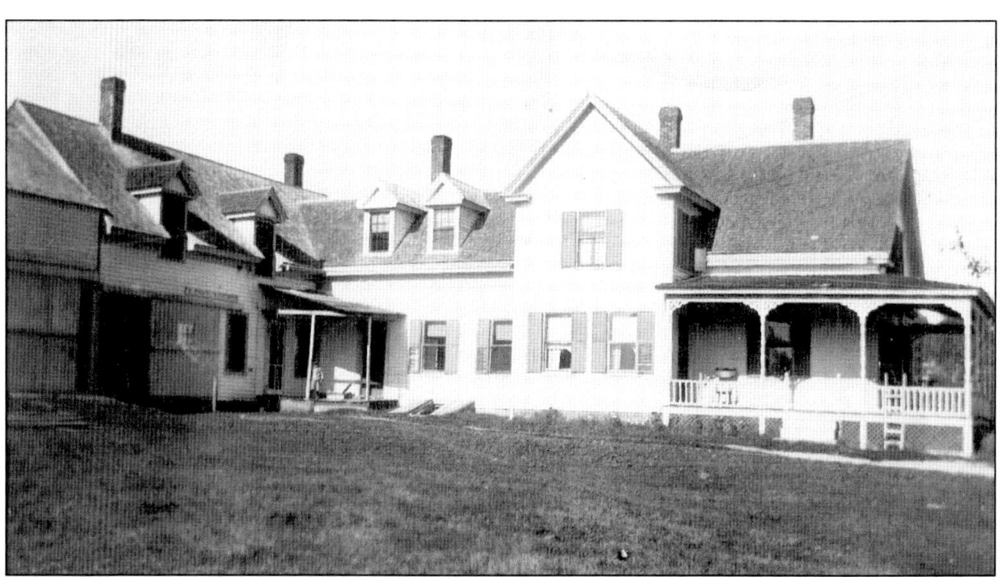

The Sherman boardinghouse is shown after Laura and Lawrence Sherman added on the ells to create more bedrooms. Laura ran the house, and Lawrence was the North Brooklin postmaster and a fisherman.

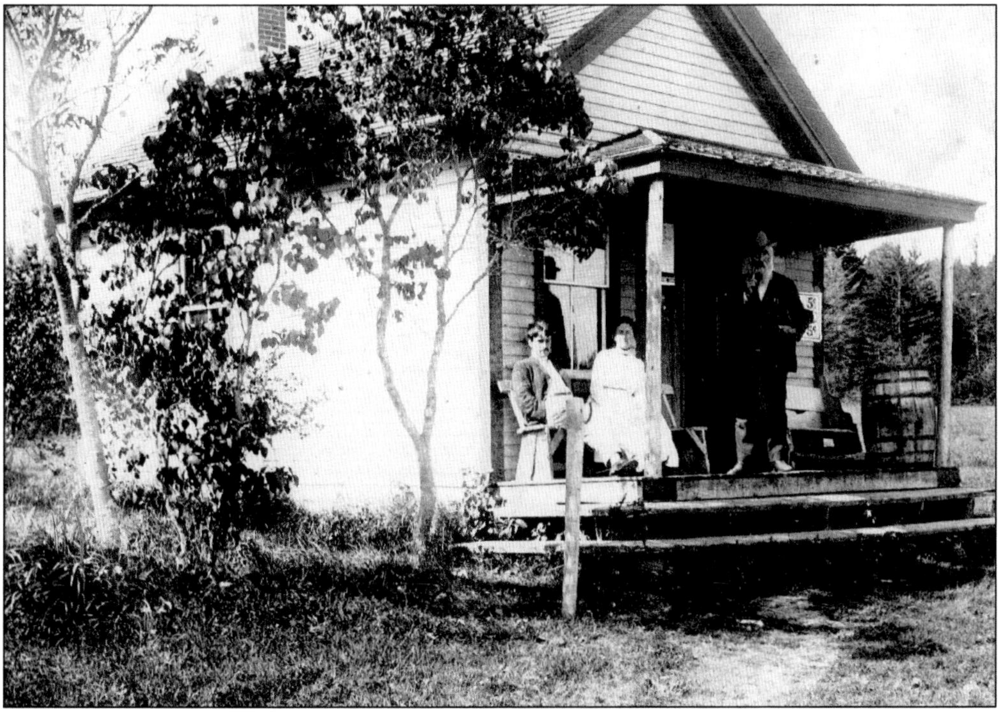

In the field next to the Sherman house was this variety store. Sitting on the porch in 1904 are, from left to right, summer boarder Harry Neville, Emma Sherman (the wife of A.H. Sherman), and Isaac Cole.

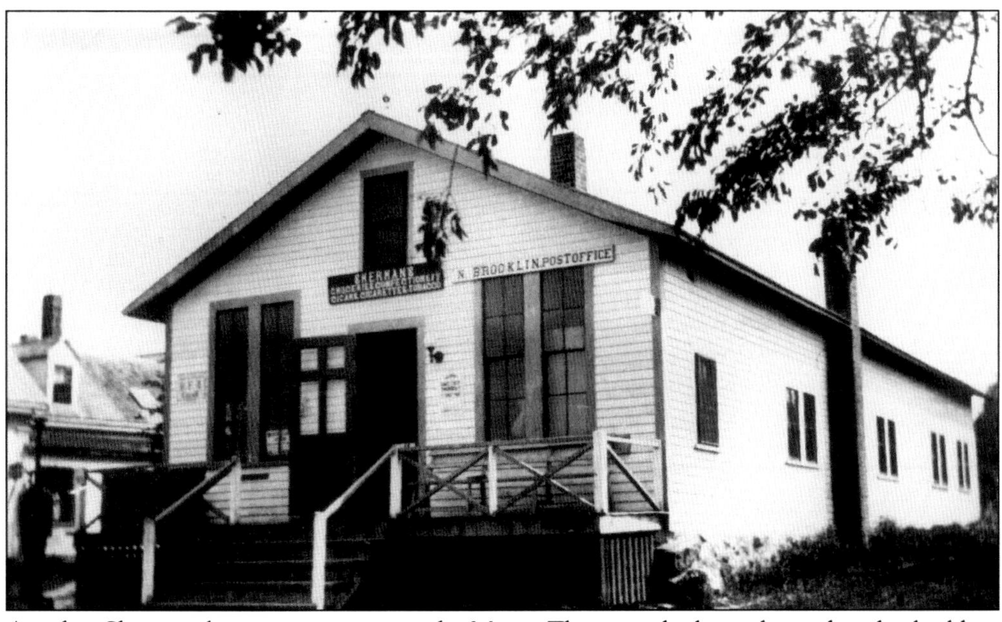

Another Sherman business venture was the Miami Theater, which was housed in this building (constructed in 1922), along with the North Brooklin Post Office and Sherman's store. Movies were shown for 25¢, and Ralston Means Sr. cranked the picture machine. The theater closed after 1928. The building was torn down, and a house on Naskeag was built from the lumber.

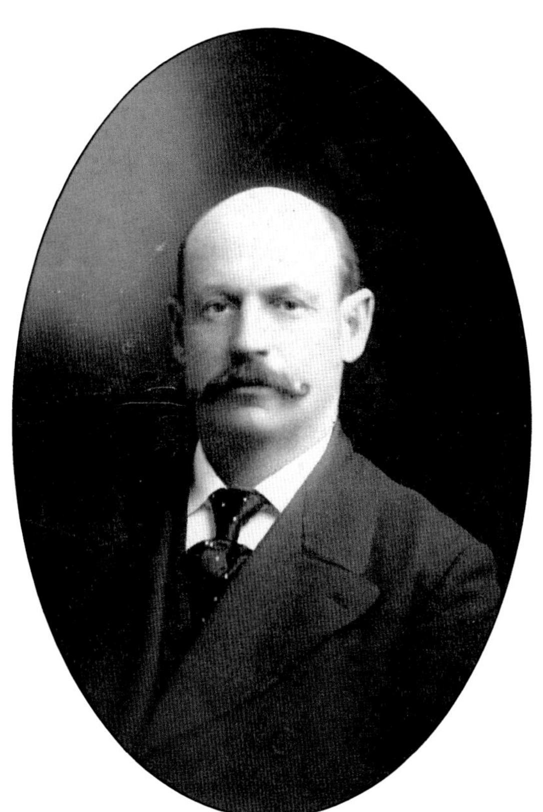

Mark L. Dodge (1855–1929) was a fisherman and first selectman (serving from 1900 to 1904). He also helped build Bay View Hall in North Brooklin. He was married to Annie M. Cole (1860–1946).

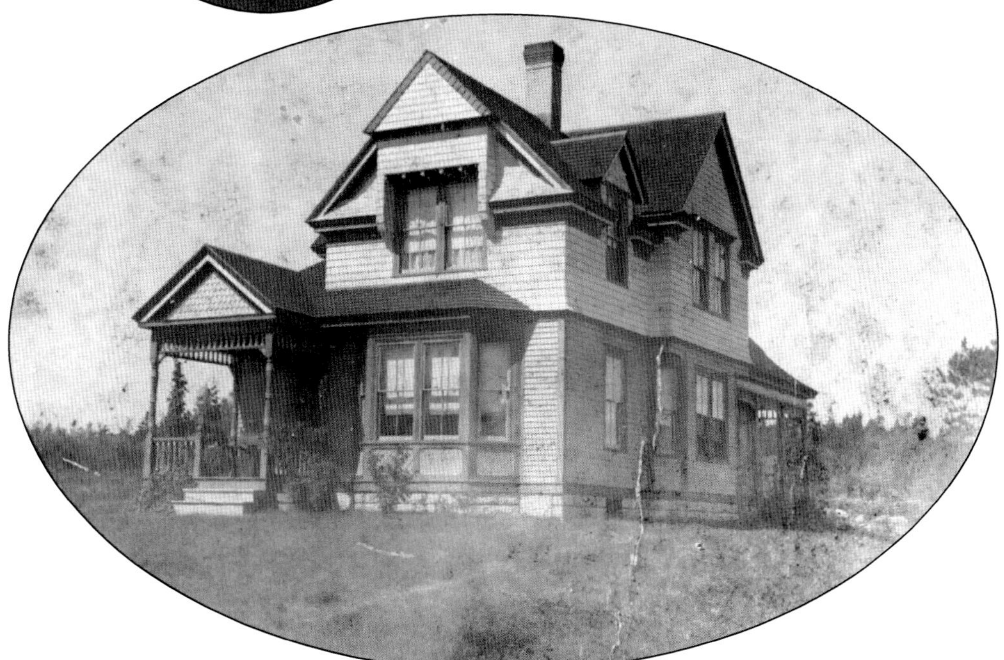

The Mark and Annie Dodge house, on Cemetery Road, is pictured as it looked in the late 1800s. The Dodges' daughter Katherine Dodge Kent lived there after her parents, and it was later the home of Dean Bingham.

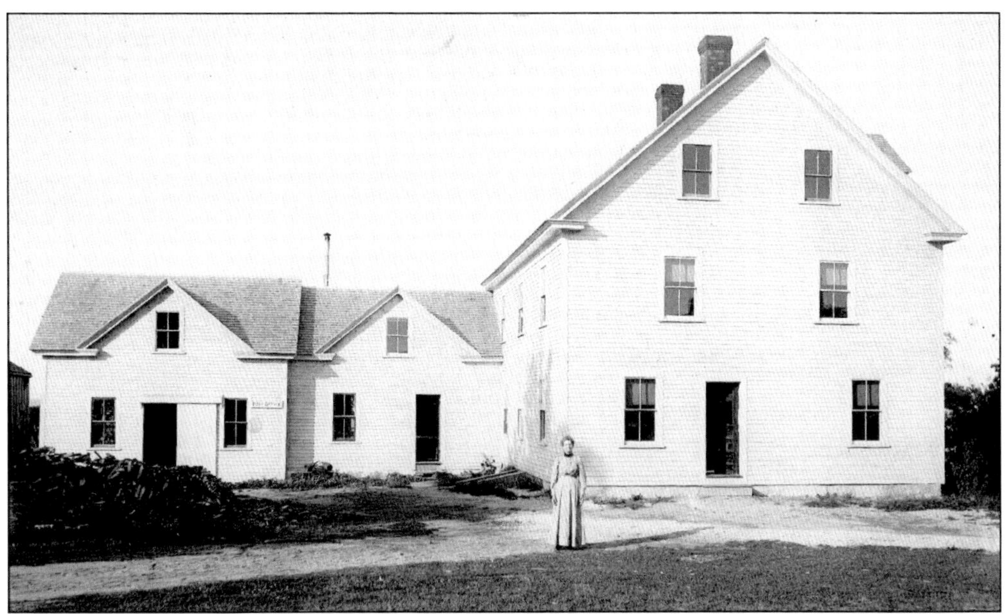

The Bay View Hotel, owned by Emery Dodge, was located near the junction of High Street and Bay Road. The land went all the way down to Dodge's Wharf on the shore. Dodge served as postmaster in one of the two attached ells of the house. The large ell is now the barn of the old Pervear house next door. The hotel was torn down by the next owner for tax reasons.

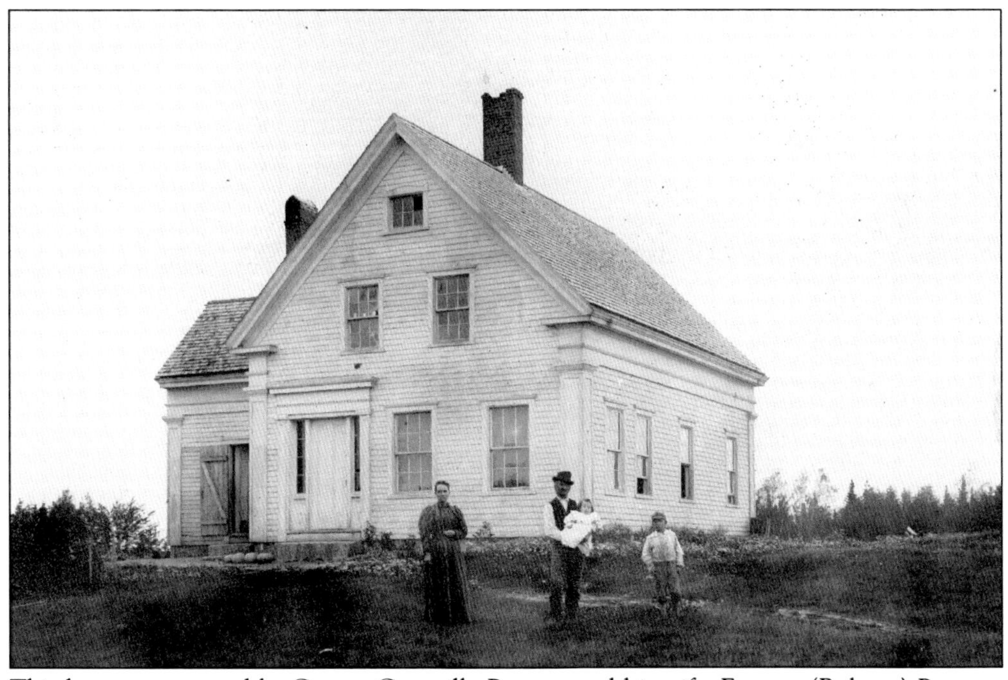

This house was rented by George Granville Pervear and his wife, Frances (Roberts) Pervear, on High Street, where they brought up 11 children. When their son George Elmer was 13 years old, he started making payments and eventually owned the house. Later, his daughter Amelita lived there.

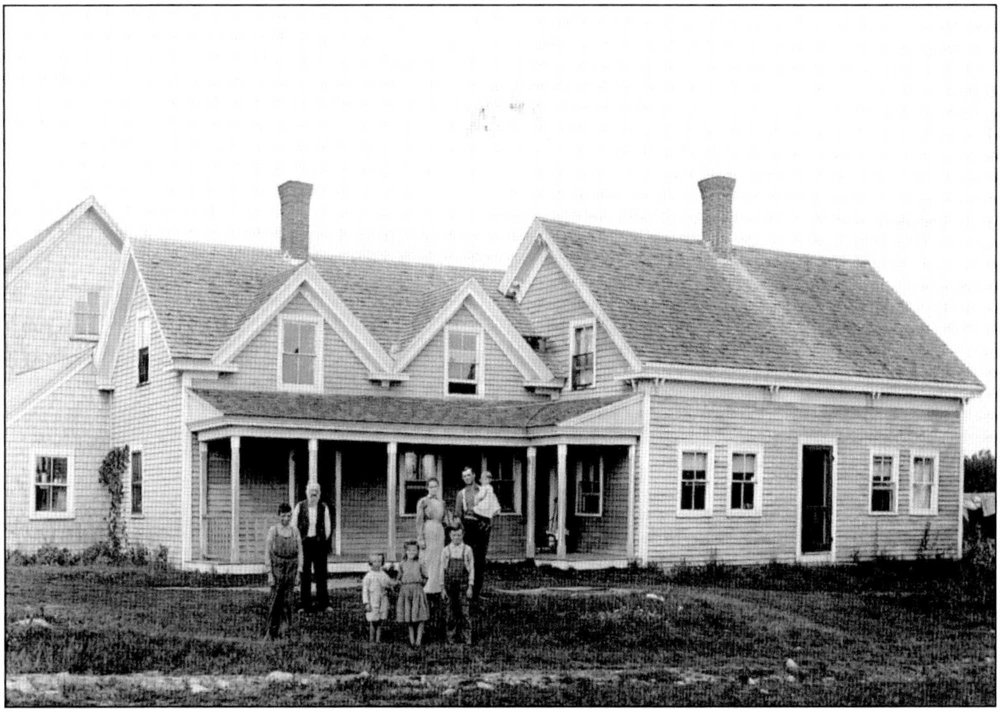

This house belonged to Mattie L. and Erastus J. Candage, who are shown in front with members of their family. It later belonged to Edna and Howard Pervear, who ran the North Brooklin Post Office there for a while before that moved to Bay View Hall.

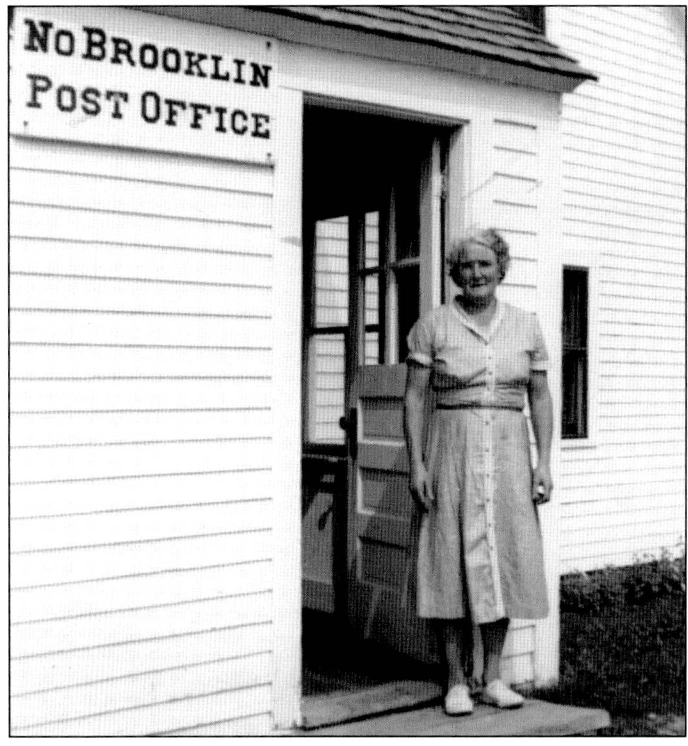

Edna (Allen) Pervear was postmaster in North Brooklin for many years. She lived on the curve of Route 175 right near the junction of High Street.

Katherine R. Pervear (left) and Harriet Pervear Tapley are shown in this photograph.

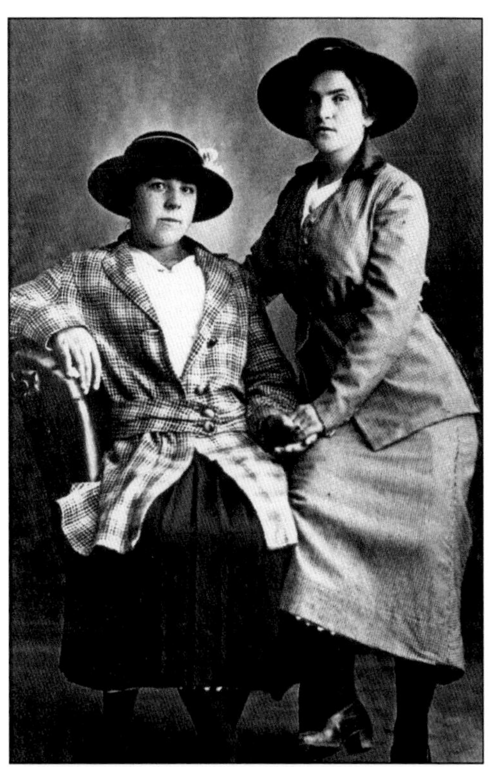

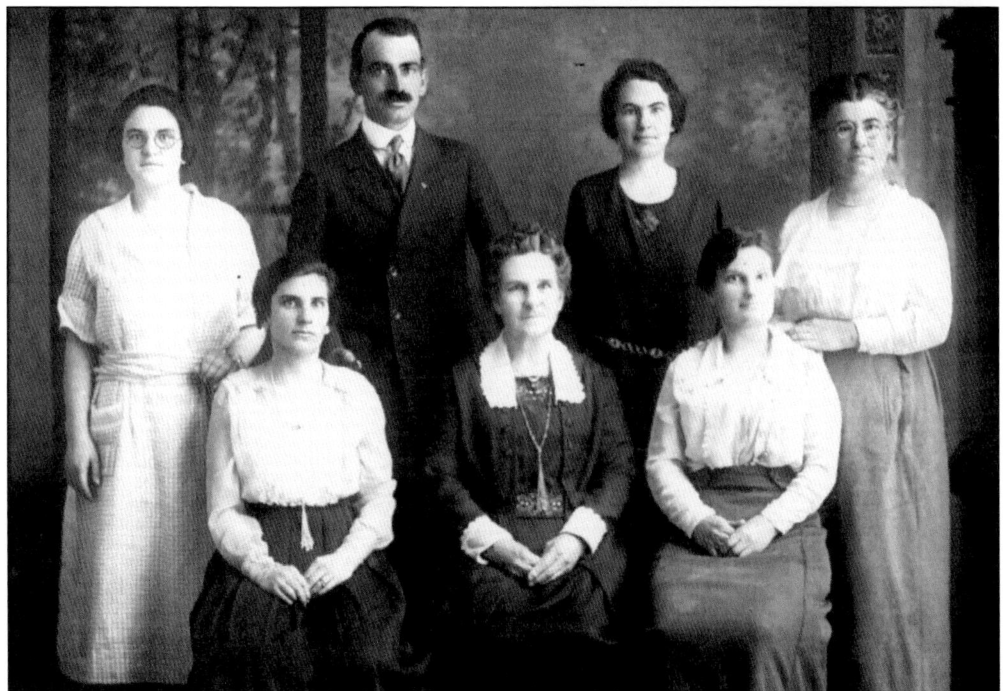

The Pervear family members shown in the early 20th century are, from left to right, as follows: (front row) Maria, Frances (Roberts), and Hannah E.; (back row) Harriet (Tapley), George Elmer, Nellie, and Ella.

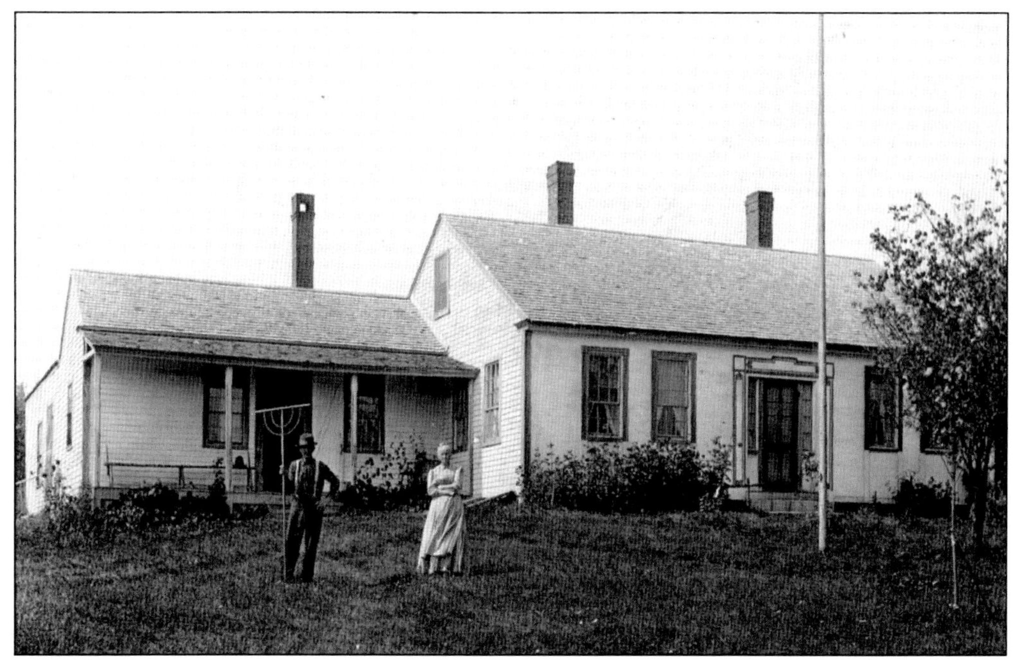

This house was built by Kenny Stanley and his wife, Elizabeth, *c.* 1816. In 1860, it belonged to Samuel Ober and, in 1881, to Peter Anderson. It is thought that Celestia and Adelbert Seavey, the next owners, are the ones pictured here. Giles and Grace (Seavey) Webber lived there next, and in 1929, it was purchased by Chester Flye.

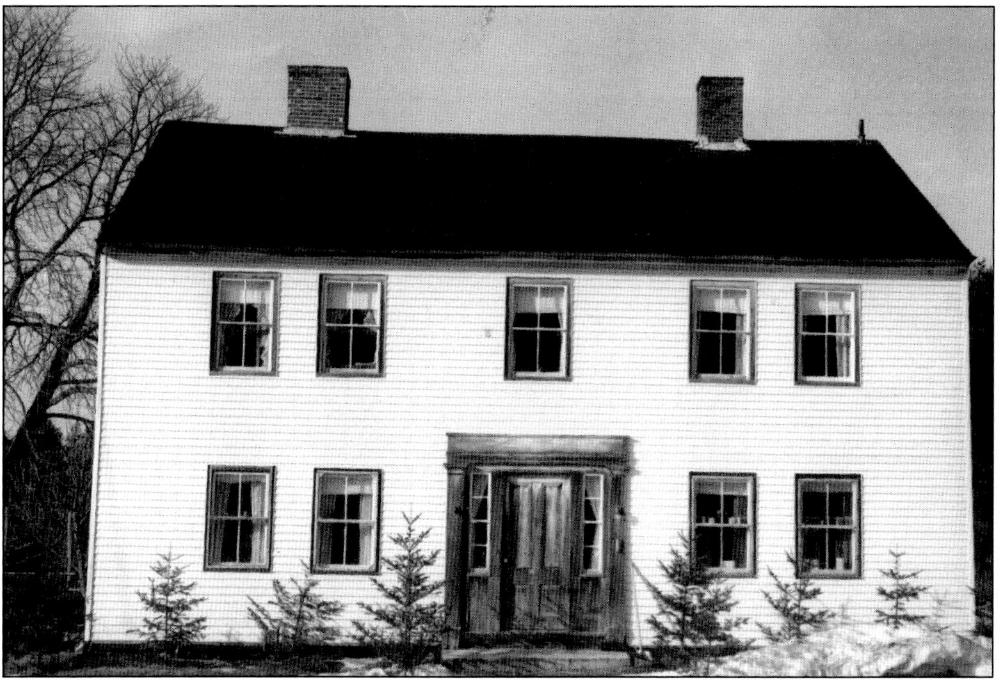

The Hooper house, on River Road, was built by Samuel and Lenny Herrick *c.* 1800 on land purchased from Ebenezer Eaton. It was built as a two-family home, with each side having a chimney. In 1955, one of the chimneys was torn down without ever having been used.

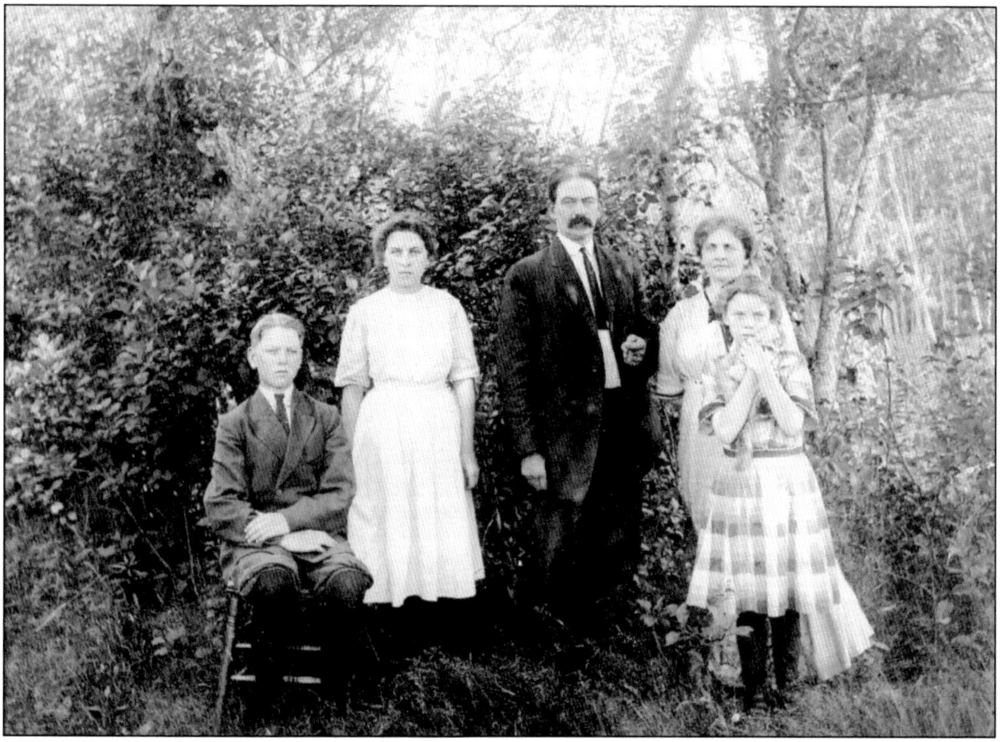

Fred L. Cole (1874–1945) and his wife, Clara Thurston (1876–1960), are pictured with their children, from left to right, Frederick L., Dorothy T., and Elizabeth Cole. In 1911, Fred was a merchant in North Brooklin.

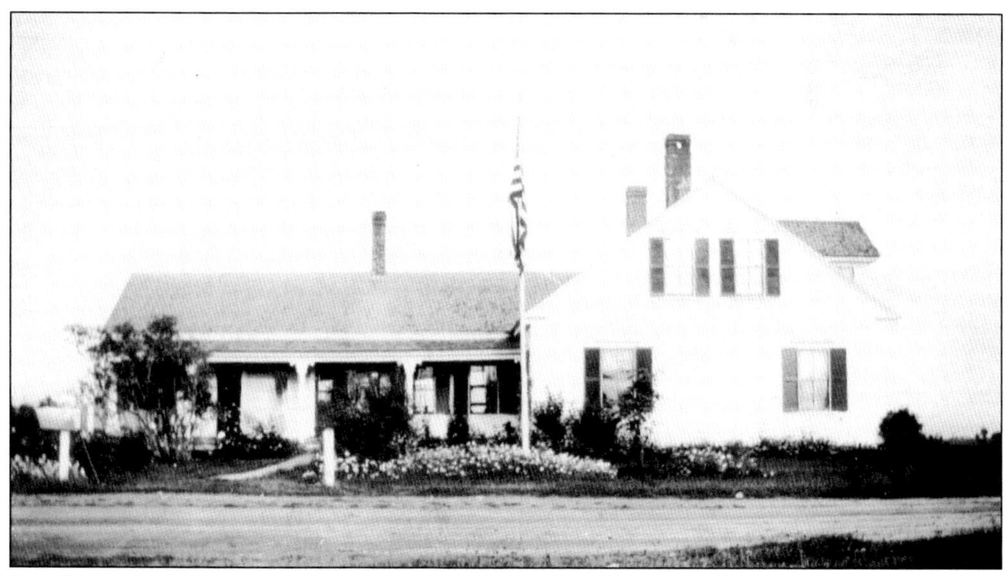

The Cole House, where Ben and Emma Cole lived in North Brooklin, is shown here. After Ben and Emma Cole, Eugene and his wife, Suzie N. Cole, lived there, and it is still in the Cole family.

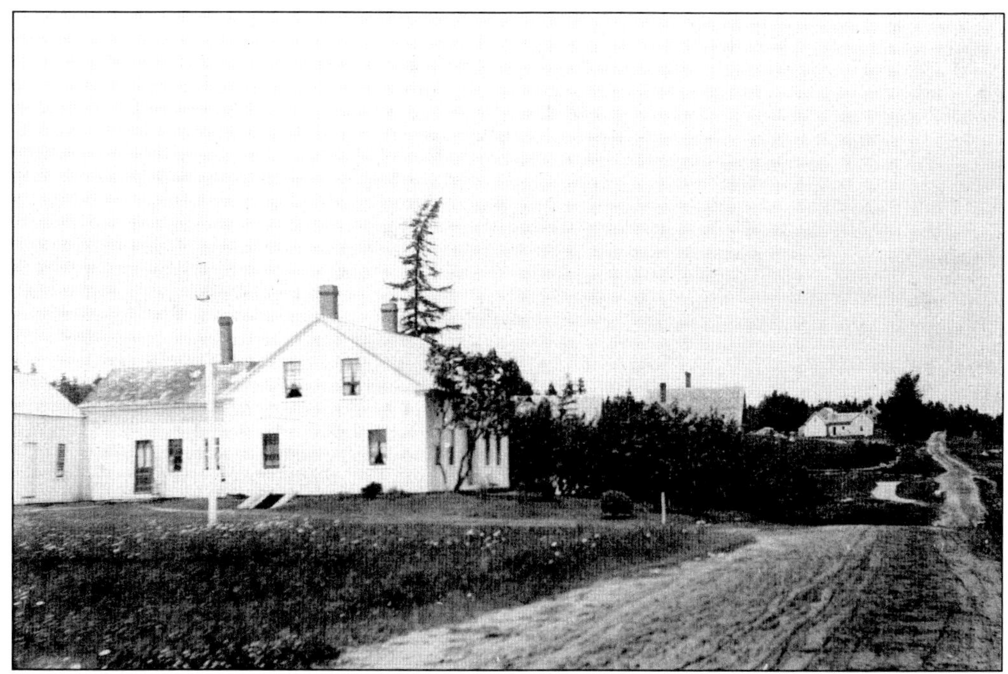

This North Brooklin photograph, taken before the roads were paved, shows the Hamilton houses shortly before the South Blue Hill town line. The first house on the left belonged to Thomas Hamilton, and the next belonged to Gene Hamilton. Gene Hamilton's house is now being extensively restored.The third belonged to Floyd Hamilton but is no longer there.

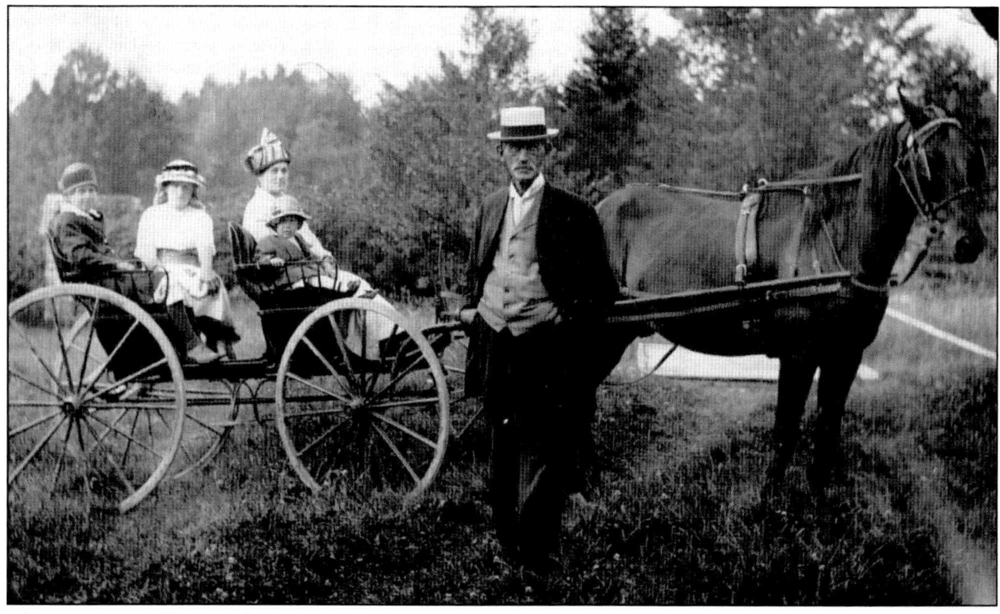

This picture shows three generations of the Freethey-Hamilton family in their horse-drawn carriage. From left to right are Ruby Freethey (Burnham), Rebecca Freethey Vial, and Winnifred Hamilton Freethey, next to young Marjorie Freethey Teachout. Standing is Fred Hamilton, the father of Winnifred and grandfather of the three children. The Freetheys lived on Harriman Point.

Eight

Schools, Scenes, and Celebrations

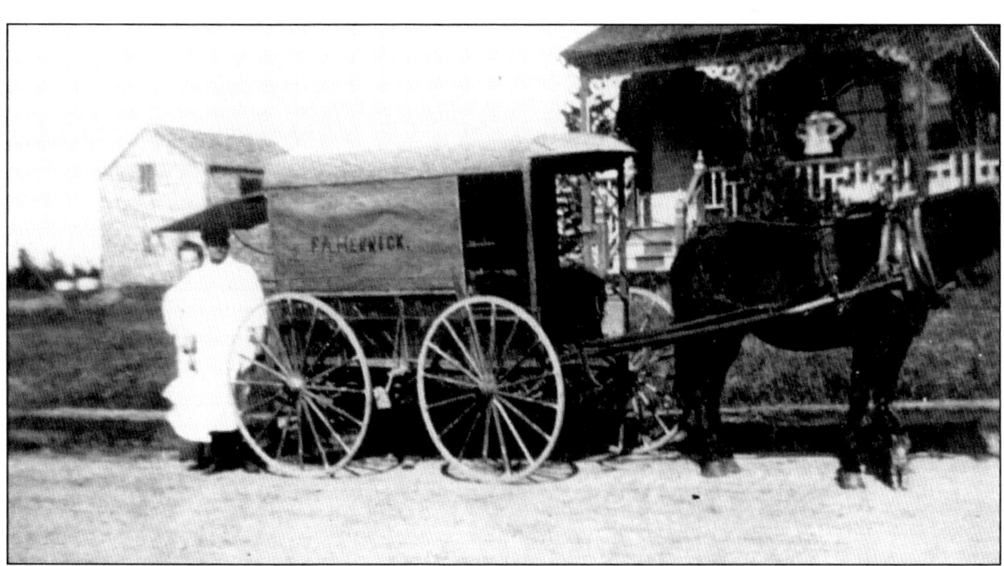

Frank A. Herrick's horse-drawn meat wagon is seen in front of a customer's house for a delivery. Frank (1876–1941) married Etta Candage (1872–1926), and they had a large family of girls and one boy, Frank A. Herrick Jr.

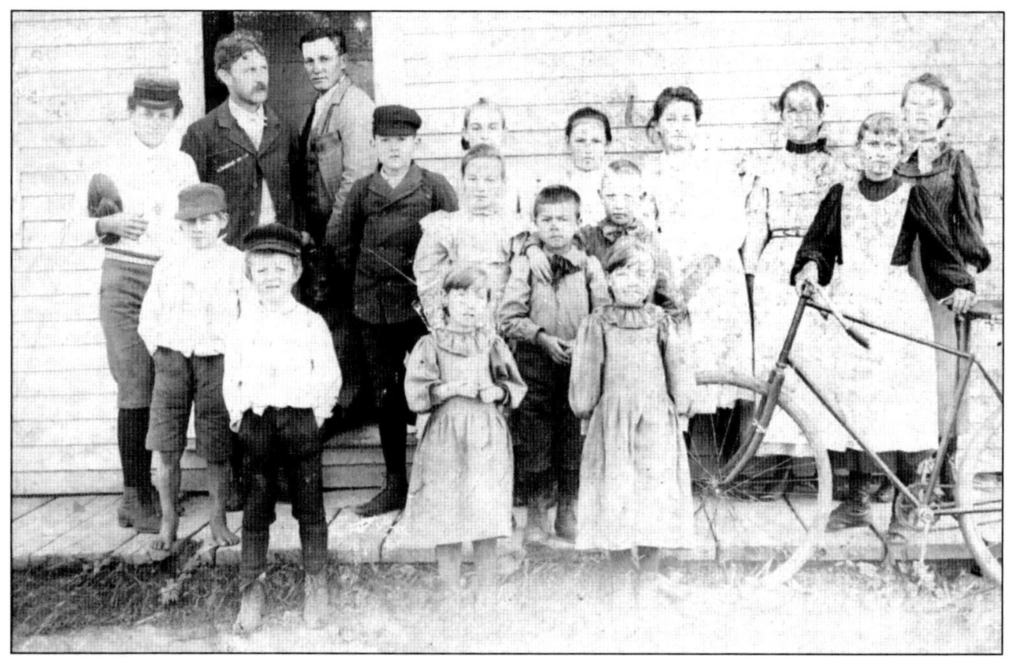

Owen Flye is one of the adults pictured here at schoolhouse No. 7 on River Road. The students are Rowland Carlton, Carol Kane, ? Day, George Torrey, Minnie Hooper, Belva Hooper, Minnie Turner, Celia Turner, Linnie Leighton, Frank Leighton, Louise Anderson, Sara Hall, Clara Carver, Bina Kane, and Alice Turner.

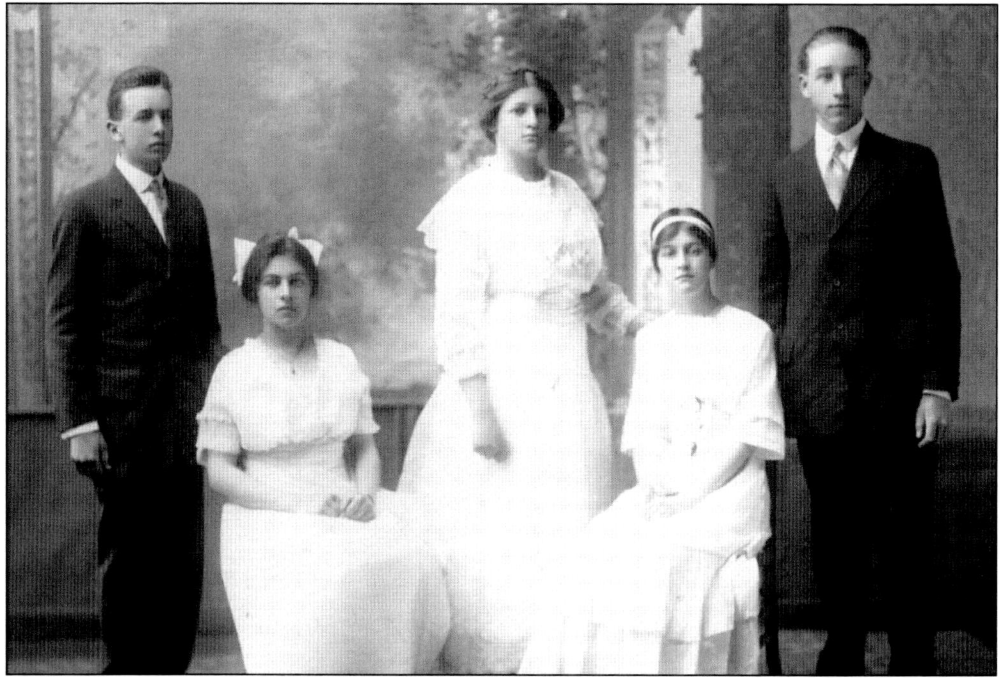

These members of the Brooklin High School Class of 1915 are, from left to right, Stanley Dority (U.S. Army), Dorothy Cole (Pratt Institute), Irene Wells (Bates College), Etta Bridges (Nevells), and Eugene Young (electrical contracting).

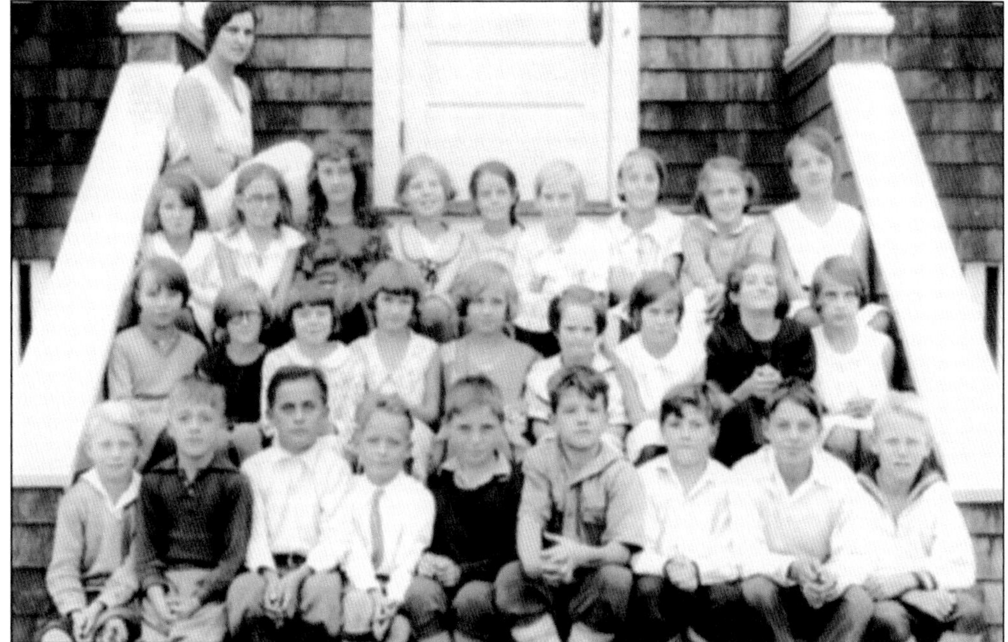

Teacher Eulalia Bridges is shown on the steps of the "Little Red Schoolhouse" with her class. From left to right are the following: (front row) Arnold Staples, unidentified, Percy Henderson, Beverly Staples, Wesley Bartlett, Clyde Cole, two unidentified, and Russell Staples; (middle row) Evelyn Holden, Natalie Smith, Virginia Tyler, two unidentified, Annie Phillips, Norma Smith, Elizabeth Allen, and unidentified; (back row) unidentified, Ruth Corbin, Glynita Flye, Elizabeth Gray, Mary Corbin, Shirley Bartlett, unidentified, Elise Allen, and unidentified.

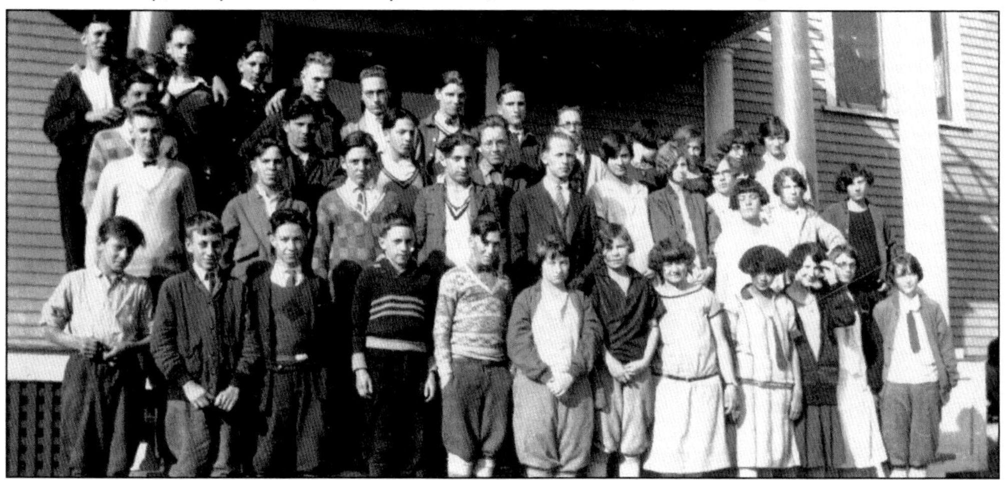

These Brooklin High School students in 1925 are, from left to right, as follows: (first row) Charles Tyler, Elmer Bent, Frank Day, Edgar Wells, Berdard Anderson, Vivian Ward, Ree Dennison, Edna Smith, Edith Hale, Jennie Firth, Emma Candage, and Effie Wardwell; (second row) Kenneth Dow, Harry Wardwell, Robert Bridges, Waldo Clapp, Keith Weymouth, Dorothy Carter, Dorothy Lambert, and Leona Howard; (third row) Elmer Bridges, Chester Freethey, Earl Firth, Cecil Clapp, Alvin Howard, Rayford McFarland, Caroline Mitchell, Elizabeth Henderson, Eulalia Bridges, and Thelma Lurvey; (fourth row) Frank Sylvester, Sumner Bridges, Wallace Tainter, Walter Staples, Walton McFarland, Basil Roberts, and Ronald Gray.

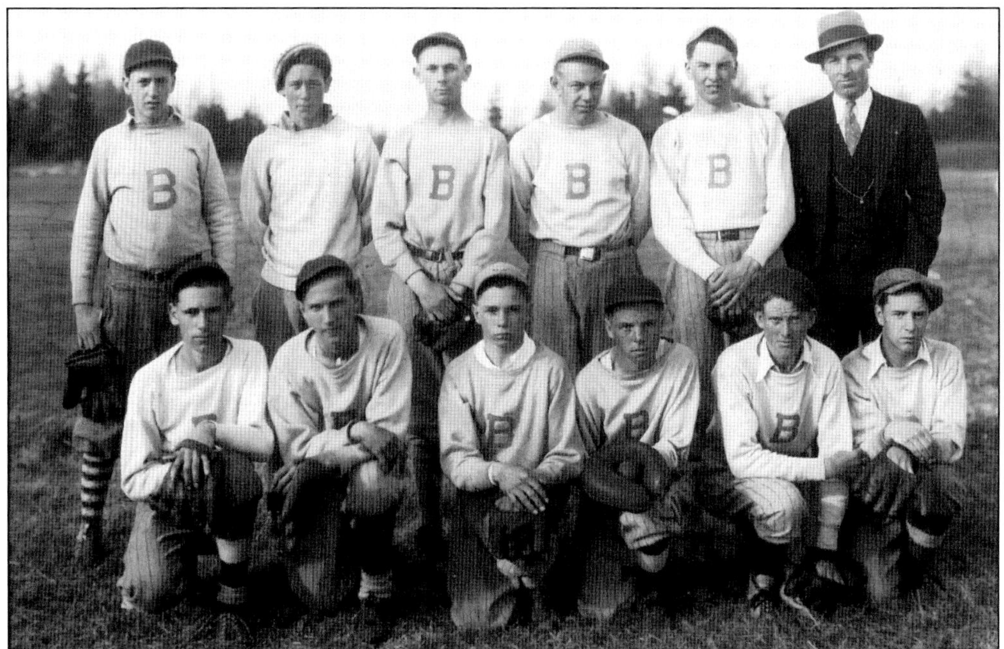

Baseball was very popular in Brooklin. Pictured here is the Brooklin High School team of 1931. The front row includes Robert Hale (far left) and Eddie Sherman (far right). In the back row are, from left to right, Roger Carter, Aubrey Allen, Clarence Bridges, Robert Powers, Donald Cole, and principal John Lampher.

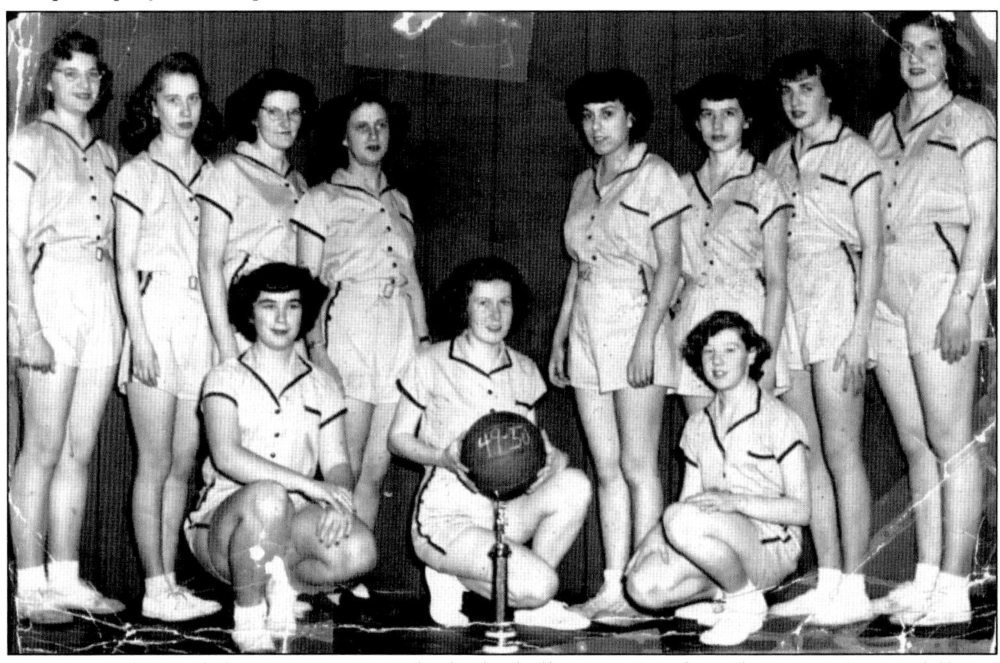

These members of the 1949–1950 girls' basketball team are, from left to right, as follows: (front row) Charlotte Cole, Helen Carter, and Sally Tyler; (back row) Patricia Flye, Roberta Staples, Velma Carter, Jeannette Pierce, Harriet Morgan, Betty Eaton, Wilma Tapley, and Kathryn Friend.

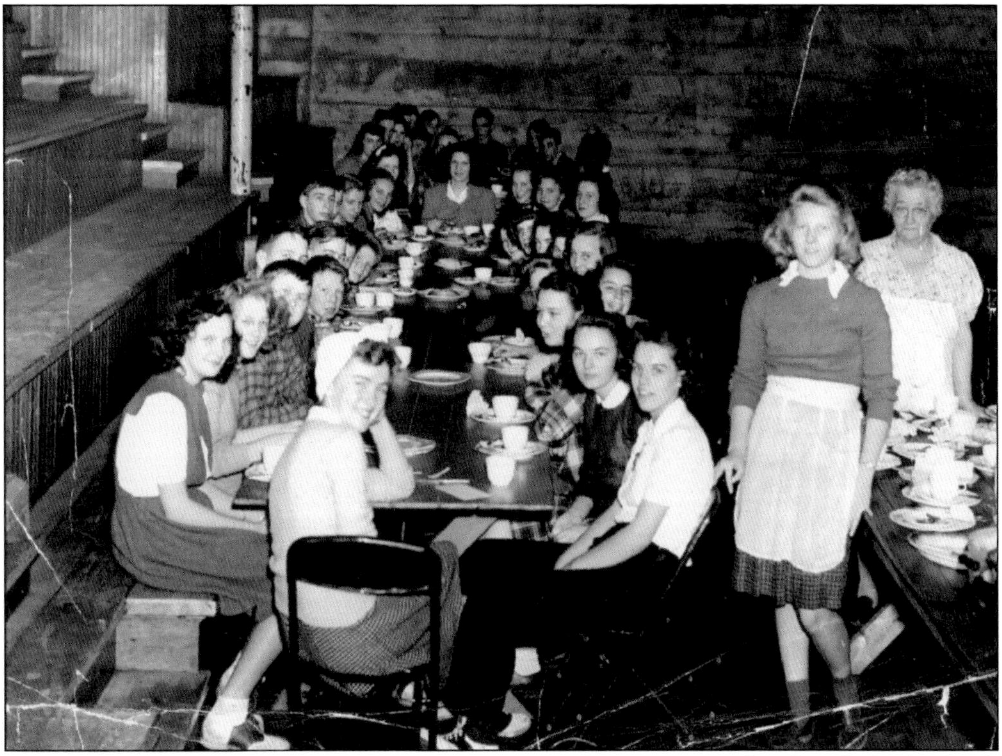

In 1946 or 1947, cooks Alice Staples and Ernestine Crockett are serving lunch at the high school. At the first table are, clockwise from the bottom, Agnes Young, Harriet Gott, Peg Staples, Ashman Hooper, Henry Lawson, three unidentified, Ken Carter, Merrill Means, unidentified, ? Carter, and two unidentified. Clockwise from the top are Kathryn Friend, two unidentified, ? Friend, Alice Schillinger, Alberta Holden, Evelyn Holden, and Madeline Smith.

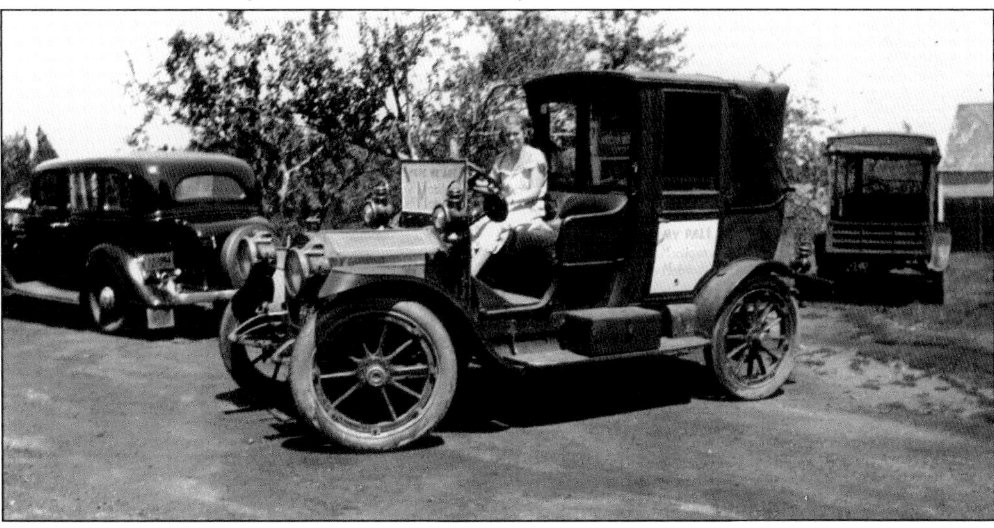

Muriel Bridges Dow (1918–1997), the wife of Kenneth Dow (1908–1984), is pictured with some interesting vehicles. On the left is a 1936–1938 sedan, and on the right is a delivery wagon. Muriel's parents, Harry and Laurel Bridges, owned a "car for hire," so that could be the one she is sitting in. Notice the right-hand steering on that car.

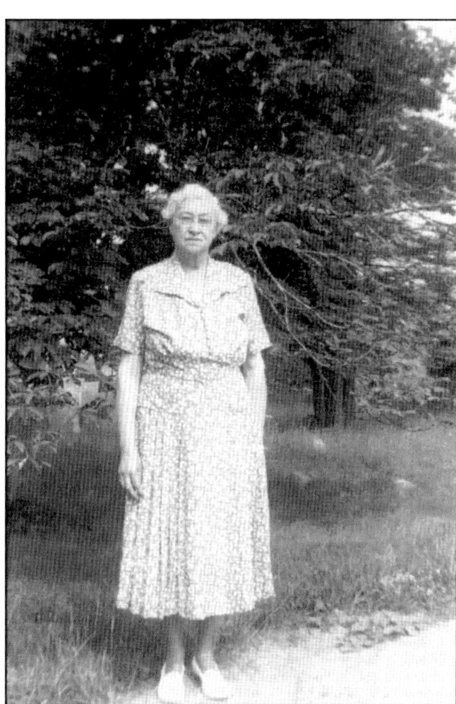

Ada Herrick was well known to many children in Brooklin, as she taught Brooklin's elementary schools most of her life.

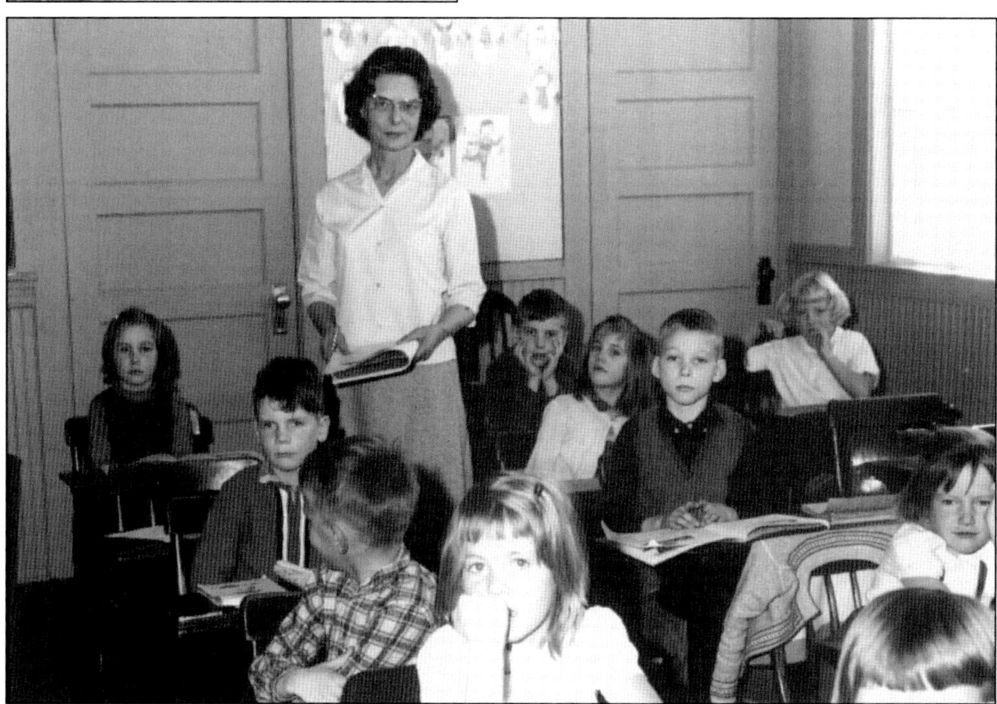

Olive Bartlett Bent, the wife of Elmer Bent, is shown here with her class in the Little Red Schoolhouse classroom. To the left of Bent are, from front to back, Diane Friend, Robert Austin, Paul Snellings, and Carrie Bartlett. In the next row to the right are, from front to back, Wendy Eaton, Randolph Grant, Sheryl Robbins, and Bruce Allen. Roxanne Allen is in the upper right, and Darlene Lawson's forehead is showing in the very front.

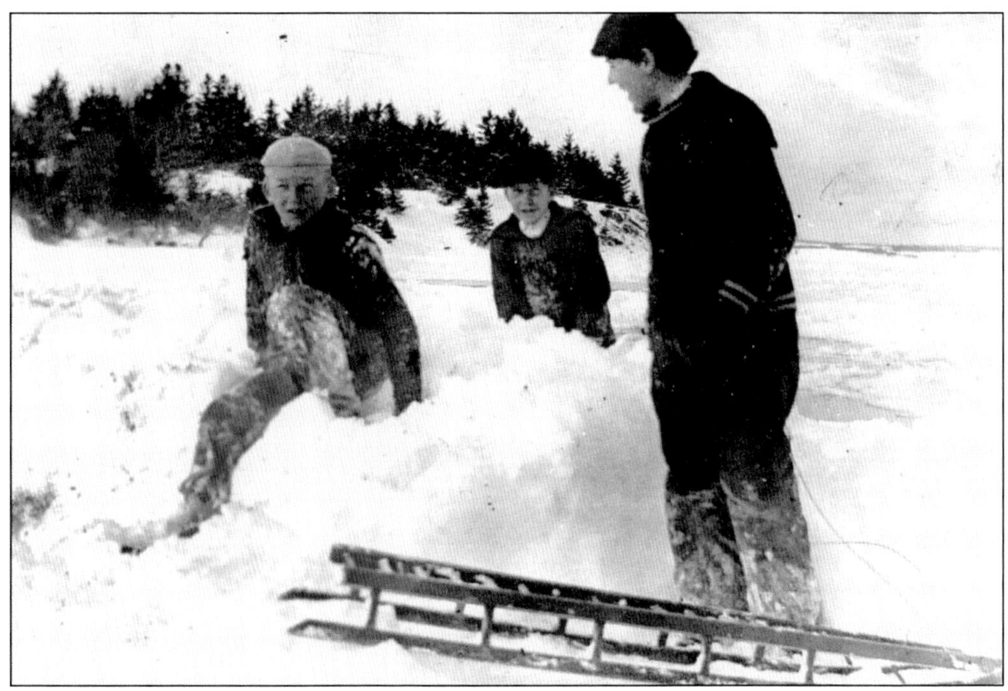

In this view, Lawrence Sherman (left), George Giles (center), and Everett Holden are enjoying a good snowfall with their Cape Racer sled.

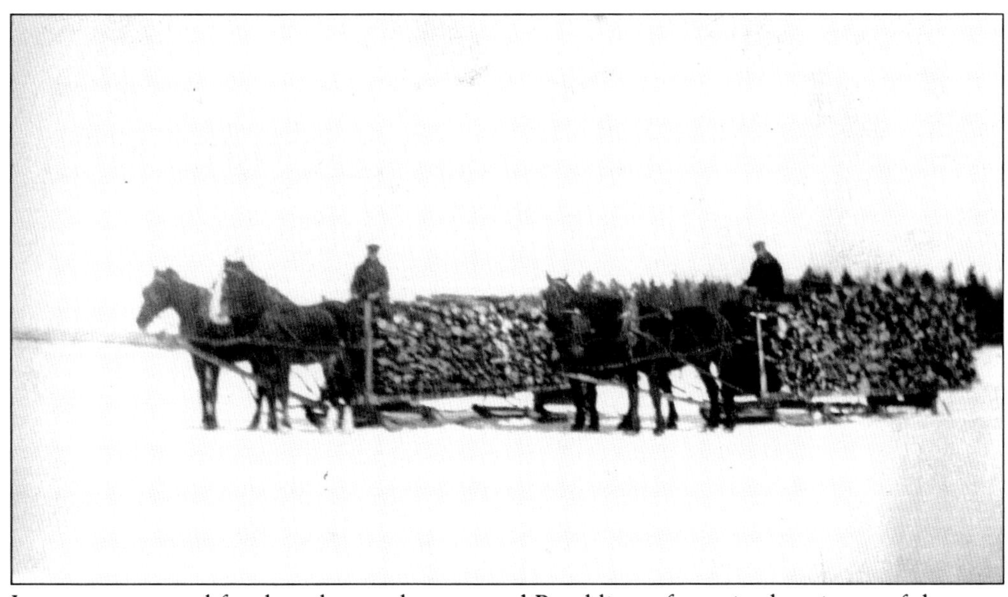

In was not unusual for the saltwater bays around Brooklin to freeze in the winters of the past, making that means of transport much easier than the unpaved and rutted roads. Here, two teams of horses are hauling several cords of wood across the ice.

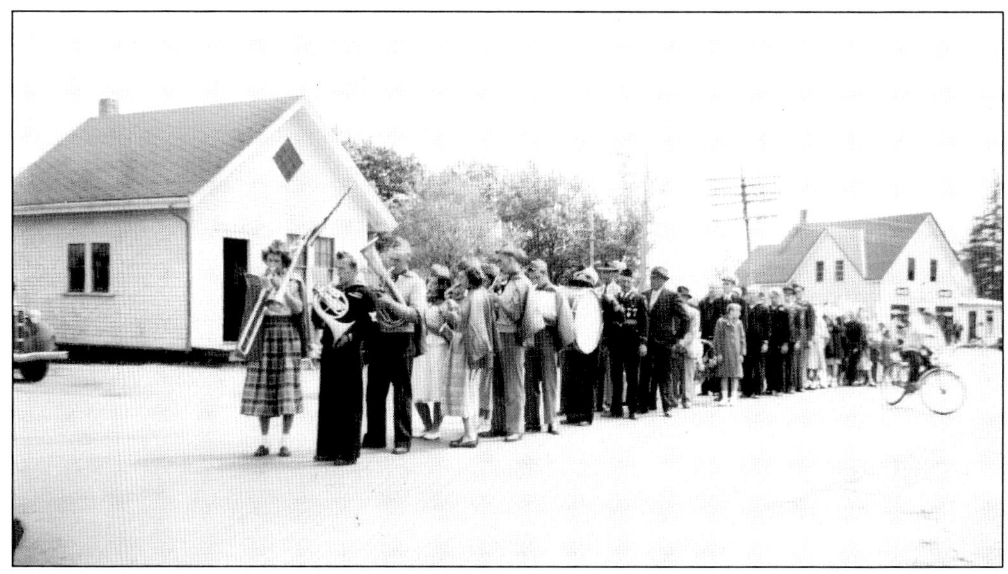

The school band marches at the Corner in 1949 for Brooklin's centennial. The building behind them has a unique history. First, it was steamship agent Lew Smith's office on Brooklin Landing and was then moved to the Corner. After that, it was moved to a site beside the Phillips House and then back to the Corner to be used as a post office with Arnold Staples as postmaster. Later, it was Victor Smith's Quick Lunch. It is now the Morning Moon Cafe.

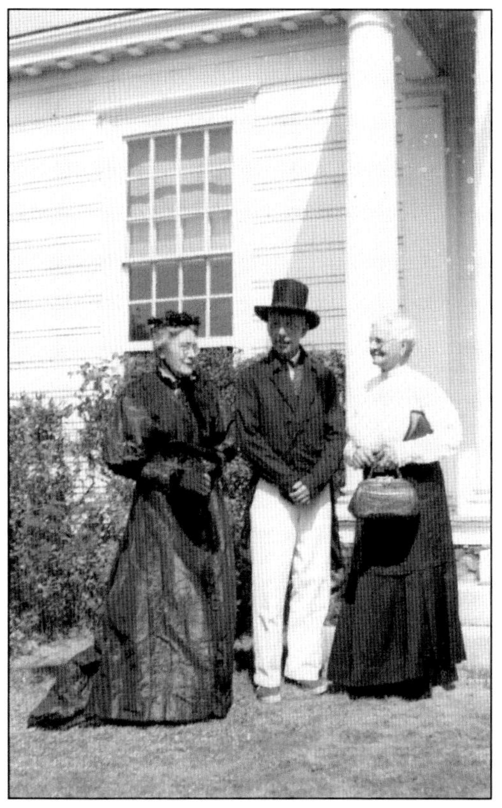

After the parade for the centennial celebration, Sadie Henderson (left) and E.B. White are pictured chatting with another costumed woman in front of the Friend Memorial Public Library. Henderson and White had taken first prize in the parade for their float, titled "Family Portrait."

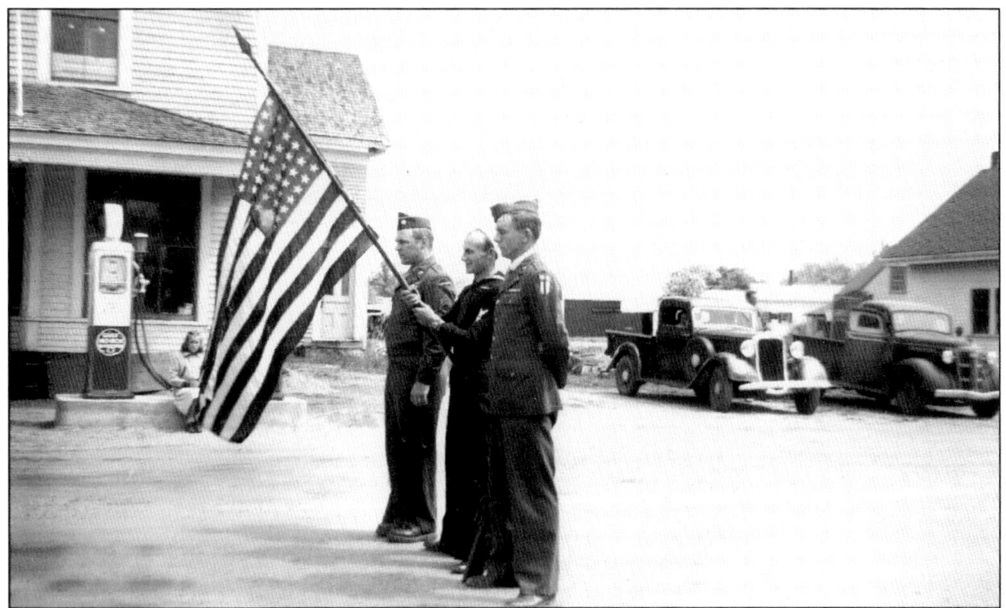

In front of Norton Smith's store are, from left to right, Gordon Smith, Robert Smith, and Steve Graham. They are in military uniform to display the flag on Memorial Day of that 1949 celebration year.

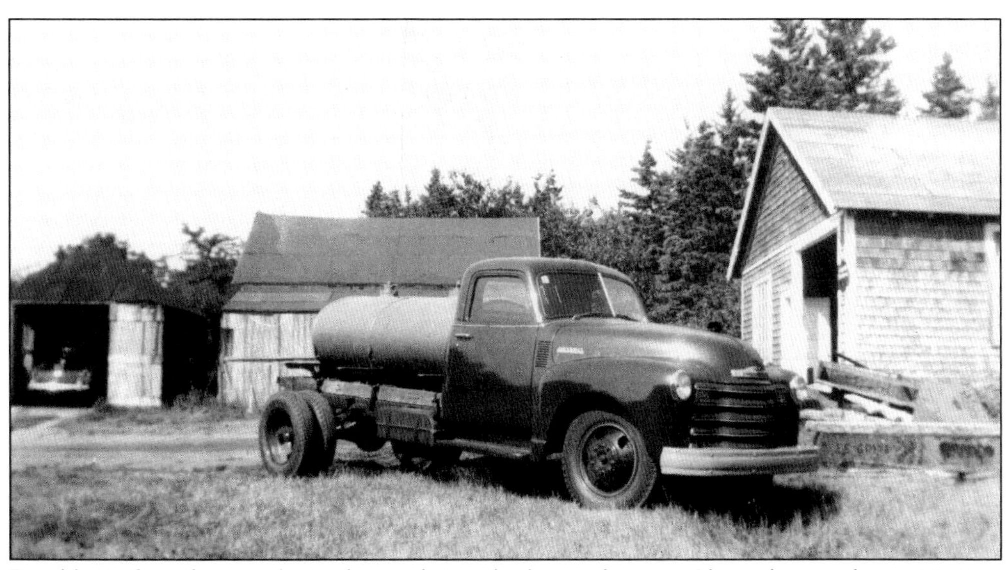

Brooklin's first fire truck is shown being built up from a Chevrolet truck in 1948 at Harry Bridges's garage.

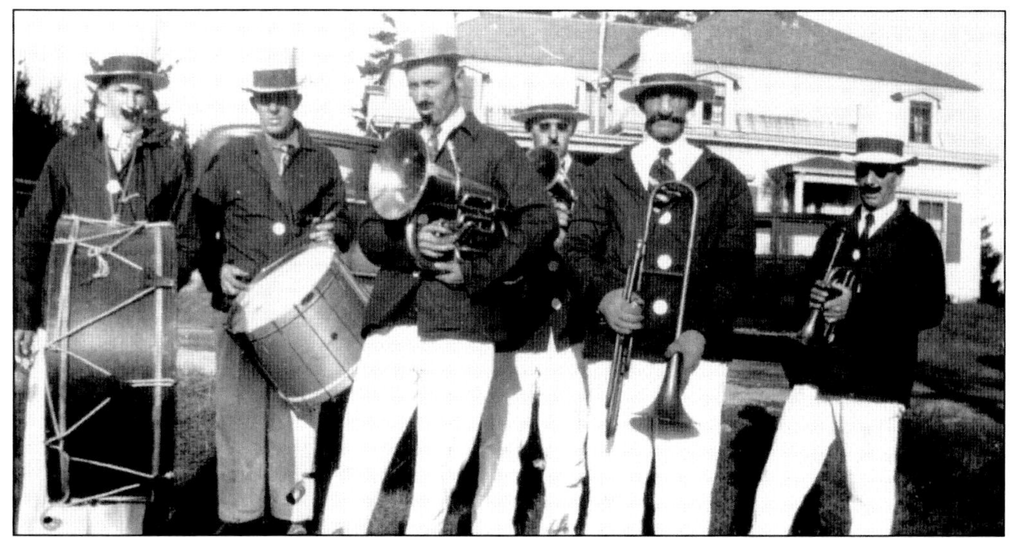

Musical entertainment flourished in Brooklin before the advent of radio and television. Members of a minstrel band are shown in their costumes in front of Fred Allen's house. Known to be in the photograph are Frank Staples, Less Mitchell, Ralston Means Sr., and David Kimball.

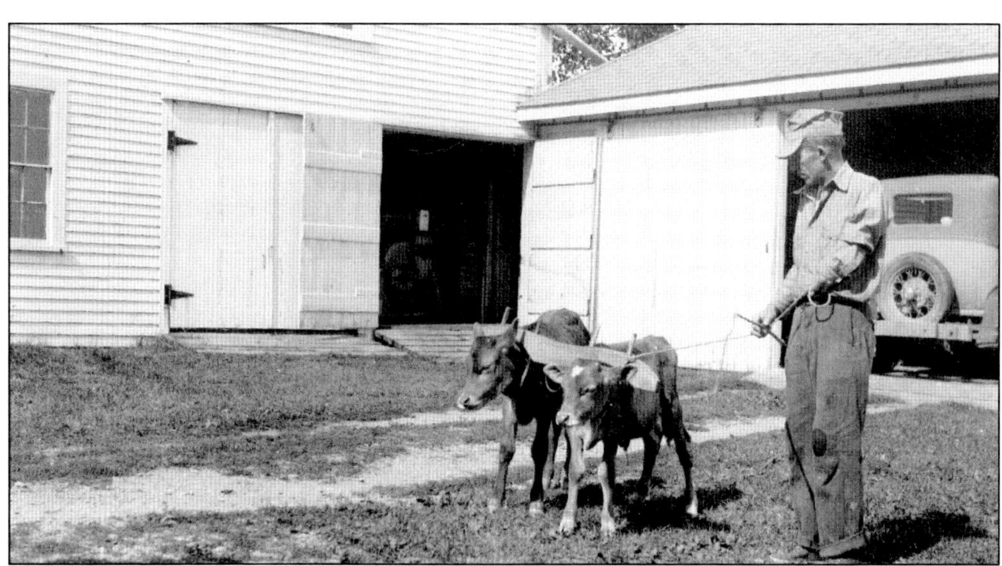

Most families in Brooklin had farm animals if only to provide for their family. In this *c.* 1929 photograph, Billy Young is training a young team of oxen for later hauling work at his place on Naskeag Road. In the garage is Ethel and Billy Young's Model A sedan.

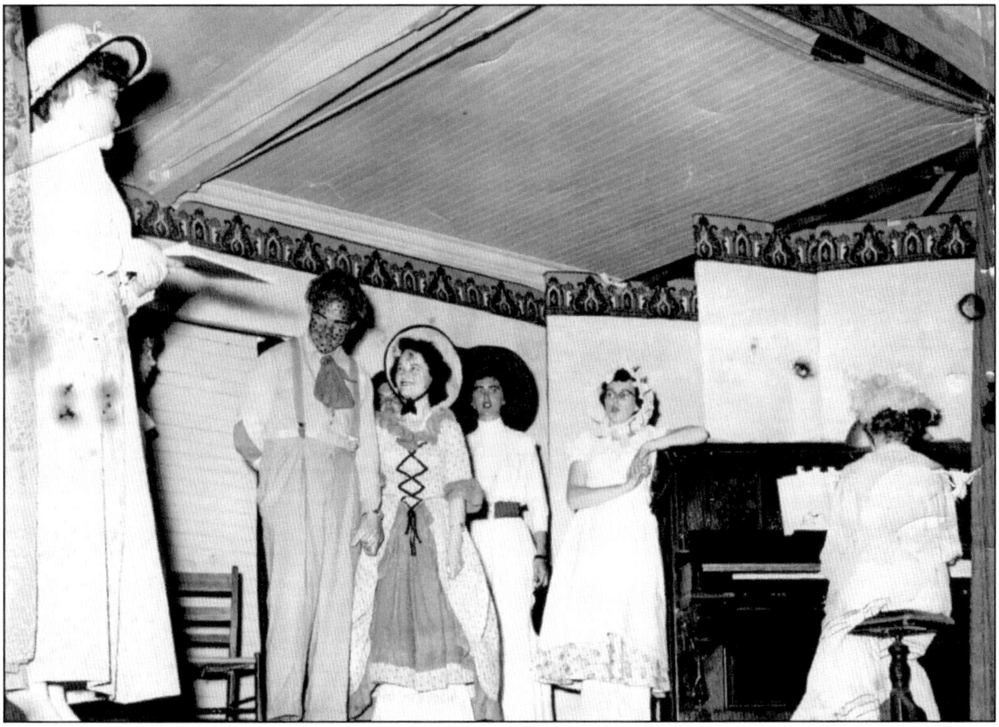

Performance of *The Bean Town Choir* has a long history in Brooklin. It was first done in 1923 and again in 1953 and 1983. In 1953, it was performed on the second floor of the Odd Fellows Hall. The 1953 cast members shown here are, from left to right, June Eaton (as Do-Ree-Mee), Gordan Smith (as Hezekiah), Anne Phillips (as Samantha), Jackie Redman Andrews, Jean Redman Graham, and Delia Tyler (on the piano).

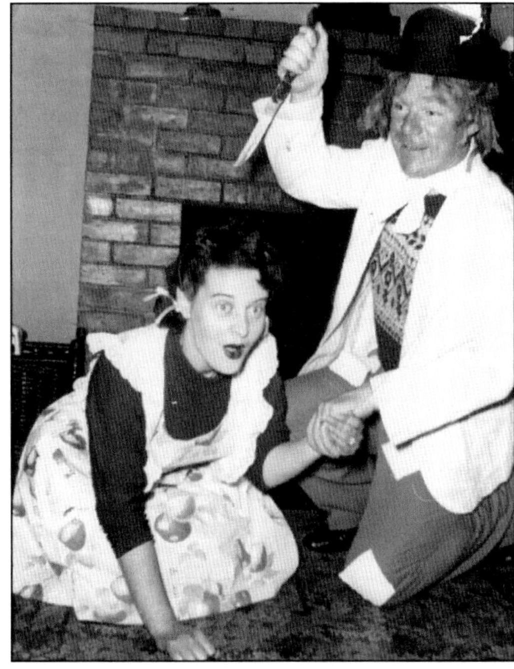

In another performance, Gordon Smith and Annie Phillips create some drama in a benefit production for the March of Dimes and the Friend Memorial Public Library.

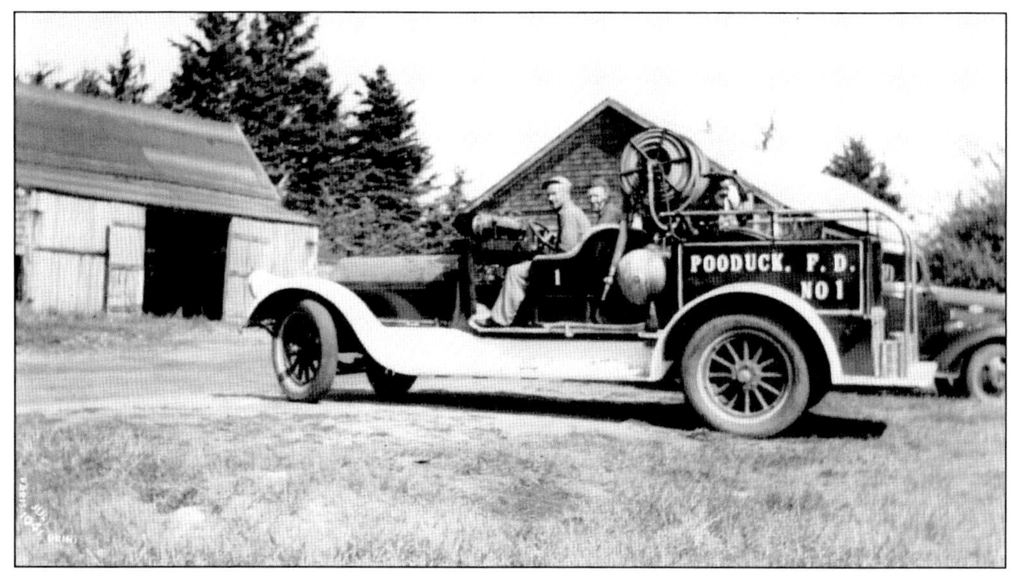

The Pooduck fire truck, owned by Alan Bemis, made a yearly appearance in the Fourth of July parade. He also loaned it to the town for putting out fires.

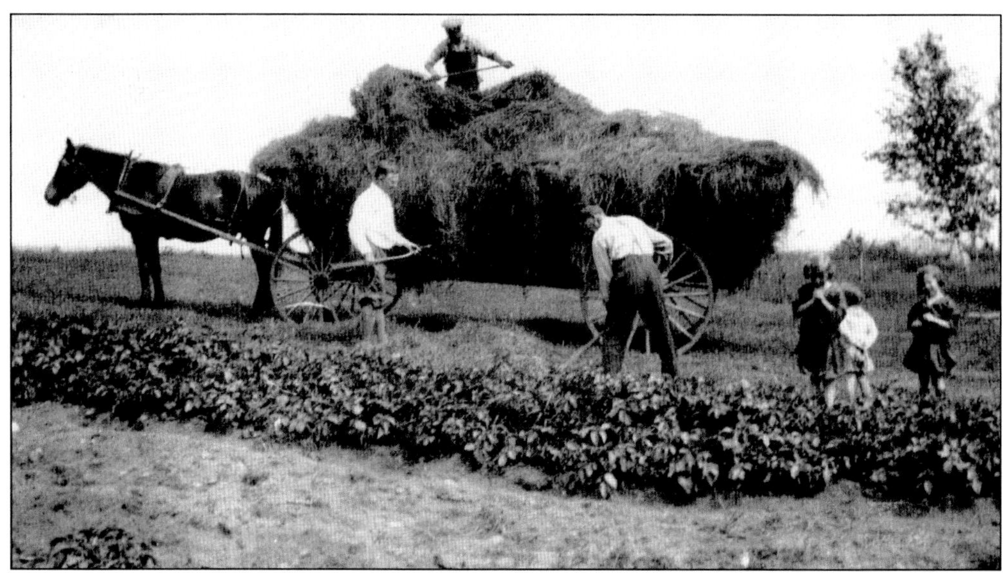

This photograph, taken *c.* 1930 near Hillside on Naskeag, shows farmer Walter Pierce bringing in the hay. "Helping" him are the Twitchell children, summer visitors at the time.

Nine

PEOPLE

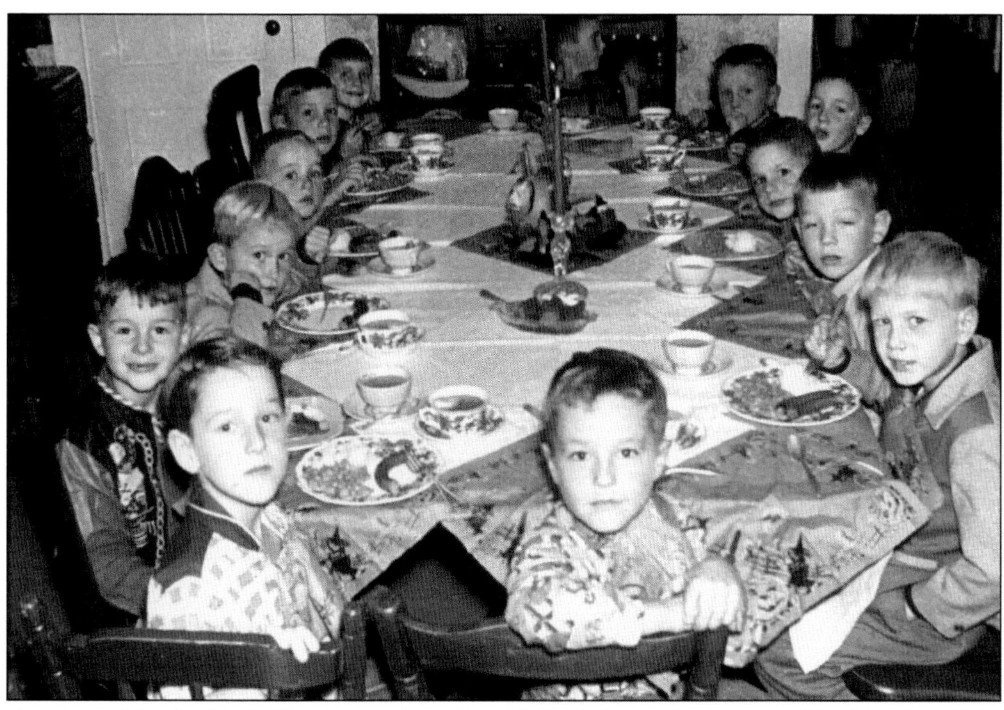

A group of Wade Dow's friends is gathered for his birthday party. Around the table clockwise, starting at the bottom, are Alvah Kane, Stephen Day, unidentified, Roland Carter, Robert "Butch" Smith, Richard Eaton, Raymond Mansfield, Wade Dow, Conrad Tainter, Billy Bowden, Townsend Rockwell, Kirby Allen, and Richard Carter.

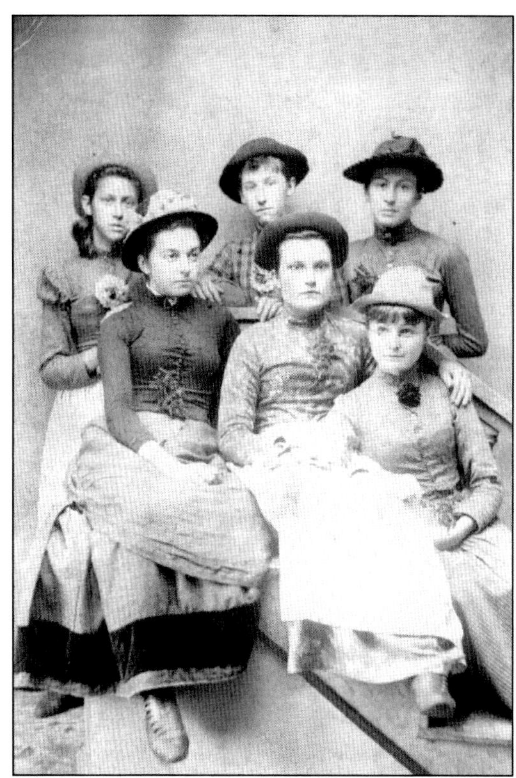

The Brooklin girls shown in this late-1800s photograph are, from left to right, as follows: (front row) Fannie Eaton Hooper, Mary Smith Sellers, and Etta Tainter Kane; (back row) Josie Nutter, Georgia Nutter, and Hattie Tainter Smith.

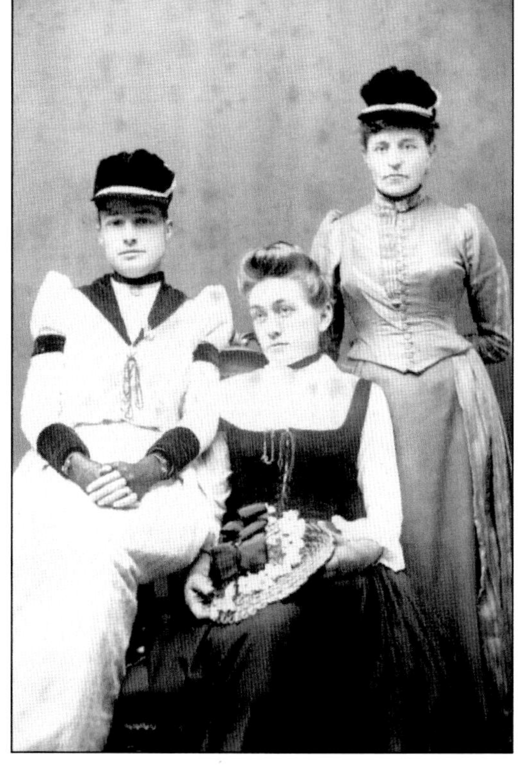

These Brooklin women from about the same time are, from left to right, Celeste A. Kane, Emina Barrett, and Rose A. Wells. Celeste later married Will Redman. Rose was the sister of Capt. Rufus Wells.

Lucy P. Allen, the daughter of Addie and Stanley, married Charles A. Choate, a yachtsman, on the day this picture was taken, May 16, 1908.

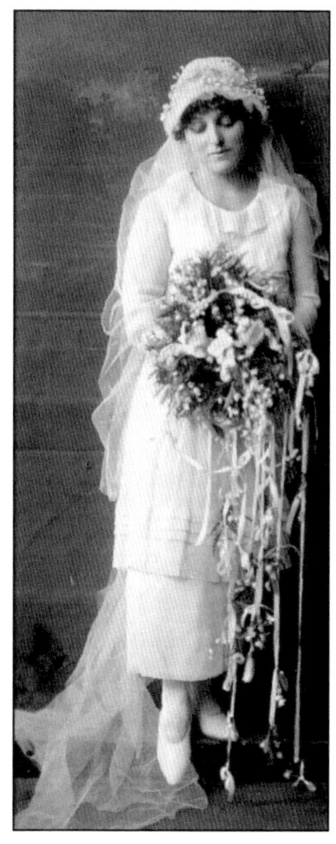

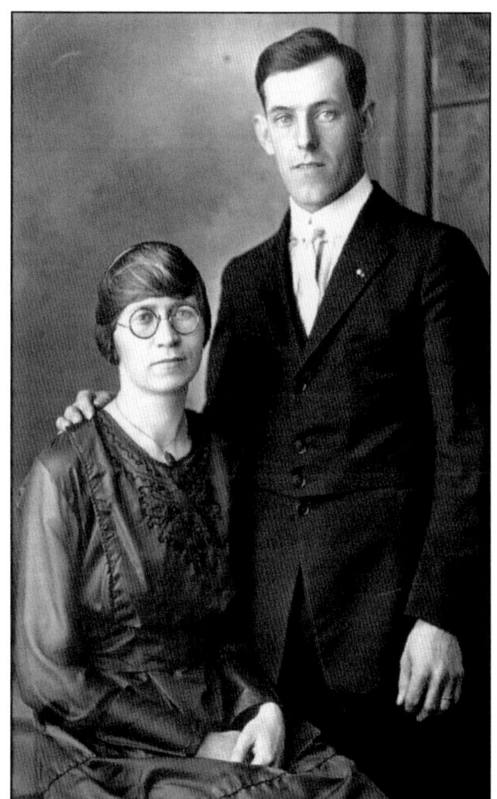

Pictured here are Hermann and Mabel (Bridges) Chatto, who lived in West Brooklin. Hermann was a selectman in Brooklin for many years. His brother Clarence compiled the census to earn college tuition and, along with Turner, published the results in 1910.

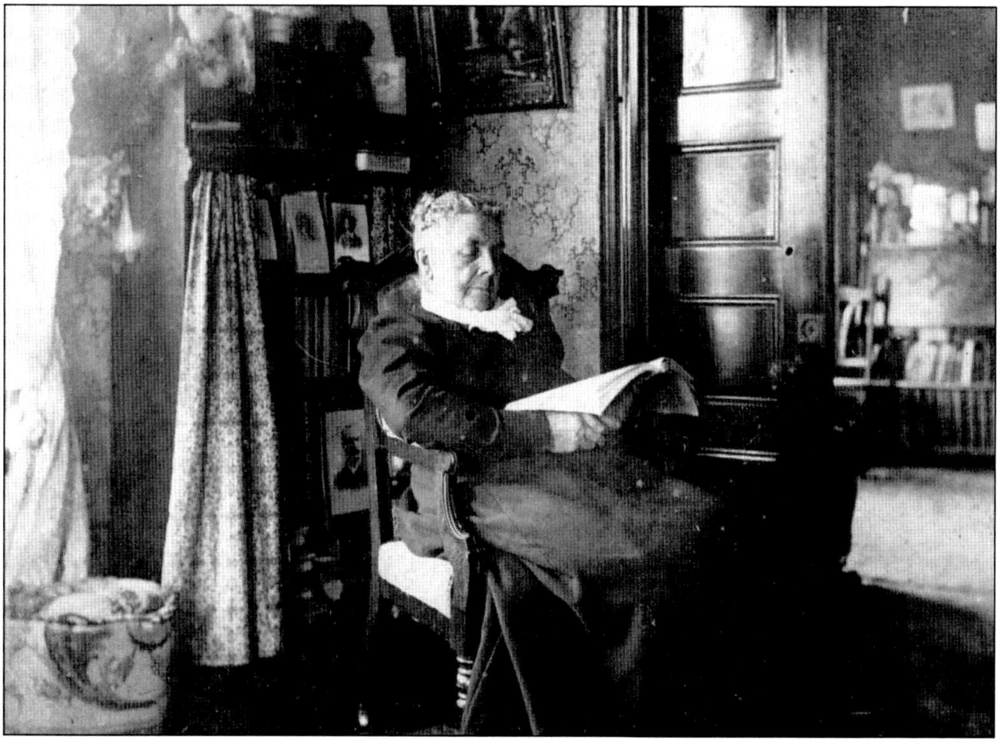

Augusta Staples (1848–1934) is shown reading in a room of Victorian decor. She was the wife of John Staples (1841–1896), a Civil War soldier with Company F, 13th Maine Regiment.

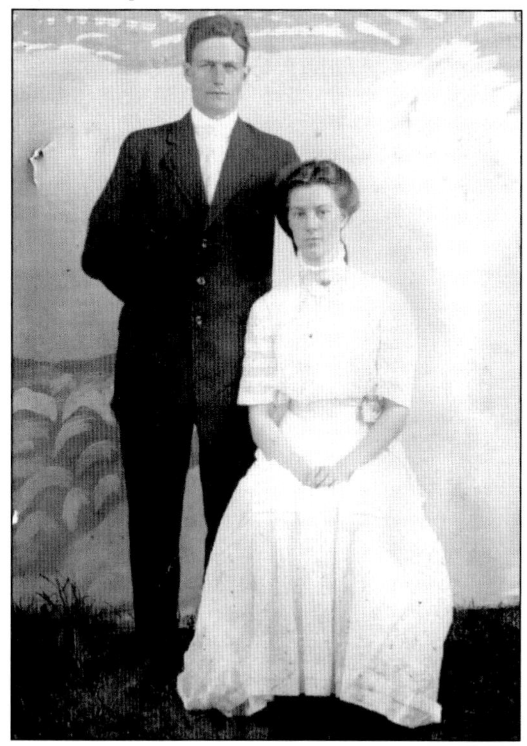

Katie Staples and her husband, Albert Hill, are pictured as a young married couple. They had two girls, Eleanor and Eugenia, but Albert died young and Katie moved back with her parents, John and Lizzie. Katie taught piano to many children in Brooklin.

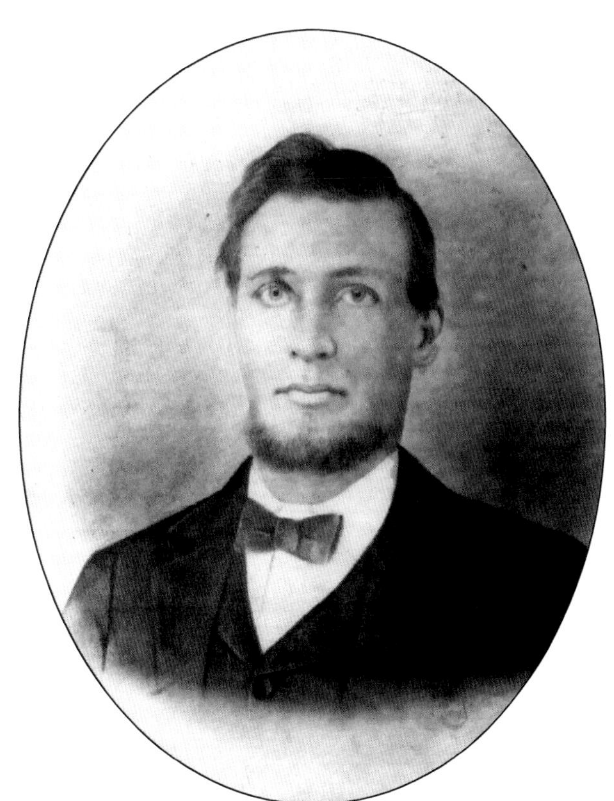

Eben Kane and his wife, Susan (Bridges) Kane, pictured here, were early residents of Brooklin. They were the grandparents of Leona Staples, great-grandparents of Alice (Staples) Allen, and great-great-grandparents of Roxanne (Allen) Sherman and Neil Allen.

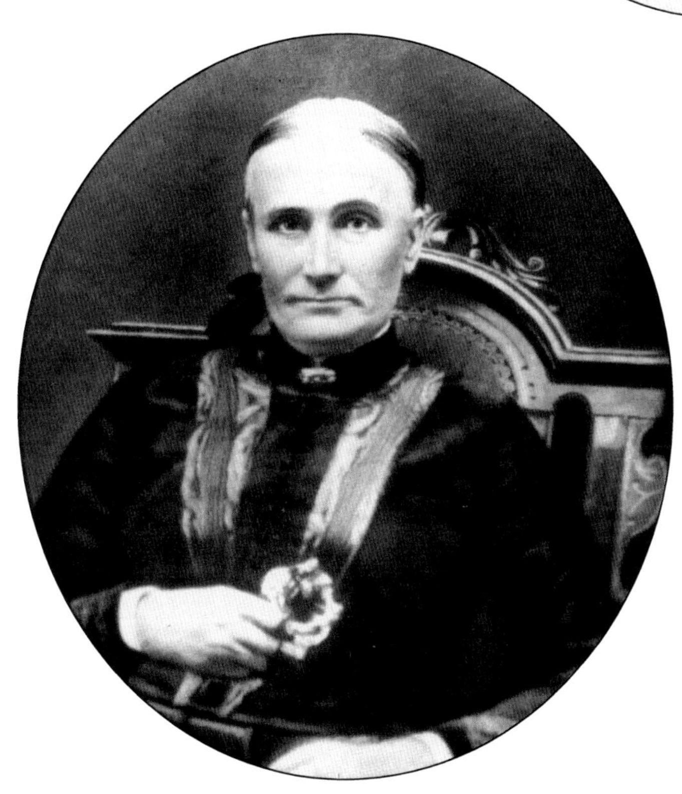

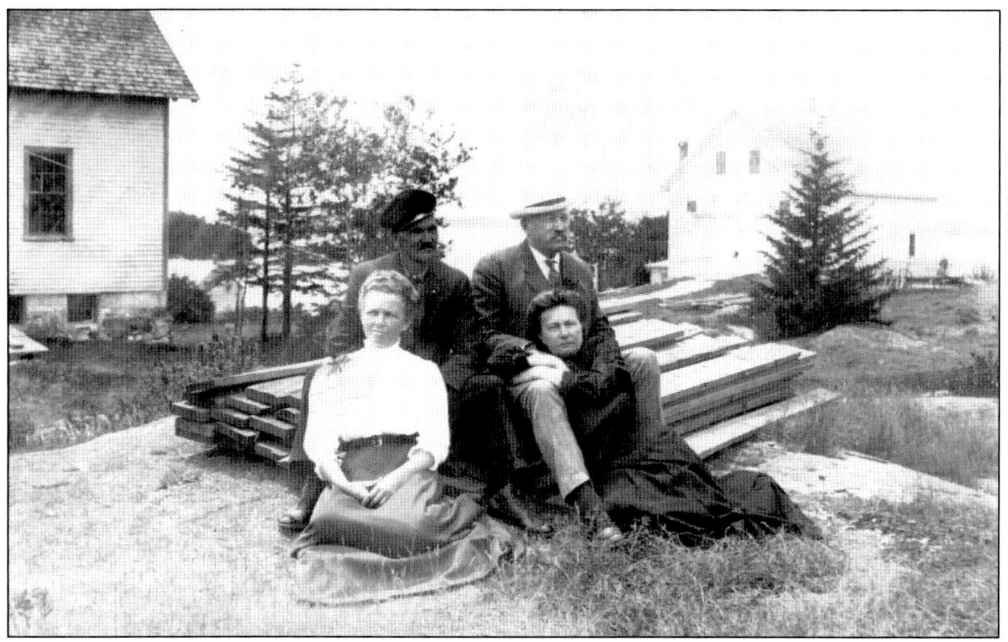

With a view of Center Harbor behind them, two couples are seen relaxing. On the left, Warren Ford (1866–1953) is sitting behind his wife, Minnie Sellers (1866–1934). They were the parents of Oscar Ford, grandparents of Mary Ford Weber, and great-grandparents of Toni Weber Smith. The other two are Franklin and Mary (Freethy) Davis.

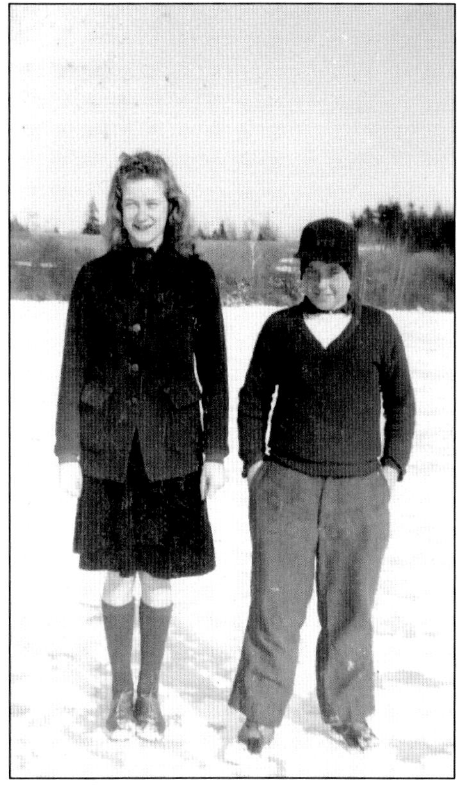

Standing on the ice in Center Harbor are 16-year-old Eunice Grey (Hardy) and her 12-year-old brother, Hollis. The Grey children lived on the boatyard road.

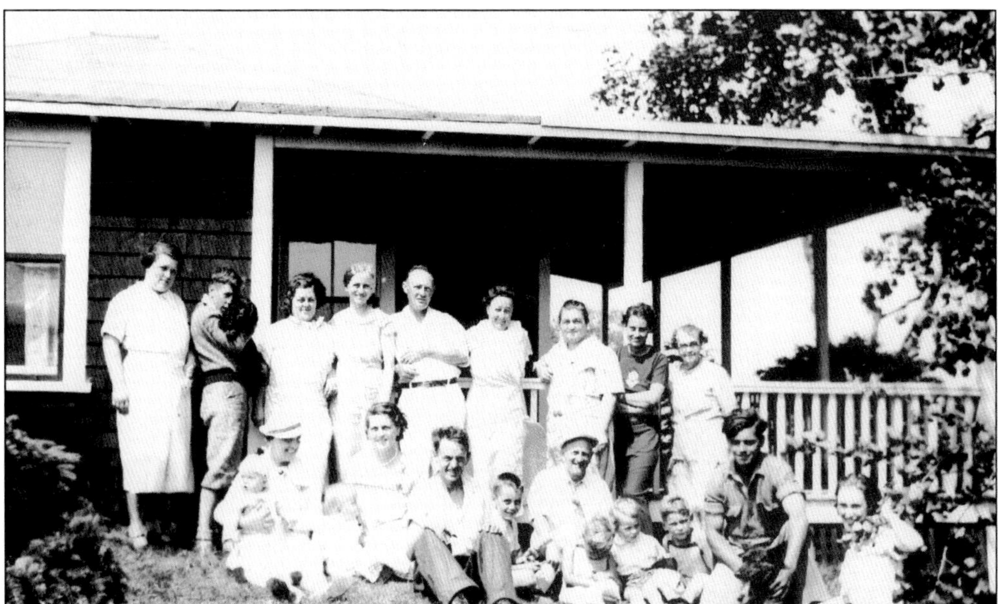

In 1935, at a family gathering at the Hamilton cottage in North Brooklin, the adults are, from left to right, as follows: (front row) unidentified, Rebecca Freethey Vial, Robert Burnham, Ellis Freethey, Raymond Bryant, and Irene Hamilton; (back row) Ruby Freethey Burnham, Junior Hamilton, Marjorie Freethey, Jennie Hamilton, Floyd Hamilton, Louise Hamilton, Winnifred Hamilton Freethey, Kathryn Hamilton Gates, and Annie Merrill.

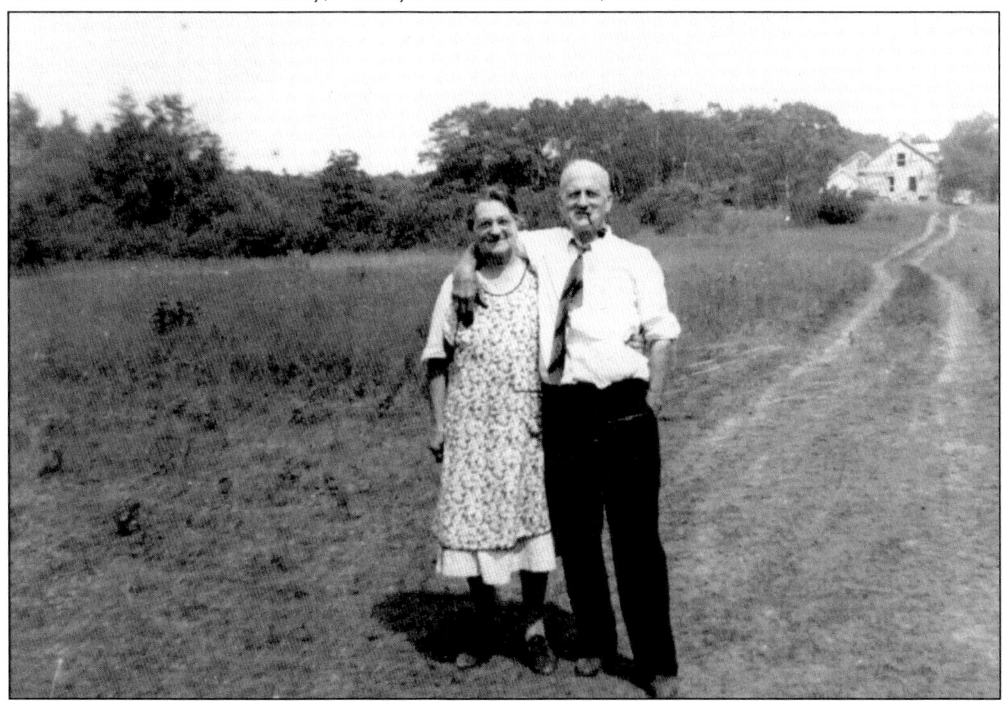

Winnifred (Hamilton) and Ellis Stirling Freethey are shown standing to the west of their "new" house, which was being built near the shore on Harriman Point. The original Freethey house burned in the early 1900s.

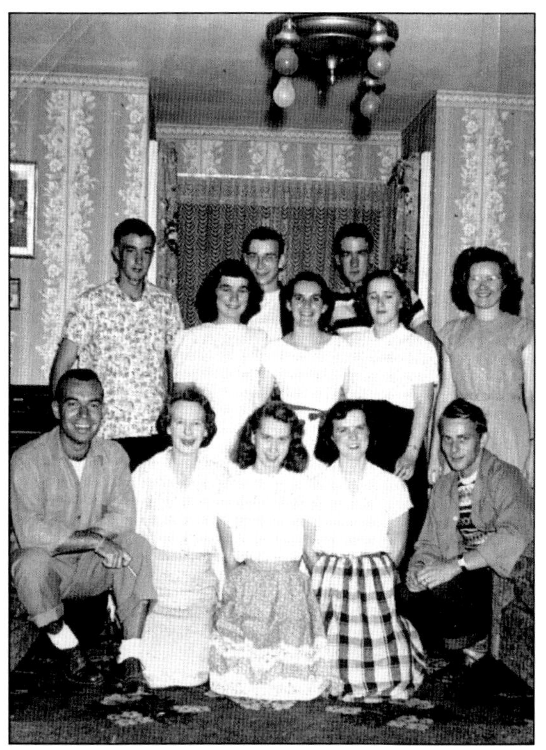

The Mountain Ash Inn staff gathered in Walter Gray's House for this picture. From left to right are the following: (front row) Andre Cote (from Old Town), Dot Keefe (from Sedgwick), Roberta Staples, Pat MacLeod (from Bangor), and Jimmie Henderson; (middle row) Carlton Gray, Charlotte Cole, Arlene Landry, Joan Thibodeau (from Bangor), and Evelyn Hooper (from Sedgwick); (back row) Decatur Cousins and Belford Gray.

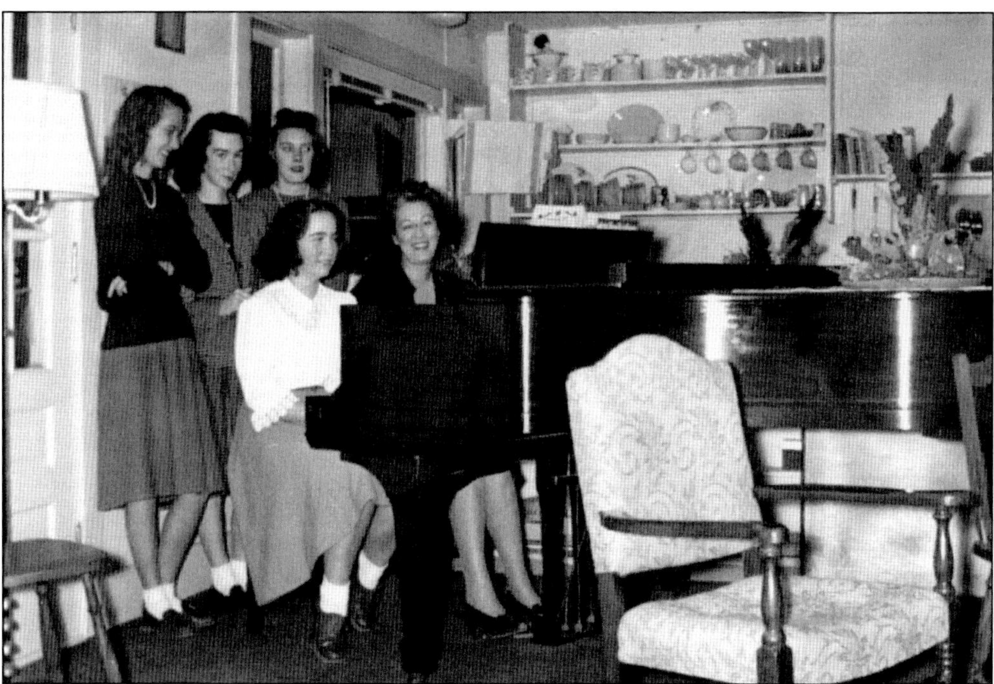

Friends meet for a sing-a-long in the living room of the Waldron home in North Brooklin. At the piano are Charlotte Cole (left) and Helen Waldron. Standing in back are Roberta Staples (left), Marilyn Cole (center), and Mary Wells. Arthur and Helen Waldron had a gift shop here and made their own pottery.

In the 1940s, Oscar Ford was the sea and shore fisheries warden for the area. The husband of Elsie Sherman, he served on the school board and lived in the house where his granddaughter Toni (Weber) Smith and her husband, Joe Smith, live now.

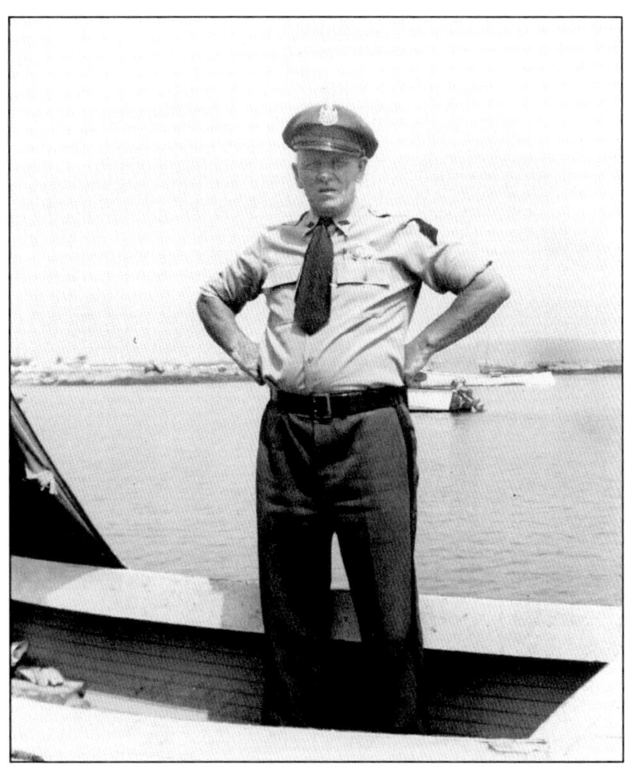

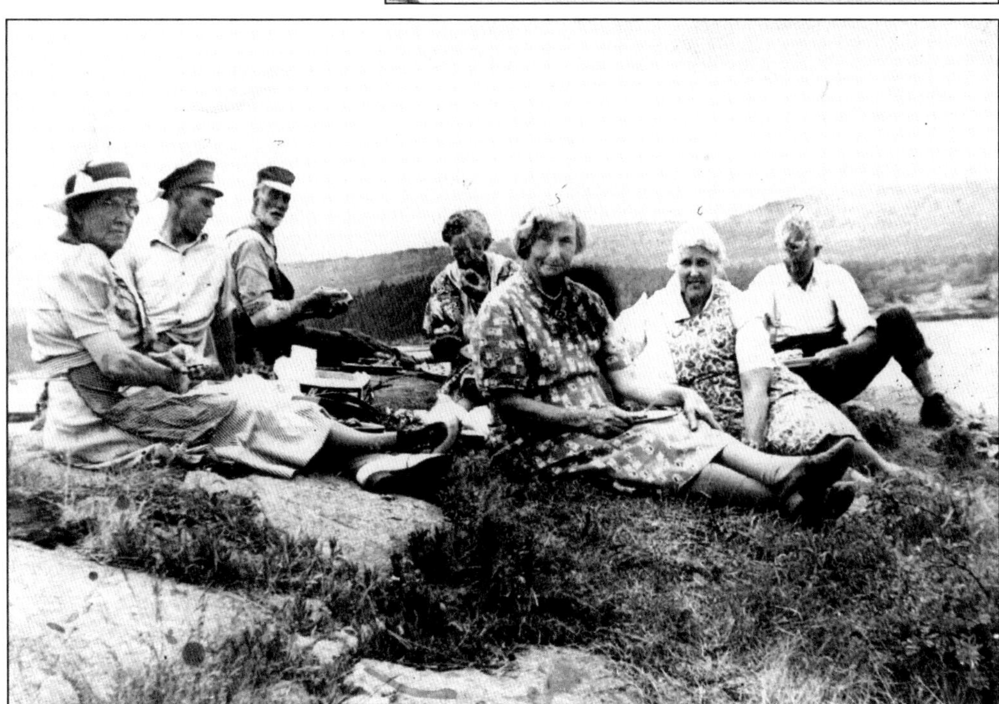

A picnic atop Cadillac Mountain in Bar Harbor is always a favorite outing in the summer. From left to right are Millie (Bridges) (Tyler) Carter, Joe Mitchell Jr., Joe Mitchell Sr., Alice Willey, Belle Mitchell, Maude (Willey) Hooper, and Ralph Willey.

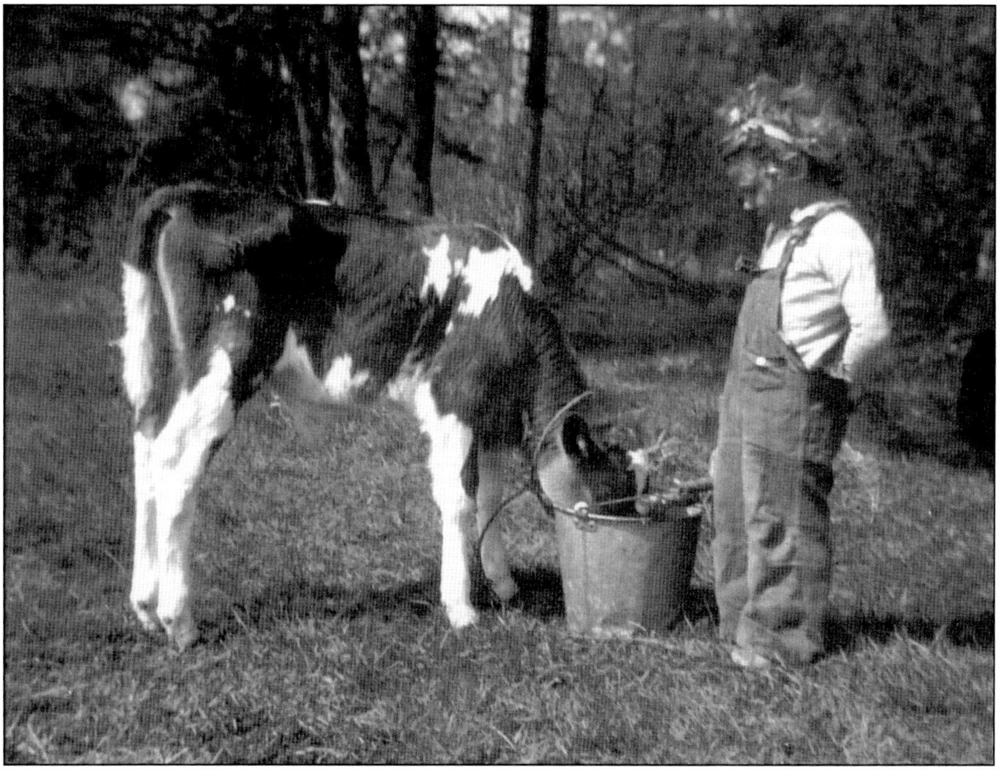

Cindy Tyler is fascinated as she watches her calf drinking from the pail.

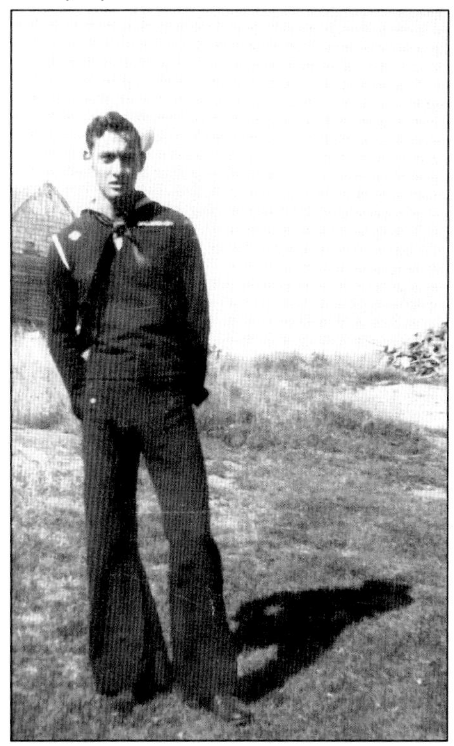

Albert M. Bridges left high school at the end of his junior year and, in 1945, shipped out to the South Pacific and served with the U.S. Seventh Fleet there. After his discharge, he graduated from high school with the Class of 1947.

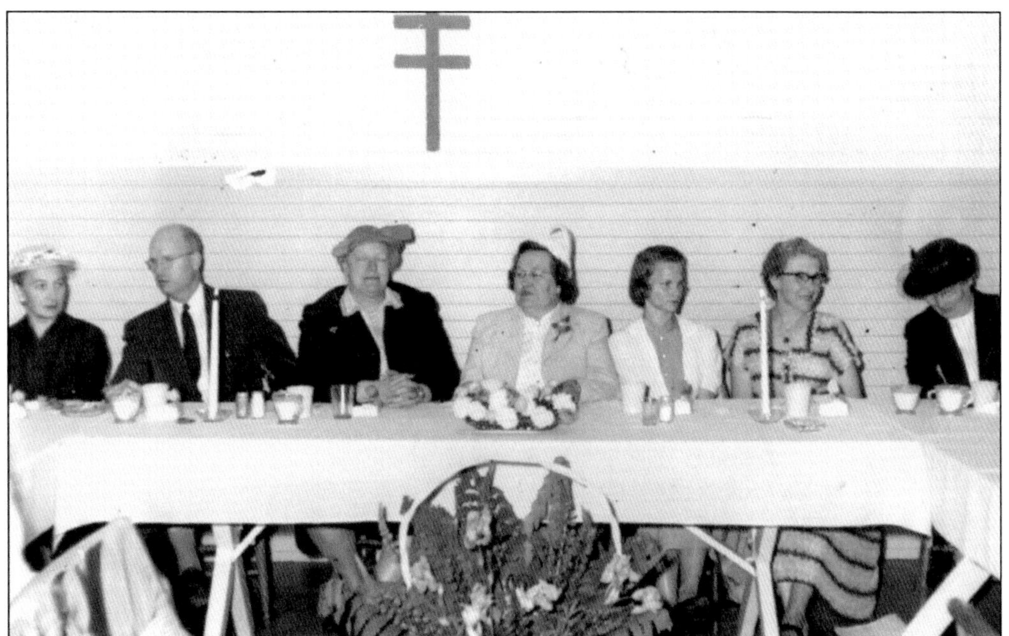

Shown in a meeting of the Four Town Nursing Association are, from left to right, Kathleen (Blake) Herrick, ? Wells (from Augusta), Rev. Margaret Hendrickson, Prudence Sylvester, Betty (Pervear) Williams, and Brooksie (Joyce) Kane.

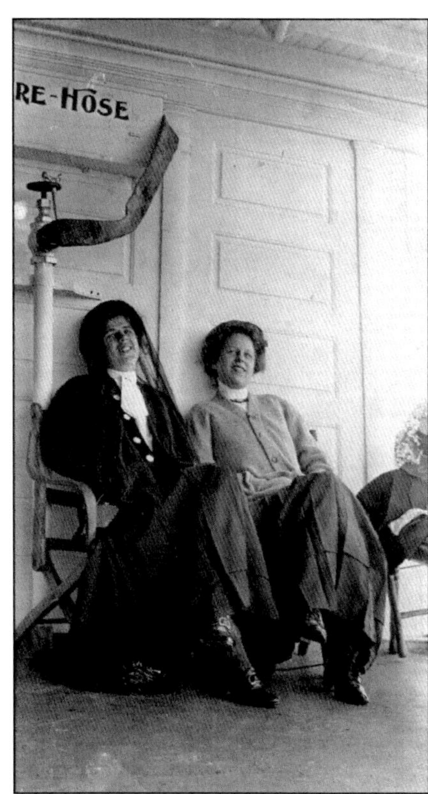

Enjoying their trip on a steamboat are Georgia Allen (the great-aunt of Susie Strout) and a friend. Georgia was the sister of Prin Allen Sr.

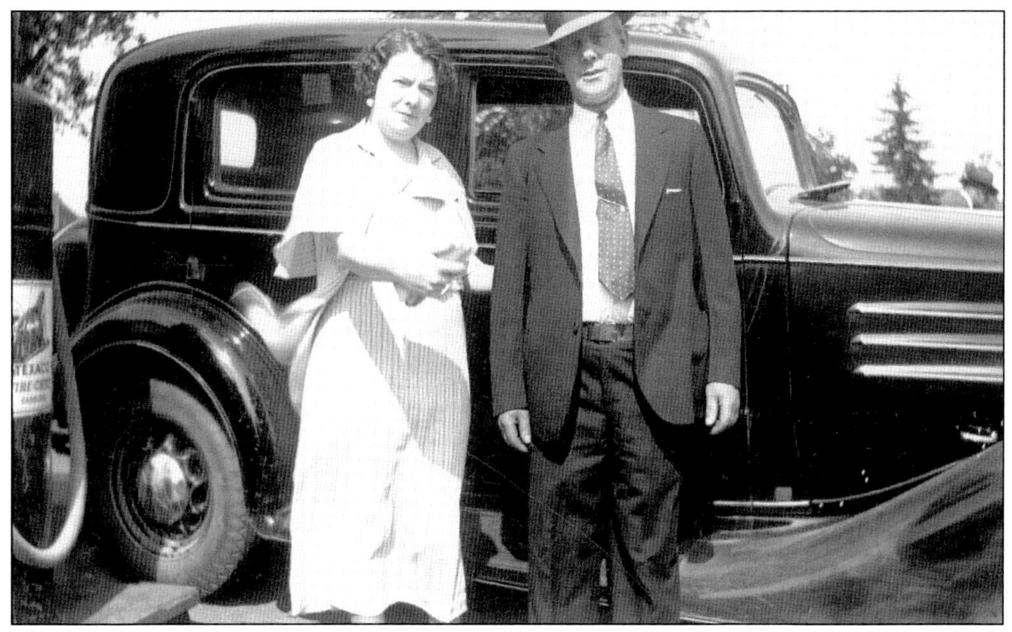

Maude and Virgil Gray are pictured at the Mobil station in Brooklin.

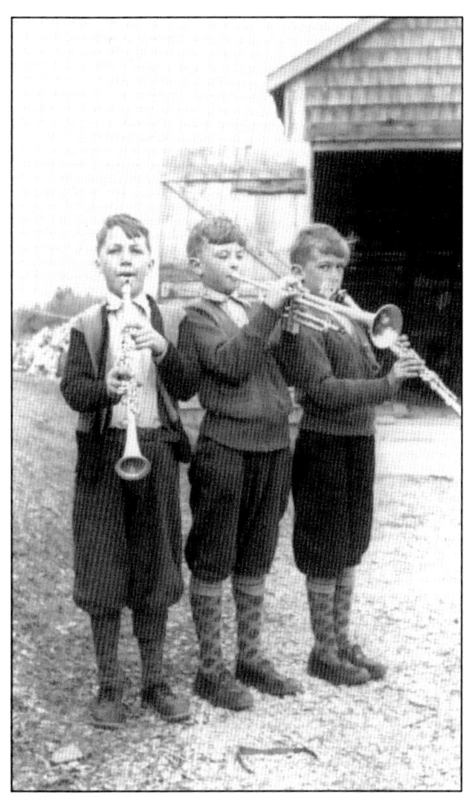

Playing their horns out by the barn are Earl Decker (left), Carlton Gray (center), and Belford Gray. The Gray boys came from a long line of musicians in Brooklin.

Ten

Boats in Brooklin

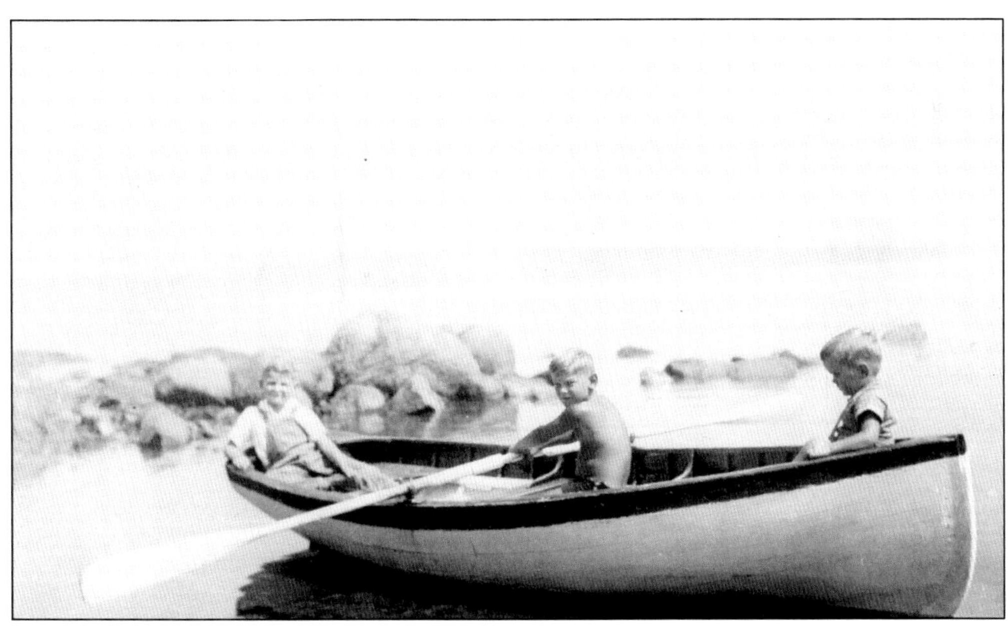

In a round-bottom rowboat in 1937, brothers William (left), Bradford (center), and Richard Viall enjoy the shore near the Hamilton bungalow. The boys are the sons of Rebecca Freethey Viall.

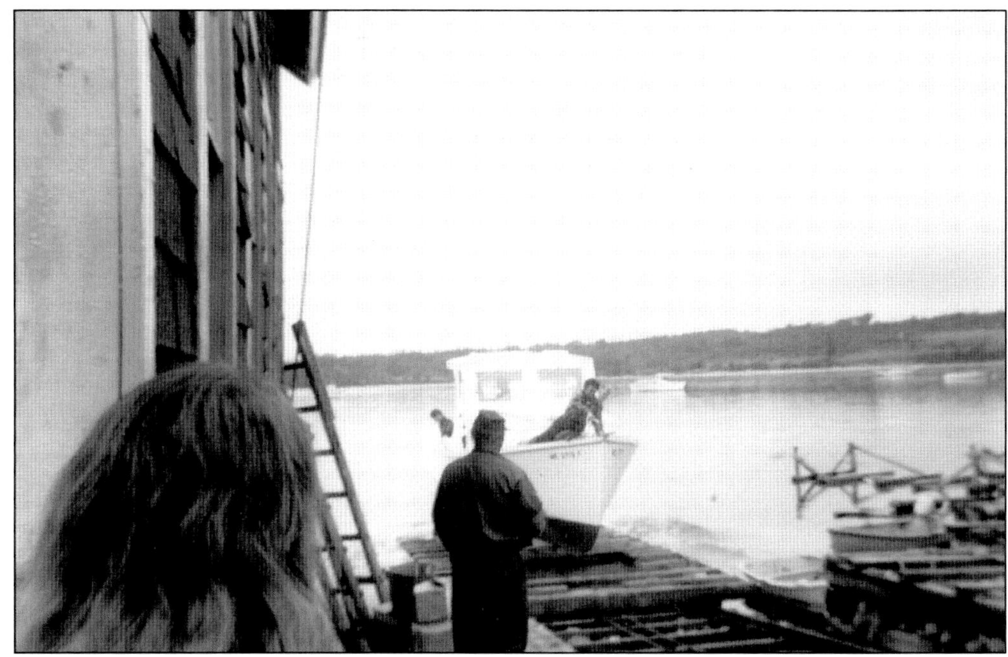

Frank Day Jr. built the *Blue Dolphin*, shown here in 1966 at the launching from the Frank L. Day Boat Yard (on the Benjamin River) for Mildred Harris. Capt. John Allen worked for Harris, as did his son-in-law, Aubrey. Harris gave Aubrey the boat, and he later gave it to his grandson and the present owner, Brian Larkin.

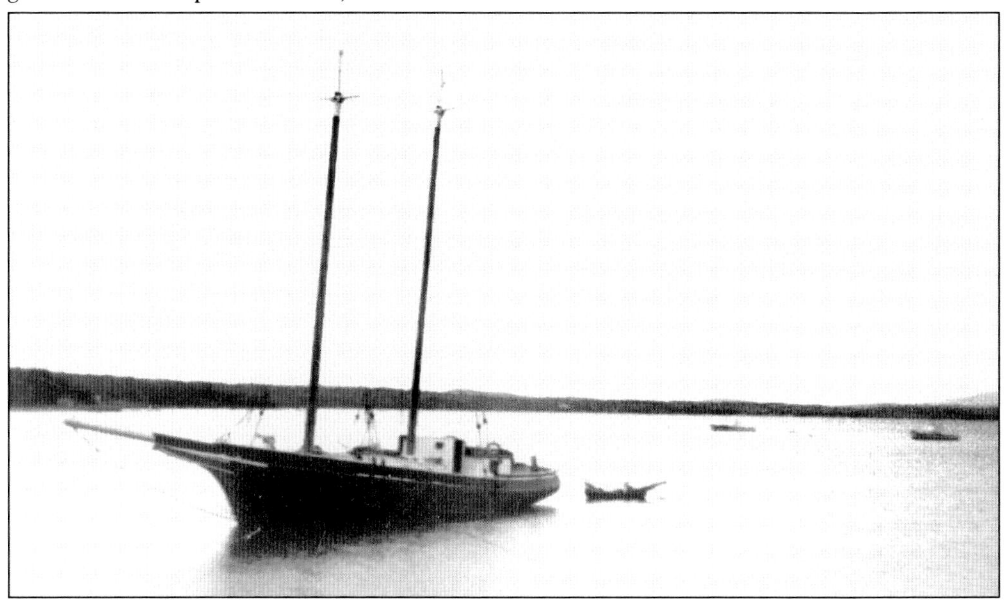

George Allen's schooner *Richard Robbins* is pictured in front of the "Deck House" on Harriman Point. Originally built in 1902 at Cape May, New Jersey, it was rebuilt in 1966 by George Allen, Maynard "Bud" Lee, and M. "Tibbs" Doake at Eddie Sherman's shore. They ran it as a tourist boat out of Rockland for about eight years. It is still in service in New York City. The Deck House, built from a 120-foot troop carrier that was floated up from Portland in 1952, was once the summer home of Maynard Grindle.

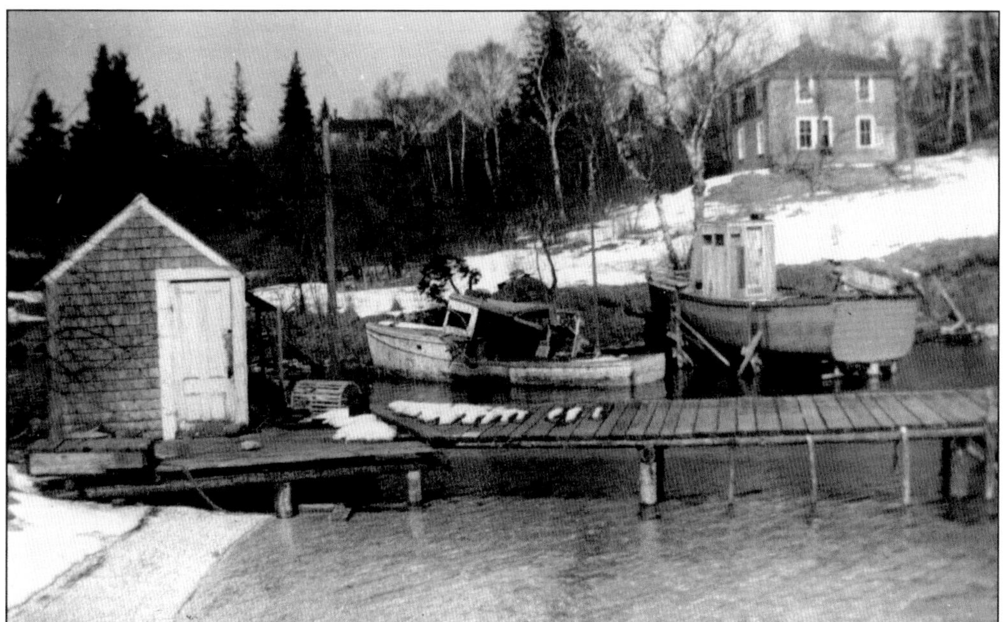

Pictured here is the old dock and bait shed in the cove on the east side of the Brooklin Boat Yard in Center Harbor. The lobster boat on the left belonged to Sheldon Torrey, and the one on the right was that of Joe Tapley. The house on the hill once belonged to Chester Kane and then to Thayer Bowden.

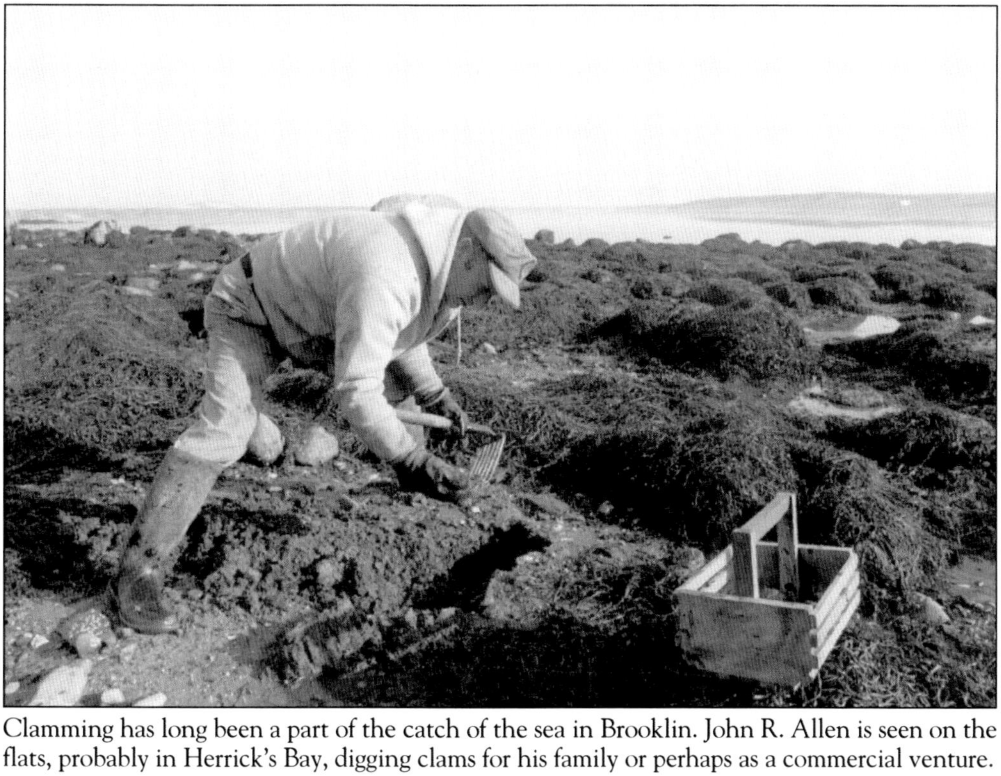

Clamming has long been a part of the catch of the sea in Brooklin. John R. Allen is seen on the flats, probably in Herrick's Bay, digging clams for his family or perhaps as a commercial venture.

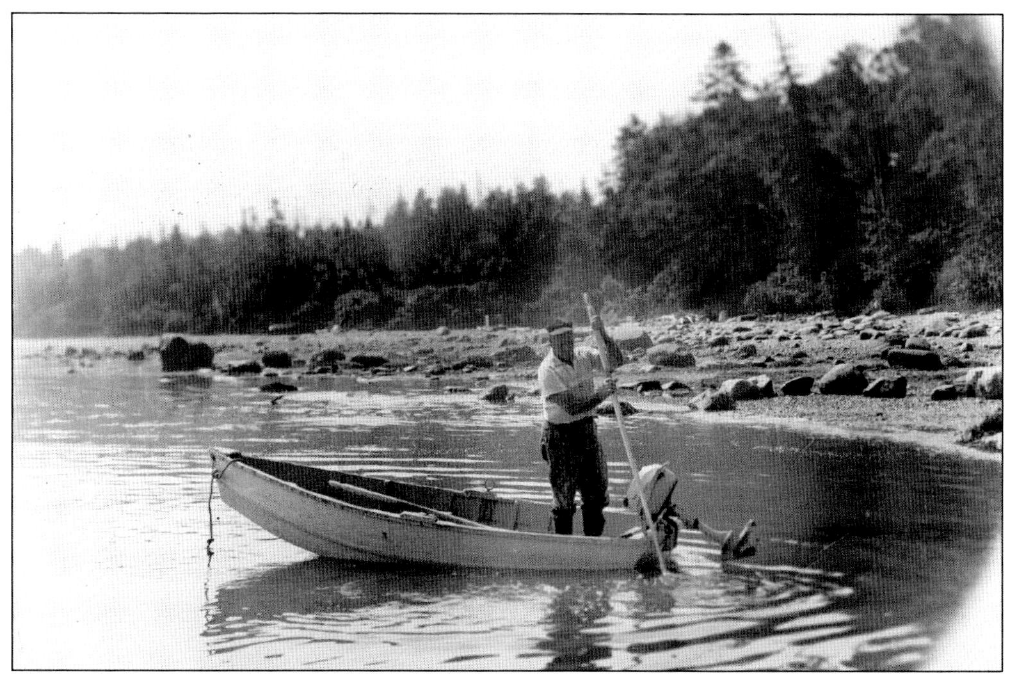

Edward Sherman is shown poling his motorboat out to deeper water from the shore in North Brooklin. A fisherman, he was the husband of Florence Grindle and the father of Michael, Reginald, Heidi, and Debby Sherman.

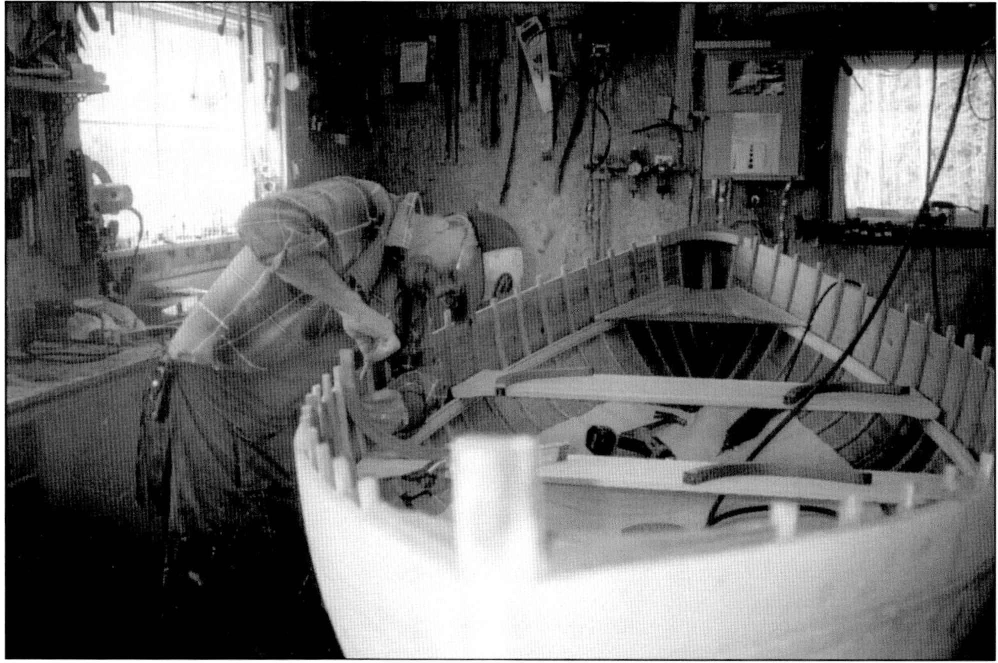

Jim Steele has been making wood peapods in Brooklin since 1965 in one of his several shops around the town. In between building houses, Steele developed a line of the swift stable rowing craft, which are often used on schooners. One of his peapods is in the museum at Mystic Seaport in Connecticut.

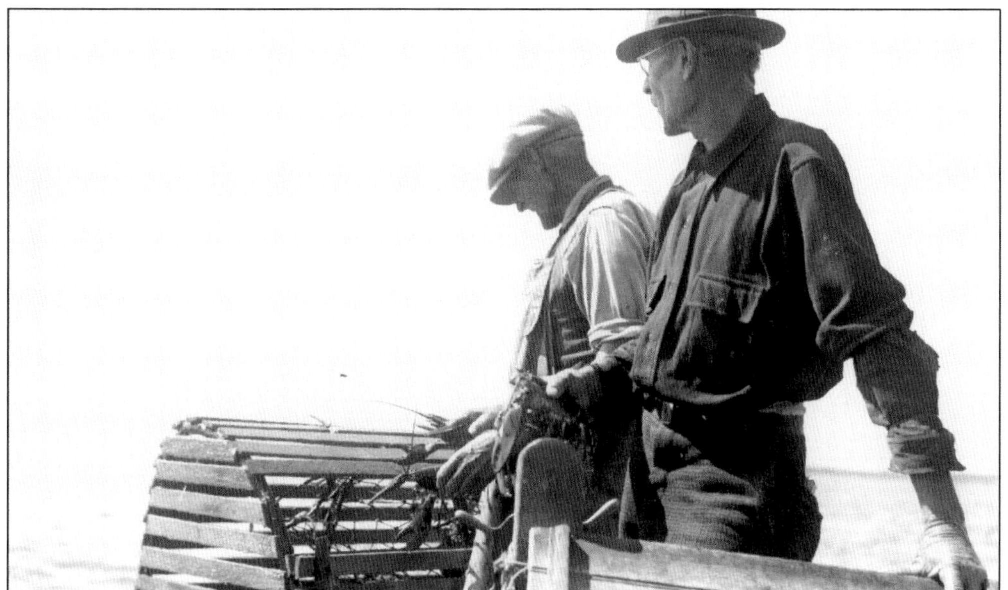

Lobstering is the backbone of the fishing industry in Brooklin. Here, Chester Kane and Gene Freethey unload their old wooden slat trap and get ready to rebait and throw it back for more.

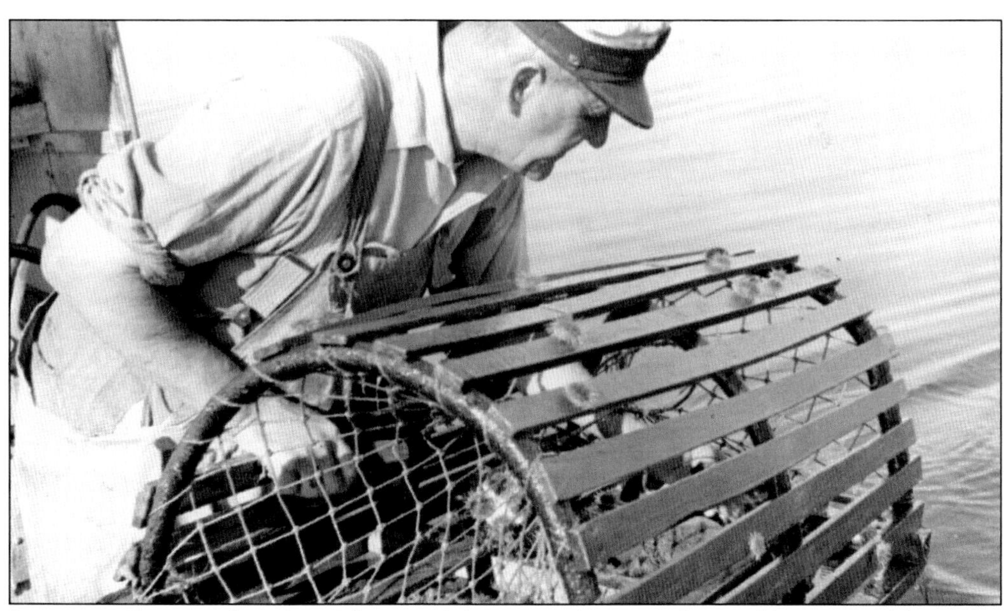

Lawrence Sherman (1885–1954) was a lobsterman from North Brooklin. Many lobstermen made their own nets, such as the one seen on the end of this trap. Sherman was the husband of Laura B. (Cole) Sherman.

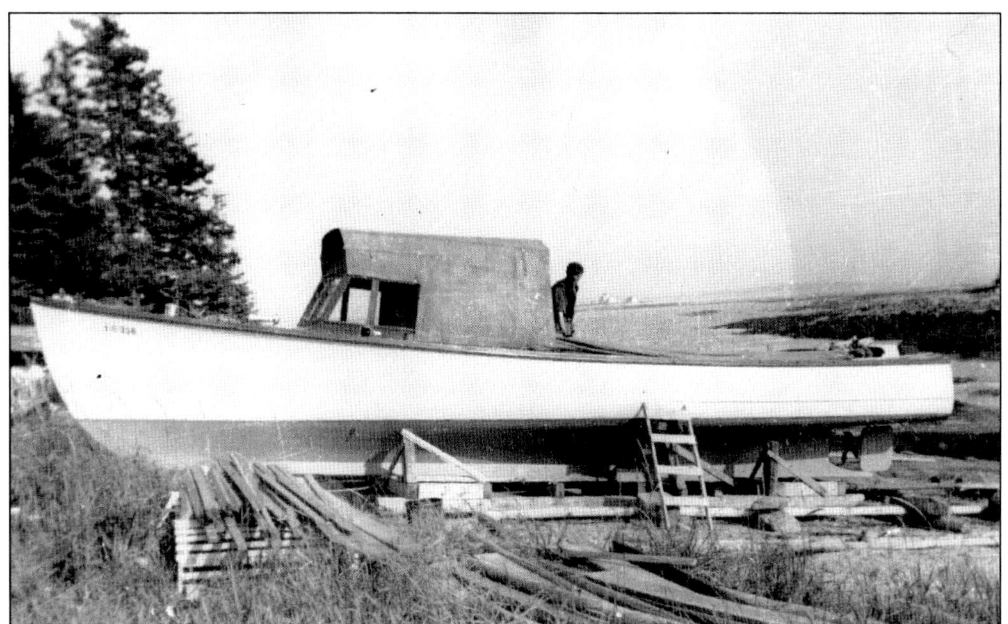

This is Kenneth Dow's boat on Goose Island, off Flye Point, in 1941. He was making the boat over for lobster fishing. The Dows made the island their summertime home.

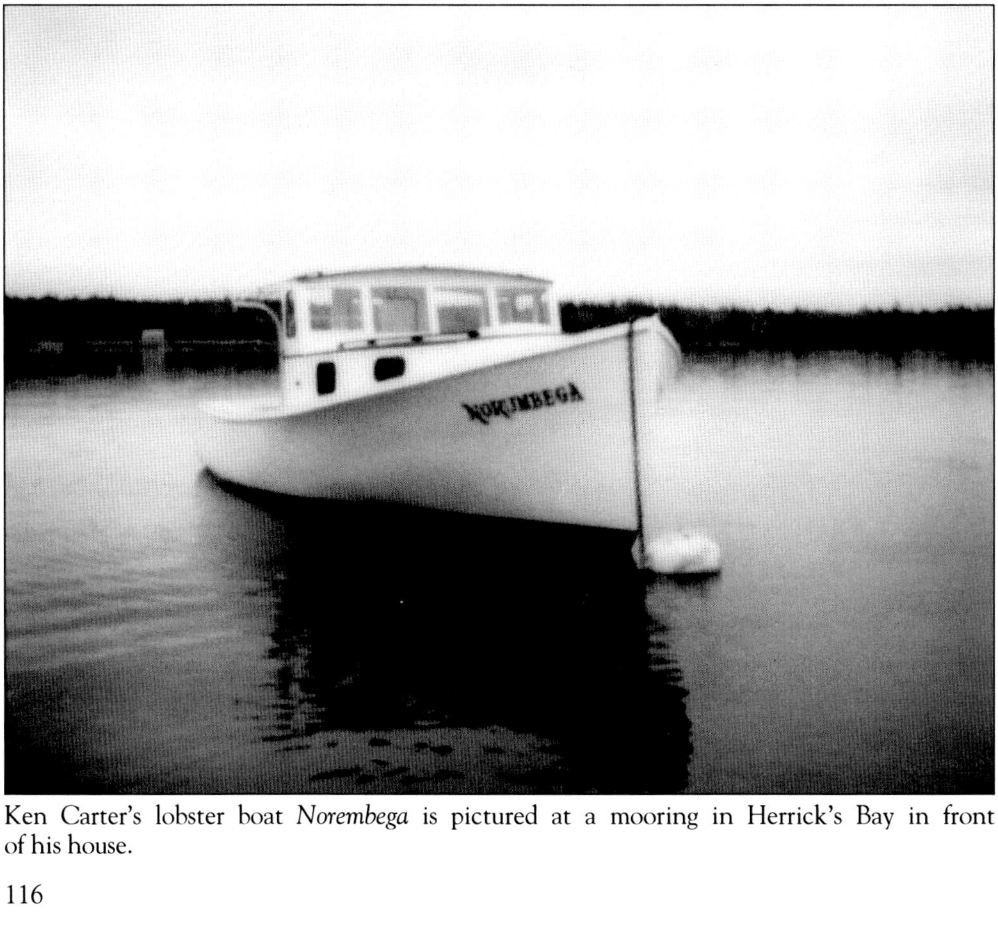

Ken Carter's lobster boat *Norembega* is pictured at a mooring in Herrick's Bay in front of his house.

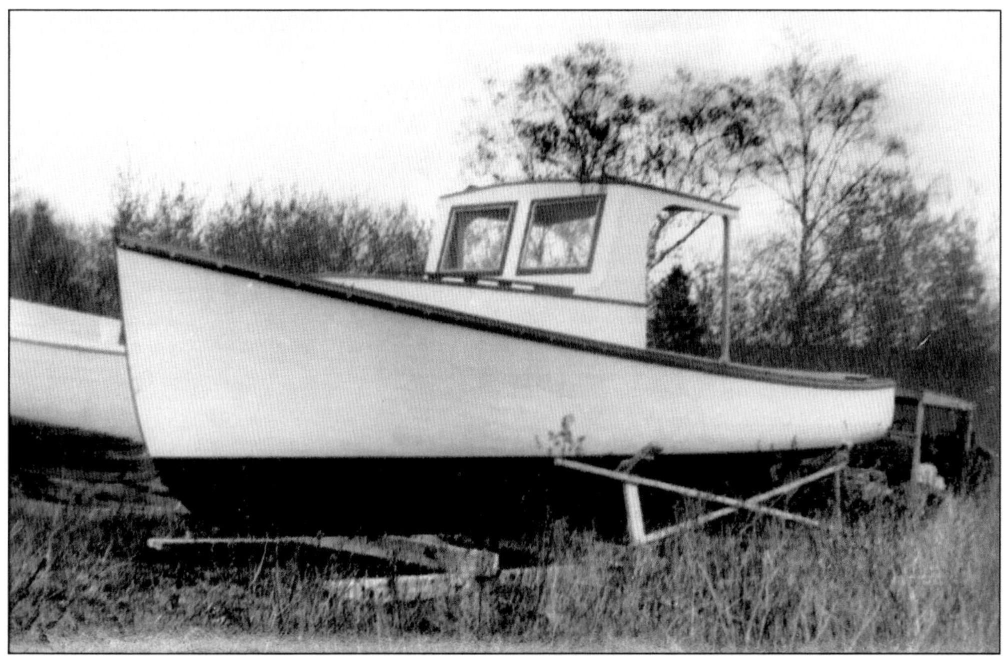

The *Evlyn M.* was built by Walter Church in the 1950s for John Faxon Bartlett. The son of Wesley and Evelyn Bartlett, Bartlett lived on Allen's Cove, Harriman Point.

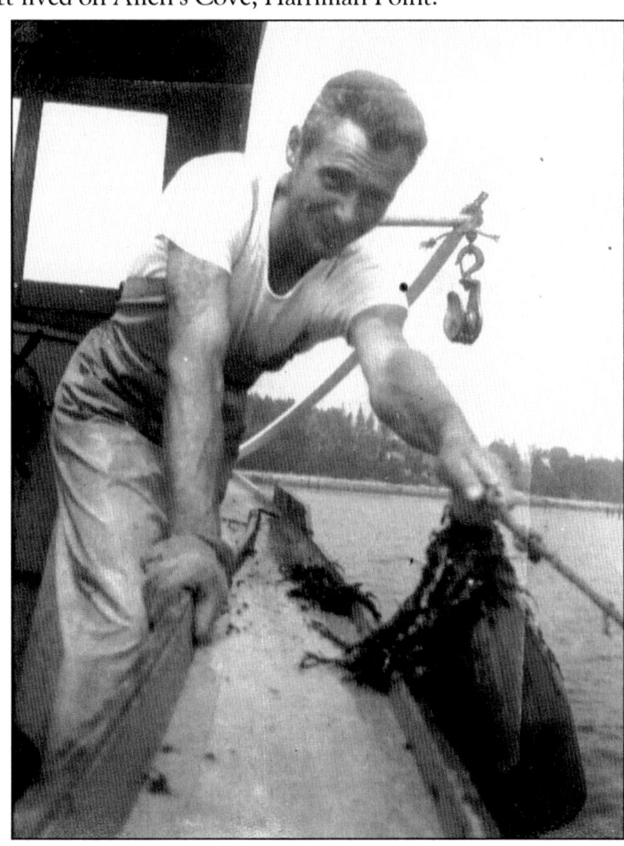

John Faxon Bartlett is pictured on the *Evlyn M.*, bringing up the wooden buoy of one of his lobster pots.

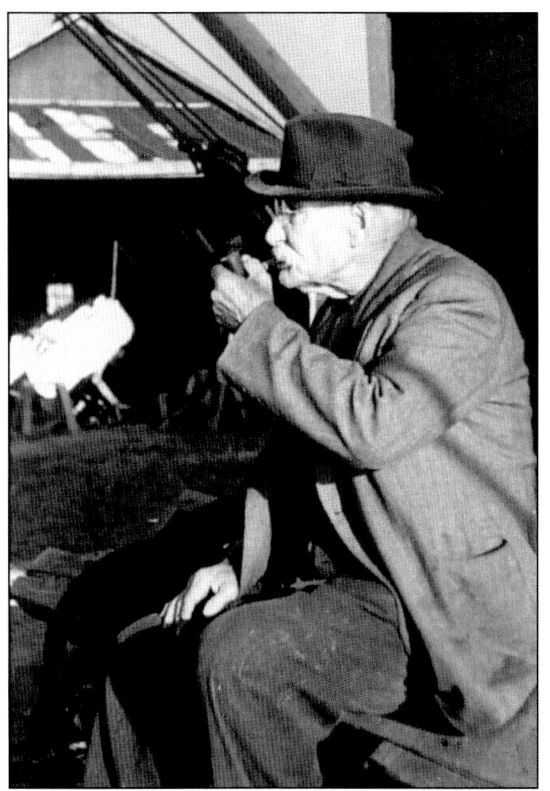

Many folks remember George Tainter (1863–1951) just as he is pictured here, sitting at the boatyard and smoking his pipe. He was known for his storytelling and love of boats. He built the 42-foot fish boat *Restless,* which he later gave to his grandson Ken Tainter. George Tainter lived on Pooduck Road with his wife, Elmina York.

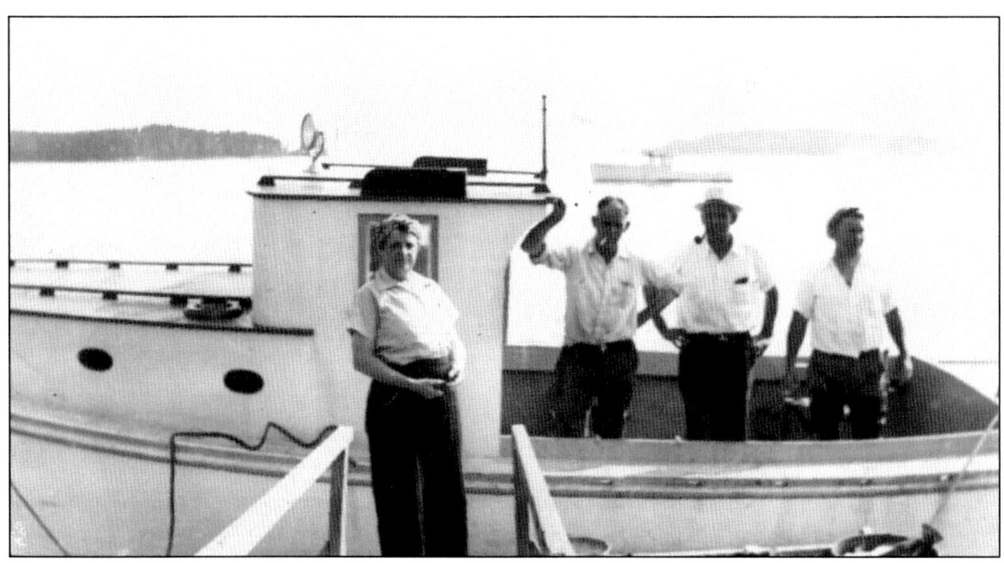

This is a picture of Lawrence Cole's boat tied up at Pooduck. Standing in the boat are Lawrence (far left) and Donald Holden (far right). The others in the picture are unidentified.

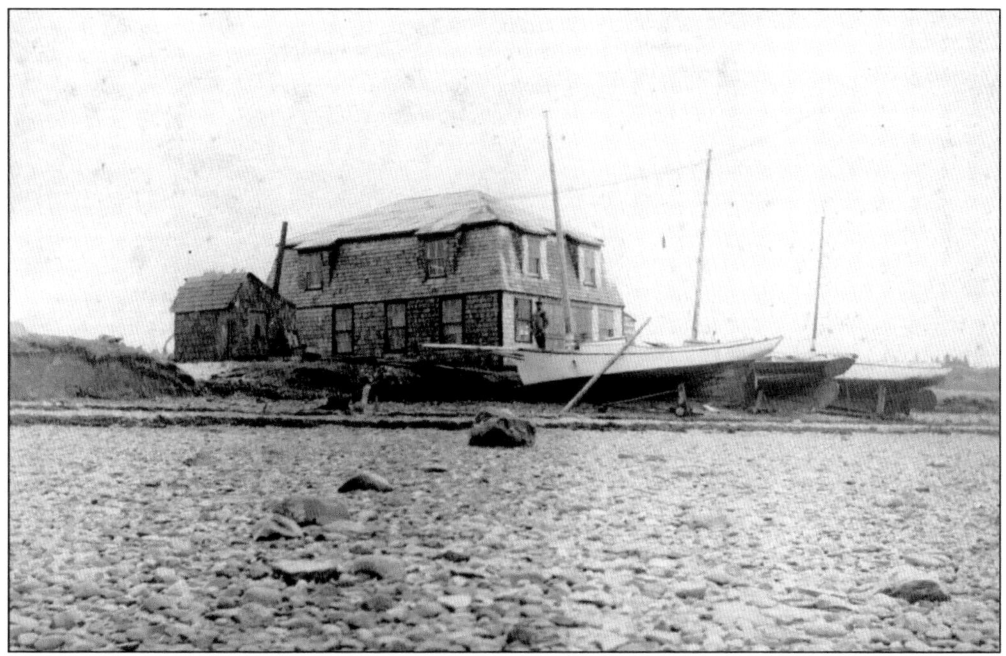

This building, the boatshop of Allen B. Cole, is pictured as it looked when it was on Long Island. When electricity came to the mainland, Cole moved this building to the shore in Allen's Cove and set up business there. The shop was later rebuilt into a private residence.

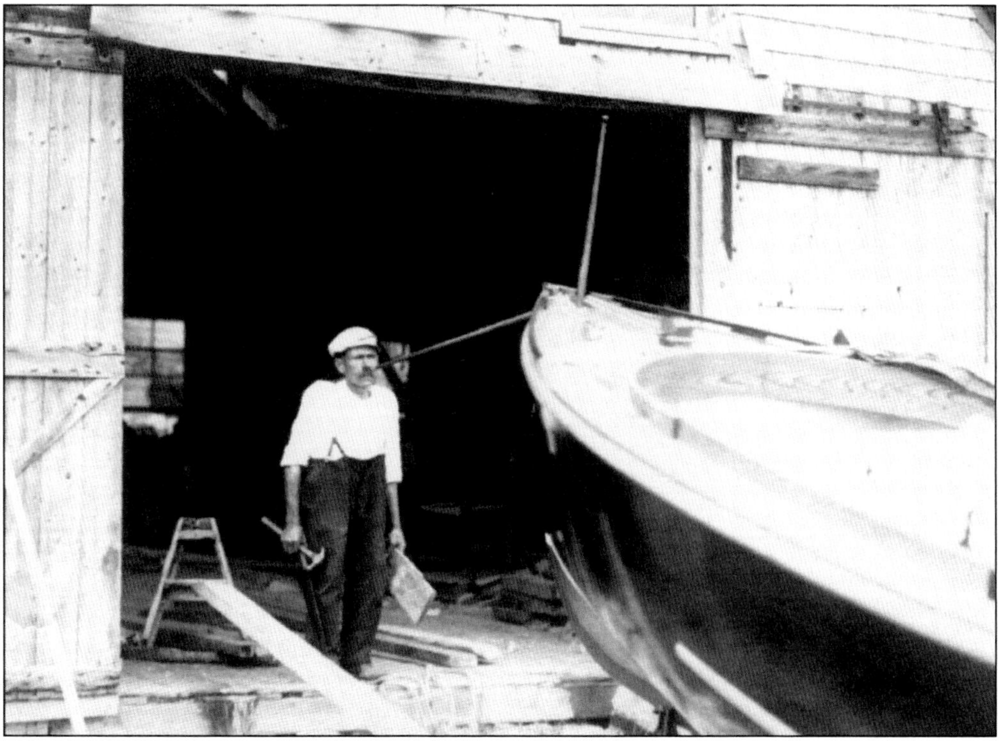

Allen B. Cole (1878–1939) is pictured here at his new boat shop in North Brooklin. A boatbuilder all his life, he was married to Margaret H. Cole (1888–1961).

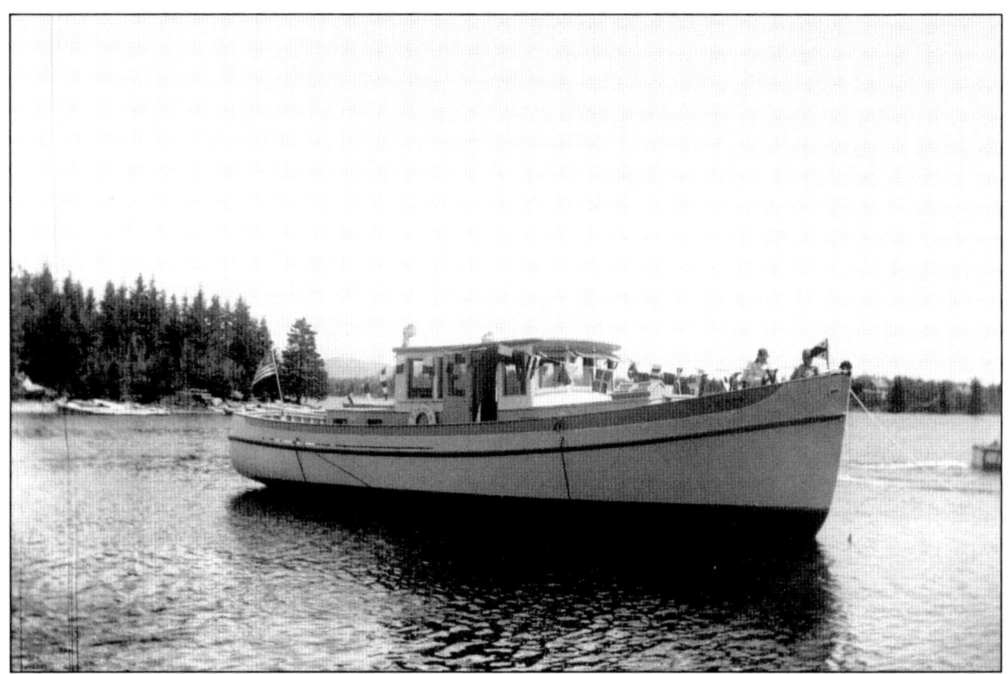

This is a picture of Bill Chisholm's boat in the 1950s. He is the owner of the John C. Tibbetts house, which was moved from Center Harbor to North Brooklin in 1948.

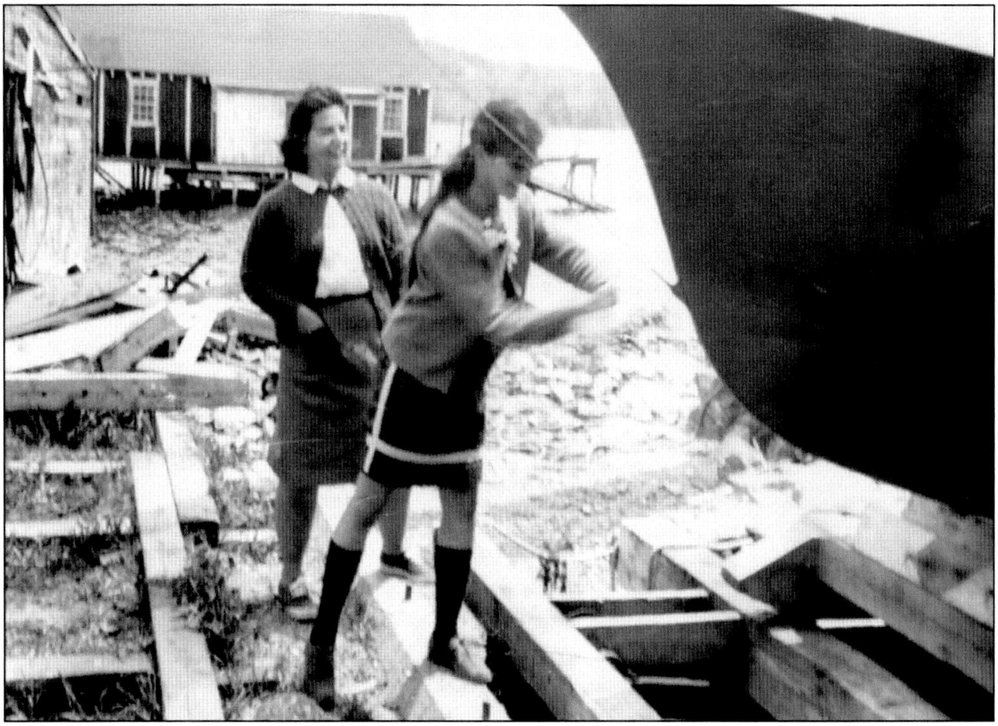

The 20-foot *Martha* was a Crocker-design cruising sloop, chosen by E.B. White for his granddaughter. It is shown being launched by Martha White in 1967 at the boatyard of her father, Joel, as her mother, Allene, looks on.

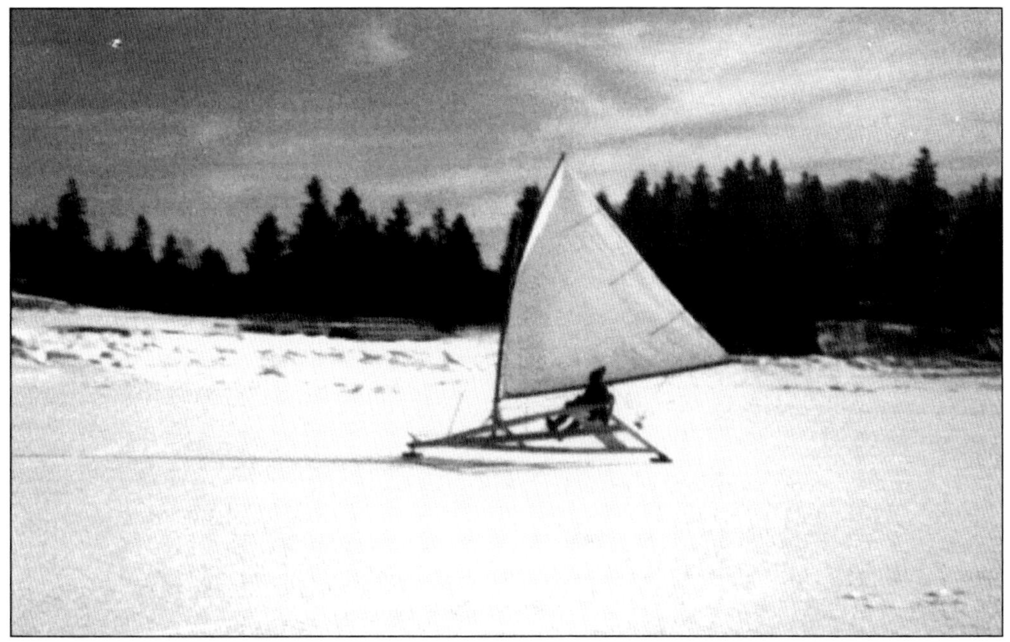

On a frozen bay, an iceboat built from a Beetle Cat by Joel White and Jim Steele is pictured as it races along in the freezing wind.

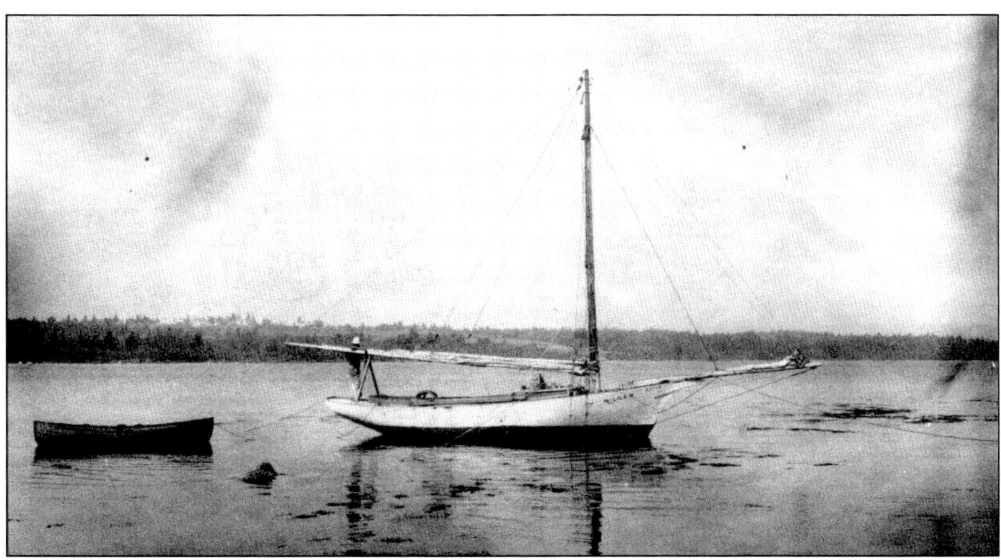

Henry Twitchell's sloop *Lila* M. was the only boat moored at that time in Herrick's Bay.

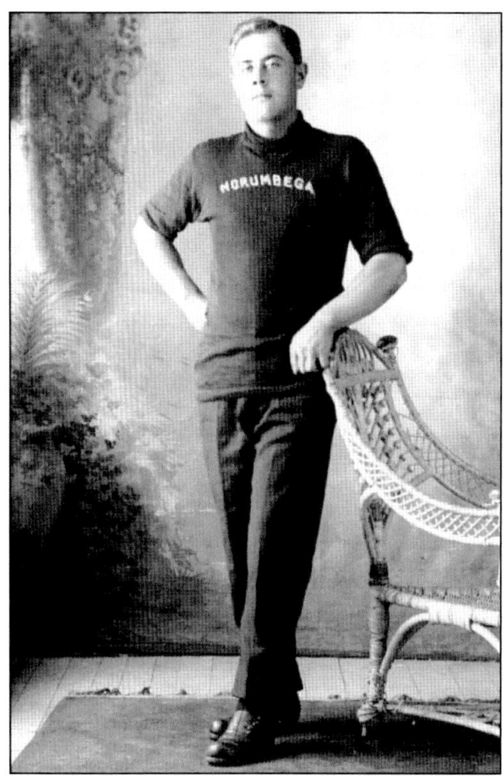

Along with fishing, lobstering, and boatbuilding, many Brooklin men went to sea on the steamboats. Gene Cole, the son of Eugene and Susie Cole, is shown in his *Norumbega* uniform. The *Norumbega,* out of Boston, ran from Rockland to Bar Harbor. Gene was known in Brooklin for his fiddle playing.

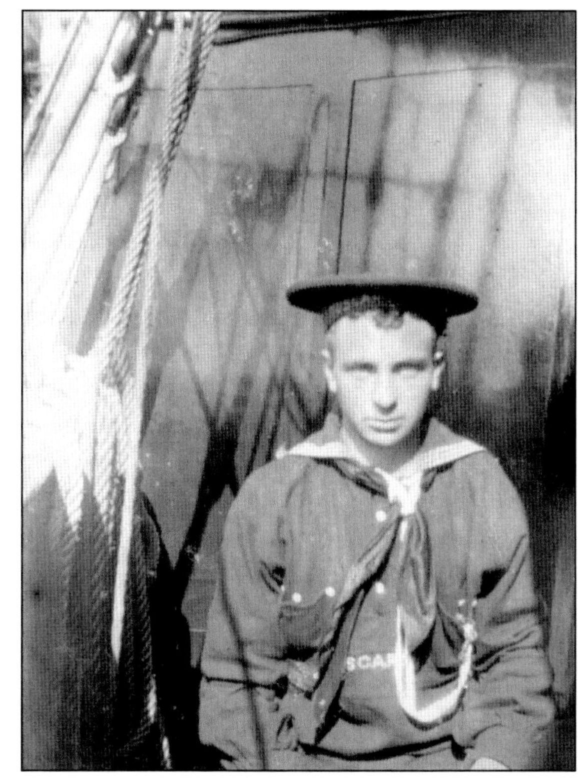

Another mariner from that era was Roswell Eaton, pictured in his uniform from the yacht *Tuscarara.* The Eva Phillips photo album of 1910 has many pictures of the crew from this yacht.

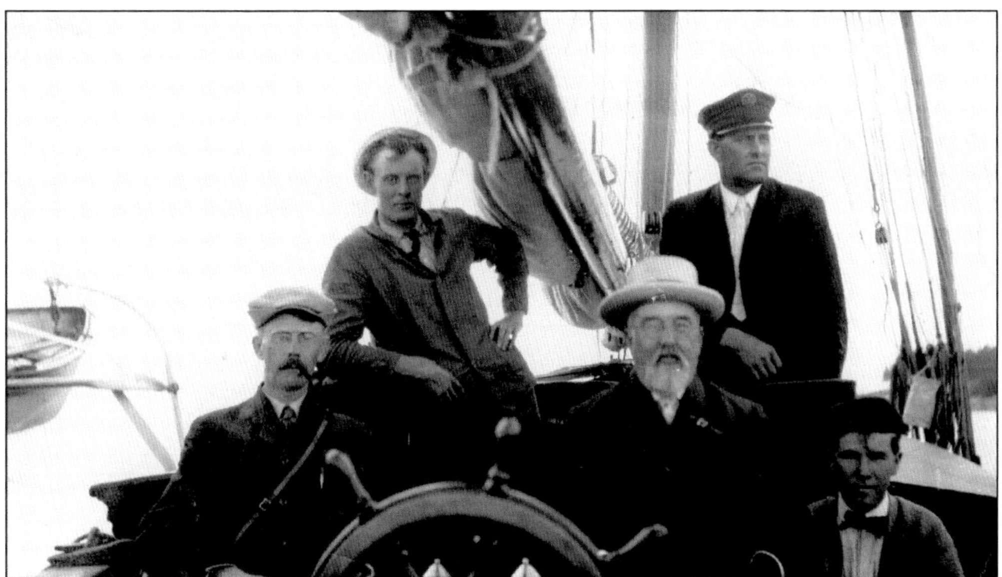

This c. 1900 photograph of people aboard the *Aurora* has an album inscription that says L. Granville Phillips and Col. W.B. Thompson are on board here. We know from the log of the *Aurora* that the famous explorer Col. Adam Wesley Powell was a daily companion to Thompson on the *Aurora* in 1900. Phillips, in the captain's cap, is standing behind the bearded man.

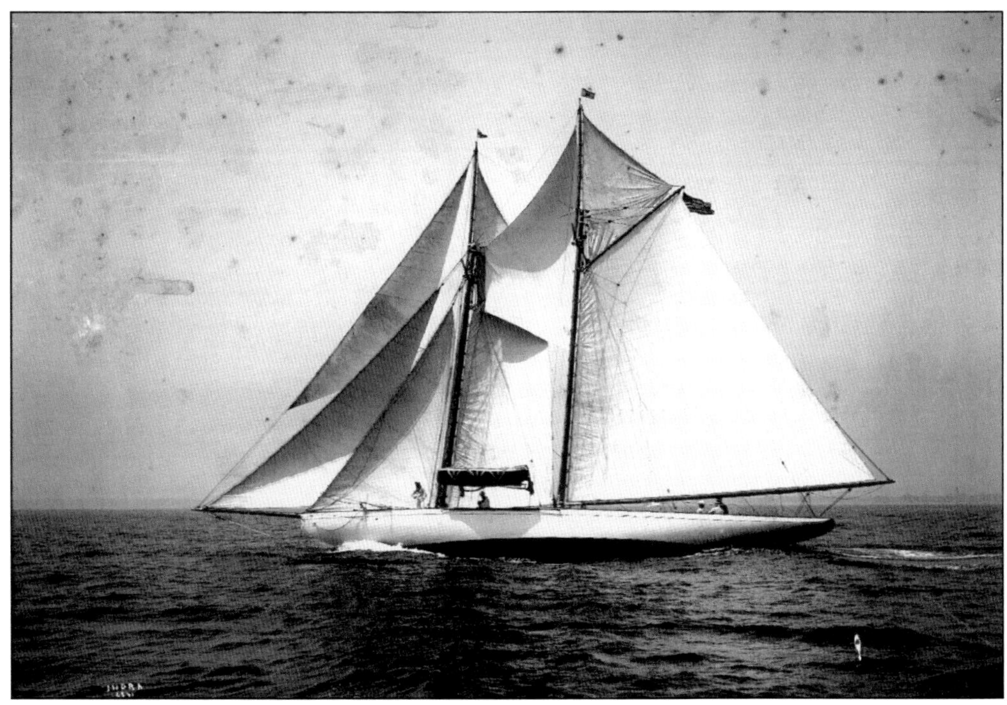

The *Indra*, a 72-foot schooner, was designed by F.D. Lawley. It was built in 1900 by George F. Lawley and Son of South Boston for I.L. Merrill of the Hotel Touraine in Boston. In 1911, it was bought by Edward Lovering, who owned it until 1925. Lovering's name appears on the Brooklin tax records from 1913 to 1915.

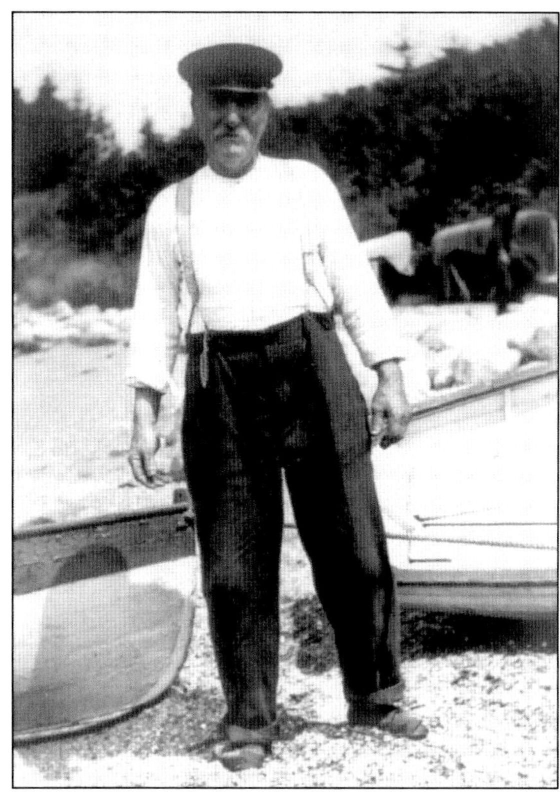

Capt. Judson Freethy had a house and dock next to Haven Colony on land the Freetheys purchased from Watson heirs. We know from the ship's log that during the summer of 1900, Freethy was the captain of the *Aurora*, owned by Col. W.B. Thompson.

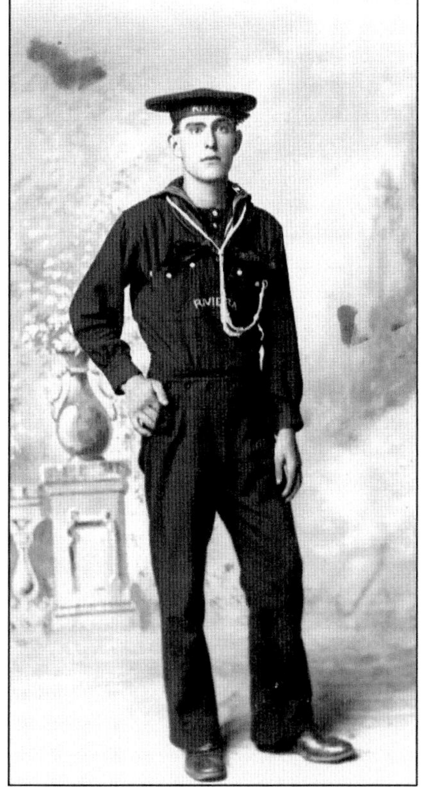

Capt. John Freethey (1881–1931) is shown in a *Riviera* uniform. Freethey lived with his wife, Bessie (1880–1964), in the home later owned by Alan Bemis off the Naskeag Road. This picture was given by the Bemis family, but little information about the *Riviera* has survived.

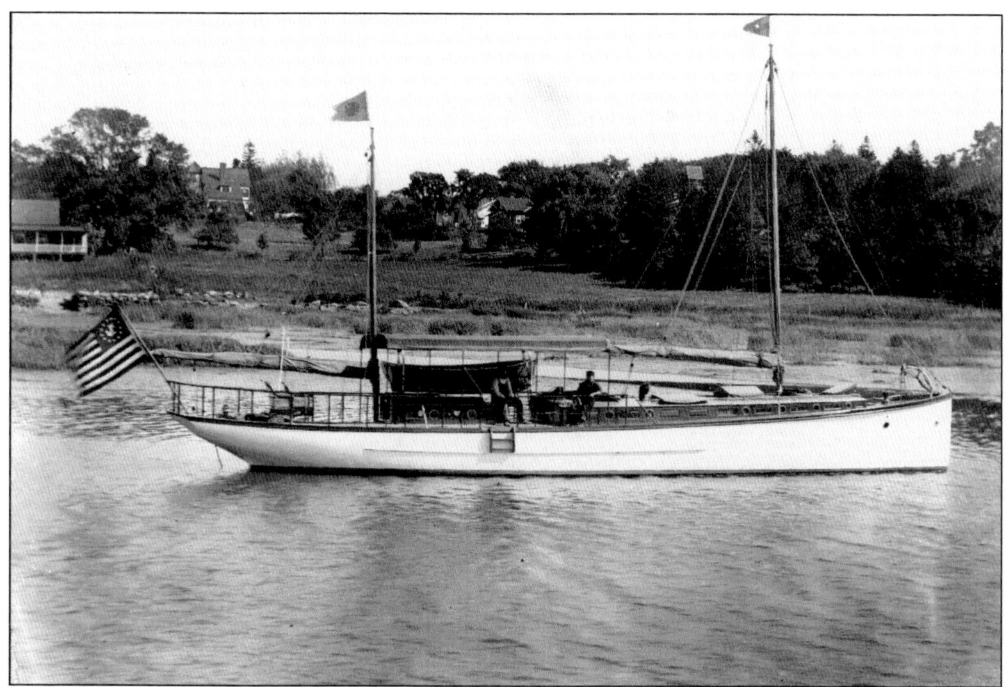

The *Maviet* was a 61-foot ketch-rigged motor sailer designed by Morgan Barney and built by J. Gaertner of Port Chester, New York, in 1913. It was owned by H. Wilmar Hanan in 1913 and Henry S. Hutchinson in 1920. The back of this photograph features an inscription: "John Freethey of Brooklin was captain of this yacht."

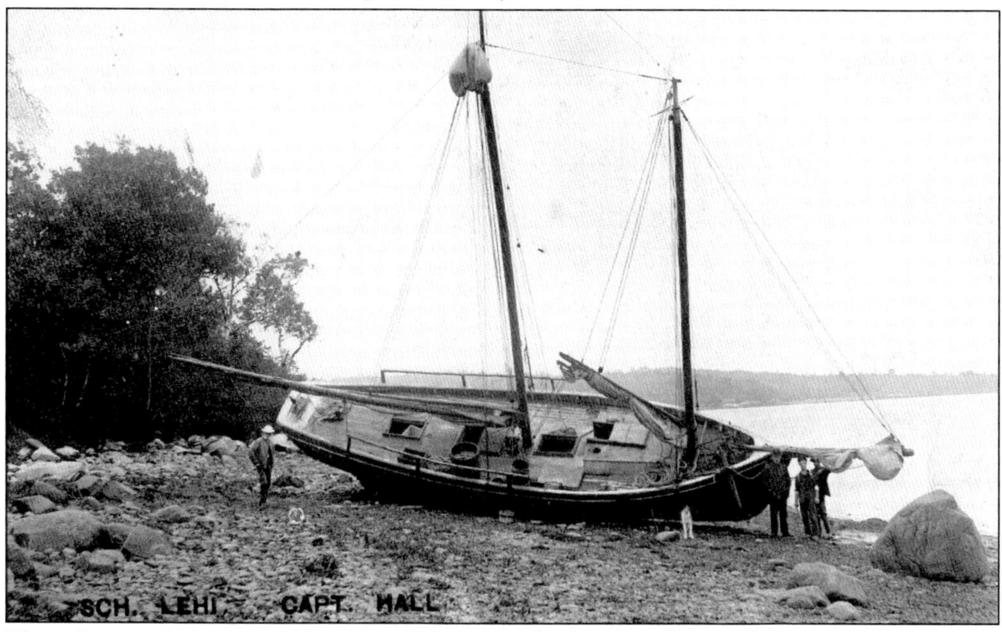

The schooner *Lehi,* owned by Capt. Edward Hall, is pictured grounded out at the shore in North Brooklin. Hall was the grandfather of Frank Day Sr., and on this boat, when Frank was 12 years old, on a return trip from Swan's Island, the captain died at the helm. The kind people of Swan's Island helped Frank, alone then on the boat, return to Brooklin.

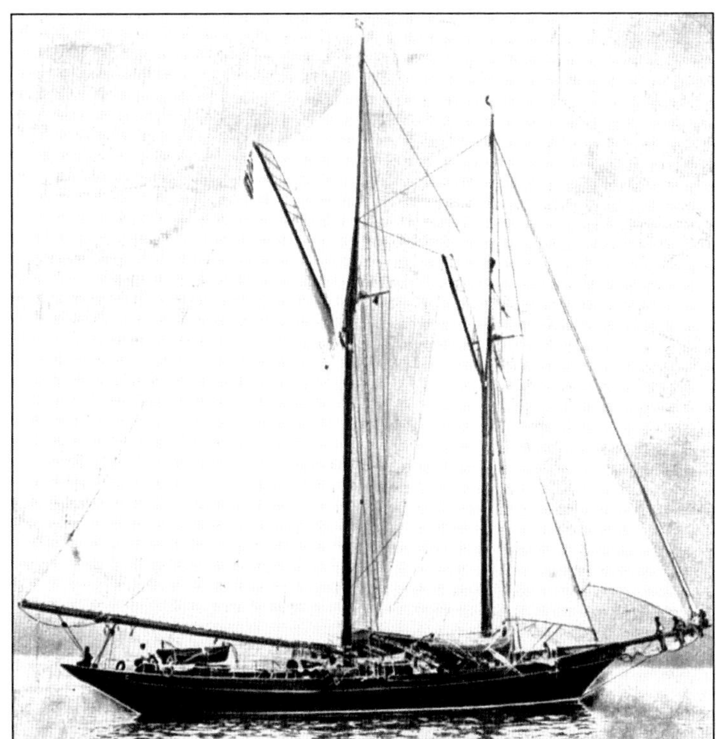

The *Palestine* was a 100-foot schooner yacht designed by A. Cary Smith and Fessis. It was built by J.M. Bayles and Company and was owned by Andrew G. Pierce Jr. The sailing master was Fred W. Phillips of Brooklin.

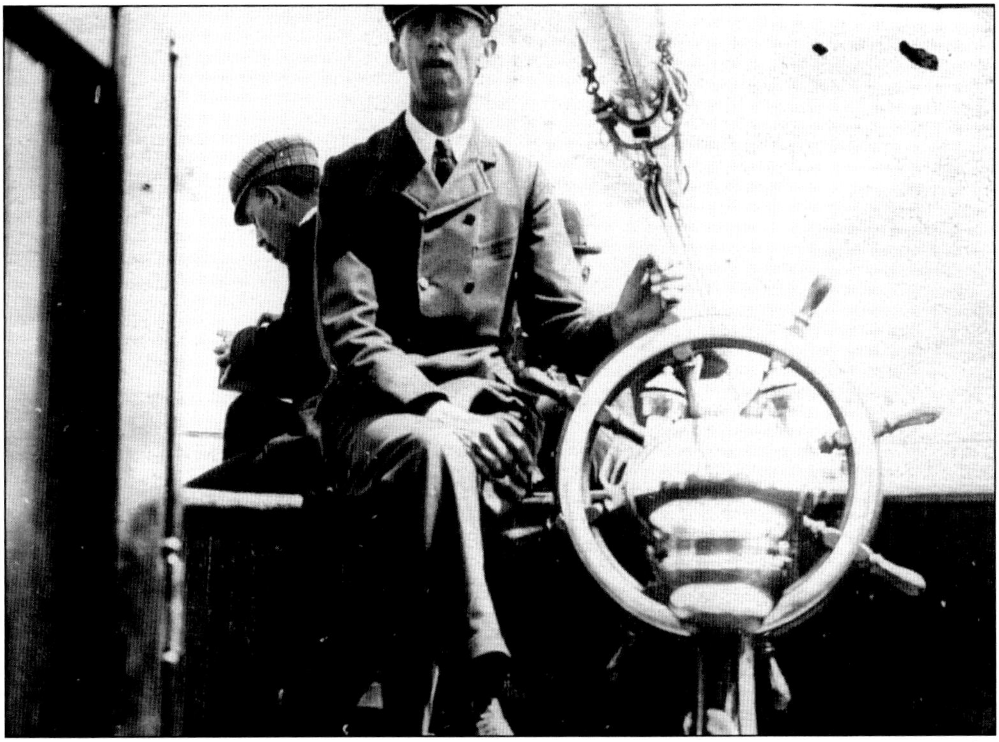

Fred W. Phillips was captain of the yacht *Palestine*, shown in the previous view. Phillips was the son of Benjamin and Edith Phillips and the brother of L. Granville.

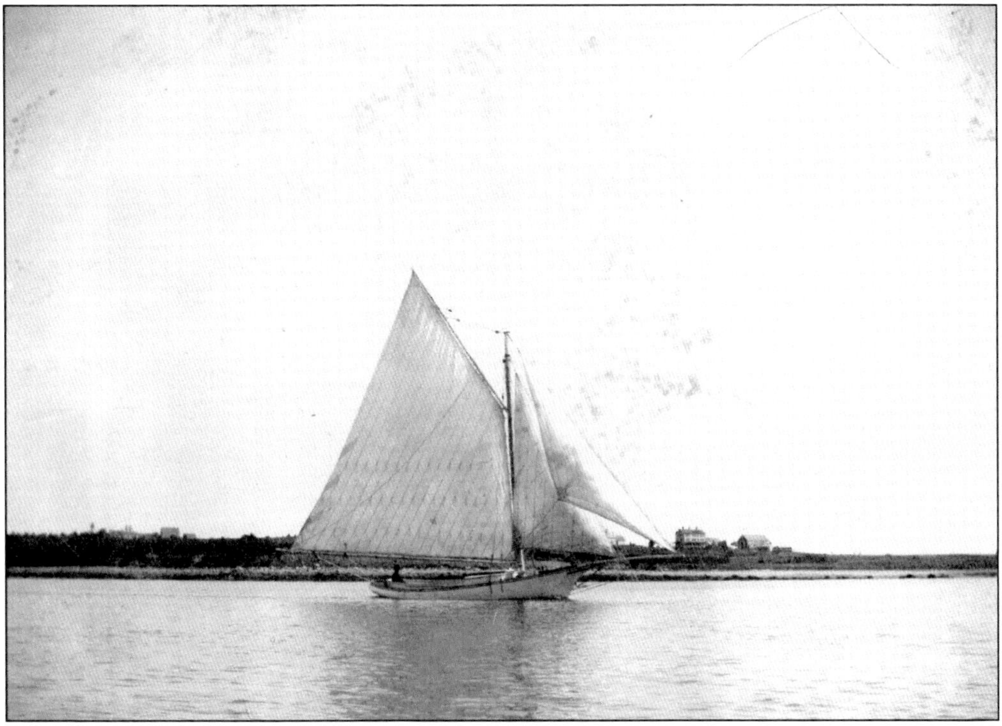

The friendship sloop *Qurita* is shown sailing in Herrick's Bay. The Lookout Inn and Flye barn can be seen in the background on the right. The Phillips House is to the left.

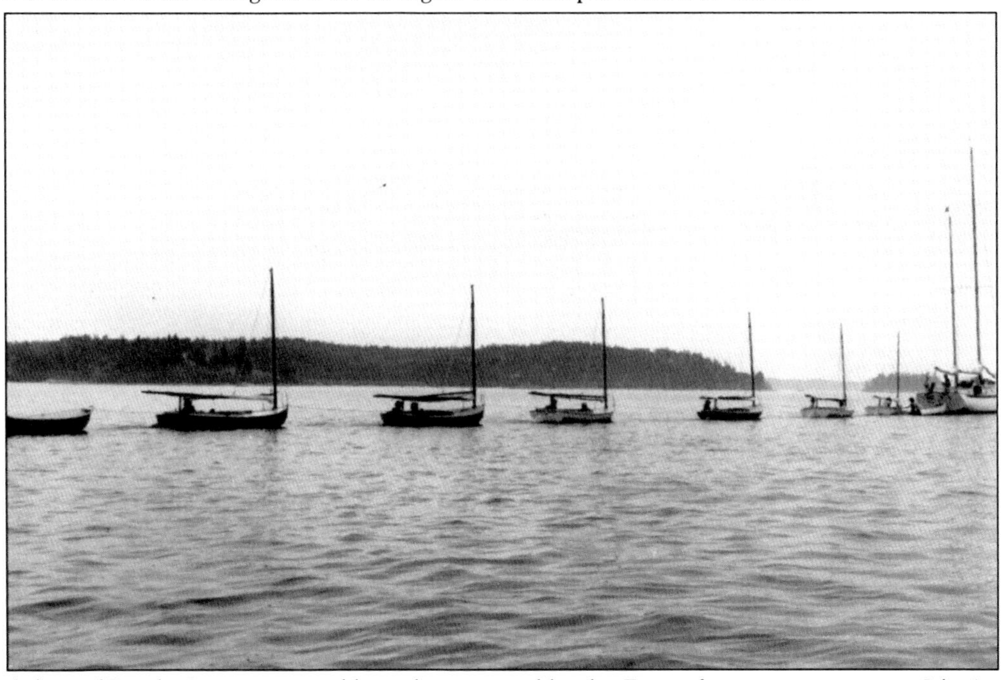

A line of Beetle Cats is pictured here, being towed by the *Freya*, for a camping trip on Isle Au Haut. The 40-foot ketch *Freya*, owned by Donald Parson, was built in 1967 by O. Lie Neilsen in Rockland from a design by Geerd Hendel of Camden.

REFERENCES

Adams, George. *Maine Register and Business Directory*. South Berwick, Maine: Edward C. Parks, 1856.

Bourque, Bruce J., and Steven L. Cox. "Man in the Northeast." Maine State Investigation of the Goddard Site, No. 22, Fall 1981. Augusta, Maine: Maine State Museum, 1979.

Brooklin Alumni Association and 1999 Sesquicentennial Committee. *Brooklin's Sesquicentennial: 150 Years, 1849–1999*.

Brooklin Centennial Committee. *Centennial Celebration, Brooklin, Maine, July 29–31, 1949*.

Chatto and Turner, compilers. *Register of the Towns of Sedgwick, Brooklin, Deer Isle Stonington and Isle au Haut, 1910*. Friend Memorial Public Library, Brooklin, Maine, 1972.

Donham, Grenville M., compiler and publisher. *Maine Register, May 1, 1898 to May 1, 1899*. Portland, Maine, 1898.

———. *Maine Register, No. 39, June 1908*. Portland, Maine, 1908.

Fiftieth Anniversary Brooklin High School: 1907–1957. Ellsworth, Maine: Hancock County Publishing Company, 1957.

"History of Brooklin," an address by Rev. E.S. Fish at Brooklin, July 4, 1876. Bangor, Maine: Burr & Robinson, 1876.

"History of the Town of Brooklin," manuscript by Mary Ford (later Weber), 1937.

Friend, Victor A., address delivered in 1950, when memorial clocks in honor of his brother, Robert A. Friend, were dedicated at Brooklin Baptist Church; copy at the Friend Memorial Public Library.

Grindle, Barbara, compiler. *Sedgwick, Maine's, Resting Places, 1789–1999*.

Hooper, Jane, and Sunny Toulmin. *Memories of Haven Colony, Brooklin, Maine*. Brooklin, Maine: Haven Publishing Company, 1985.

Howland, Llewellyn. *The New Bedford Yacht Club: A History*.

Lawson, Darlene. "A Fish Canning Industry Once Thrived in Brooklin." *Maine Life*. September 1978.

Rockefeller, James S., "A Profile." Bemis, Alan, "Flying Recollections" and "Downeast Stories." *Strut & Axle*, No. 4. Owls Head (Maine) Transportation Museum, Winter 1996.

Sherman, Bonney L. and others. *The Grovehurst Inn: A History of the Sherman Family in No. Brooklin, Me., 1774–1983*.

Sly, Roxanne T., and Clare Sullivan, compilers. *The Cemeteries of Brooklin, Maine*. 1999.

"John C. Tibbett House," manuscript at Friend Memorial Public Library, Brooklin, Maine.

Tibbetts, Emma L., "Journal of Captain John C. Tibbetts of the Brig Gulnare." *New England Quarterly*, Vol. XI, No. 1, March 1938.

Tower, Fred L., compiler and publisher. *Maine Register, No. 59, 1928*. Portland, Maine, 1928.

———. *Maine Register, No. 67, 1936*. Portland, Maine, 1936.

Wasson, George S. "Sailing Days on the Penobscot," including a "Record of Vessels Built There," compiled by Lincoln Colcord. Salem, Massachusetts: Marine Research Society, 1932.

Wells, Rufus. Papers. Sedgwick-Brooklin Historical Society.

White, Kimberly Tyler. "The History of the Brooklin Schools: 1849–1993." October 1993.